W9-ACD-814

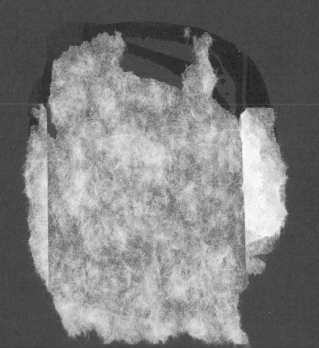

Preparation for Art

Preparation for Art, Second Edition

June King McFee

University of Oregon

Wadsworth Publishing Company, Inc.
Belmont, California

L. C. Cat. Card No.: 70-118325
Printed in the United States of America

1 2 3 4 5 6 7 8 9 10—74 73 72 71 70

Illustrated by Jean Ray Laury

To Malcolm and John

Foreword

This volume, *Preparation for Art,* is more than a revision. It presents the research developments and philosophical viewpoints regarding art education that were not available ten years ago, when the original edition went to press.

June King McFee writes about art experiences for all the children of America—the well-to-do, middle-class suburbanites and the children of the migrant farm workers, snatching their few weeks of schooling from Ohio to California. She describes with care and selectivity the sharp differences that environment imposes upon children's perceptions. She cites the research on the overbalance of intellectual concepts as compared with perceptual imagery. She portrays graphically the range of individual differences in children's reactions to visual phenomena and visual arts. Her awareness of children's insensitivities—caused by emotional neglect, by meaningless compulsions forced by adults, or by social isolation—will open the eyes of all teachers whose own sensitivity is not hopelessly blunted.

Dr. McFee gives no aid or comfort to the avant-garde of the moment nor to the nostalgic sentimentalists. Her interest is in the future, in the preservation and humanizing of man's perception of his world, and in man's aesthetic creation and recreation of the world he has inherited from his fathers. With these goals, the author has made the second edition of *Preparation in Art* even more valuable for the classroom teacher than the first edition. The scope of visual arts in experience becomes more clear to the reader. The way in which children perceive is better understood. The teacher is led logically to understand the processes by which he may enlarge his own understanding and thus push apart the barriers to a growth in perceptual awareness which realizes the promises of childhood.

Frederick M. Logan

Preface

The second edition of this book is an outgrowth of many things. Research related to behavior in art has been highly accelerated since 1961. The theory described in the earlier edition has been subjected to constructive criticism by members of the profession, particularly Dr. Arthur Efland, Dr. Richard Salome, Dr. Mary Rouse, and Dr. Gordon Kensler. Students in many classes have provided the catalyst for reanalysis of my ideas. The pressure of the times, the impact of social change, and reevaluation of the values of major social institutions, particularly education, challenge one's ideas.

The purpose of this book is to bridge the gap between research and practice, between the science and the art of art education, and to make this bridging useful to classroom teachers, consultants, and scholars in the profession as well as anyone concerned with the art development of children and young people.

Several people made very important contributions to the preparation of this edition. Frederick Logan has provided continued professional encouragement by reviewing and introducing the two editions. Two other colleagues made particularly important contributions. Dr. Kenneth Beittel and Dr. Ronald Silverman devoted extensive time and the highest levels of constructive criticism to the review of the second edition. Other reviewers also made most useful contributions to the overall perspective: Dr. Julia Schwartz, Dr. Elliot Eisner, and Dr. Harlan Hoffa. Dr. Jessie Lovano worked as a research assistant in reviewing the field. She also contributed results from her own dissertation and examples of children's work. Lucille Just DeRose, editor of the first edition, has been of inestimable help in clarifying and polishing this edition.

Many of Jean Ray Laury's drawings, which seem as fresh now as when they were originally drawn, have been retained. Barbara Kensler worked persistently to contribute lucid drawings to illustrate new materials. Ann Wills' photographs captured the essence of children's involvement.

The Portland Public School, the Honolulu Academy of Arts, Mary Jo Albright, Art Consultant in Corvallis, Oregon, all provided either slides or permission to photograph children at work.

To Dr. Malcolm McFee, with whom I share my life and work, I am most in debt.

Eugene, Oregon   June King McFee

3

Perceptual Readiness for Art   53

Your Preparation for Art

This book is designed for you who are concerned with art in the lives of children and young adolescents. Its purpose is to help you to be more effective in guiding their experiences in art so that the world of vision will have rich meaning for them. Two interrelated assumptions are made: (1) teachers who have developed high levels of visual sensitivity and have experienced the process of creative invention and expression are more aware of the possibilities for learning; (2) teachers who combine this background with understanding of the human behaviors involved and the wide range of readiness among their pupils will be more effective in helping them achieve success in art.

Art courses will give you experience in creative work and help you learn to see and to understand design, the grammar of art. The theory and research described in this book will help you to understand this experience in perceiving, designing, and creating. With this combined knowledge you will have a sounder basis for understanding individual differences among young people as they explore the world and man's experience through art.

The title *Preparation for Art* means just that. This book's goal is to prepare you to become a professional person who understands human behavior in art and art education from its foundations. Some of you have had experiences in art through your own creative work, but you may need to understand more about the diversity of children's and adolescents' readiness for art. Others of you are new to the field of art, but, by understanding art as a result of human behavior and man's need to communicate visually as well as verbally, you can see its value in education. A glossary at the end of the book provides definitions of technical terms. After each chapter are listed the research materials and references that apply to that chapter.

Attitudes about Art

Many people do not think of themselves as artists, yet when they organize things, they design and when they do things differently, they create. They make aesthetic judgments many times a day, buying, selecting, or arranging. If you lack confidence in the quality of your judgments, you may feel timid about trying to develop others' abilities. This book is planned to accompany an art activities course in your preparation as a teacher. It is designed to help you understand more about what lies behind the ways you feel and the judgments you make about art. This guided experience should help you become more confident in teaching art.

Teachers have often been observed introducing a medium they have negative feelings about. Without realizing it, by the expressions on their faces and the way they handle the medium, the teachers communicate to the pupils their dislike for it. Such an introduction will hardly encourage them to use the medium freely. In all of our actions, our feelings operate along with our understandings. In art, where individual expression is involved, understanding our own attitudes becomes particularly important. *This is the reason why it is so important for teachers to explore art for themselves as well as for teaching.*

Why do some of us have mixed feelings about art, or about some styles of art? How does a person's past experience help to determine his present attitudes? What real use does art have in the life of a child or an adolescent? These are some of the questions you may be asking as you strive to prepare yourself as a professional person.

The Function of the Book

This book is focused on the professional role of the classroom teacher or the art teacher. What is said, however, is useful to those of you who work with children in art in other situations. The purpose is to raise the professional level of your activity. By knowing *why* you do the things you do, you will be able to make intelligent judgments about the art experiences you give children.

You and your art instructor—each has a specific role to play. Your role is to be as receptive as possible to new ideas, to be patient when you find yourself resisting, to experience or to study what is suggested, and to take time to let new ideas fit into what you already know before you pass judgment on them. Your instructor has had experience with many art media and with problems of classroom procedure. Furthermore, as an artist in his own right, familiar with the art heritage we share, he has much to contribute to your understanding of the vitality and importance of art for living. He will lead and encourage you as you learn about art and school art activities.

The contribution of this book to your training is to interpret suitable information from research that applies to art education. Accounts of investigations in psychology and anthropology have been selected to help you in your own creative development and in your work with children. The materials apply both to you and to the children. Because you are preparing to be a *professional* teacher, you will want to read the descriptions of the research studies and learn to interpret them for possible implications for classroom practice.

A good teacher does not work by formulas, memorizing methods and using them no matter how the situation changes. The most exciting things about teaching are the differences among children, the differences among groups of children, the changes in a group from day to day, and the challenges to the professional teacher in responding to them.

The professional person will not simply accept the word of an authority. He wants to know *how* the authority arrived at his conclusions. He evaluates different kinds of evidence. He recognizes that teaching itself is an art form that involves both the teacher's use of disciplined knowledge and his rapport with children. The professional person questions his own basic assumptions, and he is aware of the ways in which they influence his judgment and his treatment of children.

People will use this book in somewhat different ways. Those of you who are advanced students will use the bibliographies and go to the original sources to evaluate these materials. Others of you can derive guides for teaching from the available summaries and their interpretations. The situations in which you work will constantly change, and each of you, as a distinct individual, is constantly changing. Many possibilities for good teaching can evolve from the ideas presented here. Your instructor will show you some of them. His interpretations may differ from those you read here. It is good to have more than one point of view from which to make your own judgments. Most important, the sources of your information should be as reliable as possible.

The major role of the classroom teacher is to prepare students to deal creatively and effectively with their social and physical environment and to develop their own potential. The teacher's role in the field of art is to serve as a catalyst in whose presence children are exposed to many art forms and are given experiences through which they can develop their own sensitivity for making artistic judgments. Just as we cannot know what scientific judgments our children will have to make as adults, so we do not know what kinds of aesthetic judgments they will have to make. We *can* give them a basis for judgment by increasing their sensitivity to the visual world and to design. We can help them compare what has been done, and we can increase their readiness for creative problem solving.

The Scope of Art Education

Art education is not a distinct discipline since it is linked with many fields. *First* of all it is art, a basic form of *communication*. The symbols on this page, the alphabet, started out as pictographs—pictures with which man symbolized what he thought, felt, and experienced. Language and art have both developed with the history of man. Both are necessary for civilized life. Children have to learn both forms of communication in order to operate successfully as civilized human beings. For this reason we shall study art as it functions in man's life. Anthropology will contribute to our understanding of art as it has functioned in the lives of people of many cultures and as it operates in our lives and in the lives of our pupils.

Second, the production and the appreciation of art are kinds of *human behavior*. The broad study of behavior—psychology—is applicable here, with special emphasis on individual differences in perception, creativity, and growth and development. In order to teach, we ourselves have to learn; we have to understand how and why we learn as we do. Psychology—the study of the individual—cannot be separated from anthropology and sociology—studies of the group. In every classroom there are children who vary in their responses and behaviors in art because of individual or cultural differences. Our attitudes about art have evolved from our culture, our background of experience. For this reason we study variations in art-related behavior from both psychological and social points of view. All of your college courses in general and educational psychology and anthropology and sociology are pertinent to what you are studying in art education.

Third, art education is also vitally concerned with curriculum, the planning and sequence of meaningful experiences that help children develop their means of visual communication and appreciation. Some kinds of communication can be taught; others may better be discovered by children. Children's awareness in all subjects can be sharpened by their study of art.

We are concerned with the relationship of art in school to art in the home and community. As a consumer, each person must make choices, many of which depend on art judgments. As a citizen, each person's contribution to community planning is affected by his aesthetic viewpoint. As a member of a democratic society, each person needs preparation to preserve individuality as well as take responsibility for what he contributes to the views of others.

Aspects of Art in Art Education Art education is concerned with art in its broad sense. First, art is in the environment. Every individual contributes to a personal environment, his home. By his actions he contributes or detracts from the community environment. By the choices he makes he helps to create order or disorder in the appearance of his neighborhood. By the conditions of his way of living he communicates to himself and to others his values and attitudes. These are primary art forms. Judgments about what is order and what is not, what is pleasing and what is ugly are somewhat relative. But a person who has never explored the elements of art—the forms, the lines, the textures; the shapes and shades of things as they change in changing space and light—is ill equipped to make judgments, to take responsibility for or evaluate his contributions.

In school, emphasis is placed on conceptual learning. Even in art education, teachers have stressed symbolic "self-expression" without also encouraging students to learn to see visual reality—textures, lines, edges, shapes, three-dimensional forms, the myriad hues, tints, and shades of color in their experience.

Understanding of the language of art—the design that orders the lines, shapes, textures, and colors—is needed for even the primary aspects of art, the ordering of one's personal environment and community.

The second aspect of art is creation—producing symbolic expression in drawing, painting, and modeling, or producing functional objects in potting, weaving, and metal smithing. The person who produces art must have the abilities to make symbols from memories of past perceptions or from present perceptions, to manipulate tools and materials, to perceive, to order, and to evaluate what he has done.

A third aspect of art grows out of the first two—it is the whole range of visual arts in the visual world. Children need preparation to evaluate the whole range of art, not just what is called "good" or "fine" art, or they will not develop the qualified evaluative skills needed to make judgments as citizens. Children do not live in visual isolation. Television and other mass media display a wide range of objects. Children's habits of judgment and response are learned early. Television fosters passive acceptance. Education in vision and design should help children to become capable of making aesthetic judgments relative to and independent of mass media.

Meaning of Aesthetic Judgment

As used in this book, aesthetic judgment means the kind of qualitative response an individual makes to aspects of a work of art beyond merely recognizing and naming it. Aesthetic judgment is dependent neither wholly on the characteristics of the object nor on the abilities of the individual. It is the result of the transaction of the individual's capacity to respond with the qualities inherent in the object. An object is said to have high aesthetic quality when there is some agreement on its excellence among people whose readiness to perceive art forms is highly developed. This collective judgment is a result of their individual transactions with the properties in the work of art.

An aesthetic response may be a person's perception of the interactions between the organizations of colors, shapes, spaces, lines, and textures that stimulate his need for and response of pleasure to various phases of order and variety. An aesthetic response may be a person's reaction to the way the art elements (shape, line, color, texture, and space) are related to the qualities of the medium, such as light projected through images on film, three-dimensional and transitional spaces created with plastic, or visual illusions of space and form created with paint on a flat surface. An aesthetic response may be a person's feelings of tensions and countertensions as he reacts to these organizations. An aesthetic response may be made to the emotional message as it is related to the forms that are used to express the message. Almost everyone can make some degree of aesthetic response; and everyone can increase his capacity to respond, to understand the aesthetic processes, and to make more analytical judgments.

Ranges of Art   In contemporary society, children are exposed to art forms in the full range from the superficial, commonplace, repetitious, and gaudy to the intrinsic, unique, divergent, and refined. Examples of each of these qualities can be found in all of the major visual communication systems:

in those arts that are traditionally called the fine arts;

in all product design, from the handcrafted to the mass-produced;

in all advertising, display, and packaging;

in architecture, city planning, and urban renewal;

in television, publications, and moving pictures;

in interior design;

and in costume design.

Art exists in the conditions of neighborhoods, villages, cities and towns, representing many periods and copies of periods in assorted states of preservation or decay. *The whole broad face of the world expresses values and attitudes through the nature of the art forms and their state or condition.*[1]

Preparation for independent critical evaluation of what is said through this broad language of vision is as necessary as understanding written and spoken language. For both visual and verbal language are used extensively to influence people's ideas, values, and behaviors. Both condition and contribute to the quality of lives being lived.

The scope of art education begins with the foundational abilities of seeing and designing. These are used in the creation and evaluation of the personal and community environment. They are used in response to the broad array of designed visual information—the symbolism and form of cities (Figure 1–1), advertising, products, and the fine arts. The quality of a child's or an adult's experience depends

Figure 1–1. Symbols of Values in the Environment

upon the capacities he has developed to perceive, to evaluate, to make aesthetic judgments; to organize and design, to express, and to symbolize. A person may live in a bland, uninteresting environment because he responds to little. He may be a passive uncritical receptacle for the projections of mass media. Or he may be visually sensitive, highly appreciative of order and variety in his environment. He may contribute significantly to the quality of art and environmental design because his capacity to respond aesthetically enables him to evaluate critically the choices he and his society make.

Concepts of Teaching Art

The way one teaches art depends upon what one considers art to be and what one's assumptions are about children. Some people in art education stress strongly the concept of child art as inherent in the child. Others believe that almost everything should be taught to them.

The arguments for and against mainly child-centered versus curriculum-centered art education often do not include the assumptions underlying each point of view.[2] Before the merits of one type of training over another can be evaluated, the assumptions involved need to be considered. Though there are many teachers who are not so extreme, let us analyze the two opposite views to make the differences clear.

Proponents of completely child-centered art experiences for children appear to make the following assumptions:

1. Child art is an emotional expression of the child's unique self. The role of the teacher is to reduce environmental influence as much as possible so that it will not interfere with the child's work. The appropriate teaching method then is to provide the child with a wide variety of materials so he will have avenues of expression that will appeal to him.

2. Children go through age-based stages of biological development which mainly determine their behavior in art; the environment has little or no effect upon their work. Thus no sequential training is necessary because the child himself will select what is appropriate for him to do.

3. Furthermore, the field of art is so subjective that no guiding principles or directives need to be taught to children, either in the production of art or in their responses to art.

Proponents of a formal sequential program of curriculum planning, lesson by lesson, tend to make these assumptions:

1. Children are empty containers into which knowledge must be poured.

2. Child art is dependent upon learning of specific art skills and compositional principles. The content of what is taught has much more influence on art behavior than do developmental differences among children. The same curriculum will work for most children at each grade level.

3. The principles of art are definite and well established. There is agreement as to which methods are correct and which are not.

4. One can judge the quality of art by perceiving how well the artist adheres to these principles and how well he uses correct methods.

Resolving the Conflict

One of the basic steps in resolving these differences of opinion is to come to some agreement about the nature of children. Group *one* assumes that the child is a complete, genetically patterned, developing self who only needs opportunities for expression. Thus the sequence comes from the child and needs no planning. Our question then becomes not whether we should have sequence or not, but where the source of the sequence should be — in the child or in the curriculum. Group *two* assumes that the child is a "tabula rasa," a blank slate, who, through discipline and training, can learn the established body of skills and knowledge of art through drills and lessons.

The assumptions of these two groups lie near the poles of the continuing heredity-environment, nature-nurture argument. Some resolution of the conflict in ideas can come from contemporary biology and genetics. Neither of these extreme points of view (that behavior is determined mainly by heredity or mainly by the environment) is generally accepted in these disciplines today.

De Beer says that rather than arguing for heredity or environment " . . . it is necessary to regard both nature and nurture as cooperating." He adds, "There is no such thing as a character that owes its existence solely to heredity or solely to environment."[3]

Dobzhansky emphasizes what he considers to be one of the most important facts in considering the biological basis of human personality: whatever may be the genetic potentialities of an individual, they are realized through the lifelong interplay of his genotype and his environment.[4]

Thus we may say of the many behaviors involved in art — perceiving,

11   **Your Preparation for Art**

imagining, image-making, organizing, manipulating, judging aesthetically — all are the result of the interplay of individual genetic potential with influences from the environment — culture patterns, reward systems, education, and opportunity.

The importance of classroom experience in stimulating each child's potential to develop his readiness for art becomes critically evident. The school can be a strong force for developing his artistic abilities. To make art education more effective, the teacher must recognize other kinds of learning outside of school that may be in contrast to goals for education in school. How do the mass media direct a student's perceptual development? What is he being encouraged to pay attention to? What styles, values, and attitudes about art and the man-made environment is he learning?

In working with a young child, a teacher soon recognizes that the child's home environment is a strong factor in his education. Is he encouraged to imagine? Is he allowed to daydream? What are the resources of his image-making? Does he react to the activities of his peer group with inventive play or manipulation of tools and materials? Do the values of his background society encourage or discourage independent work? Is conformity to the behavior of others very important? Is the living situation itself so coercive that independence is impossible? Or is social change so great that the child needs to seek stability in what is known? How do home influences on a child's aptitude for art influence his responses to and judgments of art?

Nature of Art   Similar extreme concepts are found concerning the nature of art. Some persons believe that art is so subjective that its processes cannot be analyzed nor its appreciations shared; thus it cannot be taught. They may believe that learning has little to do with art experiences because they have failed to recognize that thinking and organization of thoughts play a major part in the creation of art works. The ingredients of thinking include images as well as concepts. Images are not necessarily dependent upon words — written, spoken, or thought. Signs and symbols, changes in form, line, color, and texture, all the variations possible in visual expression evoke thought to those who have learned to understand visual communication. Krech and Crutchfield, in an analysis of the research on images and thinking, say that "much of our experience as we think . . . consists of images."[5] If art is a symbolic language, as the evidence suggests, then in some degree it can be analyzed, shared, and taught.

The other extreme attitude is that art is solely objective, with clearly defined principles which must be taught in order for appreciation and participation to take place. The middle ground of this controversy, that art includes some of both of these extremes, seems more tenable. All of art experience cannot be put into words, cannot be shared. But the process of exploring principles of art can be used to nurture the art experience of a student, provided the *way* the principles are taught leaves room for the unique vision, the individual response of the student. Individual expression and aesthetic judgment can be strengthened by learning; yet originality need not be stifled.

Emerging Trends

At the present time, we are moving away from the extreme assumptions about the nature of art, children's behavior in it, and what the scope and content of art education should be. A middle point of view seems to be emerging. Barkan has shown evidence that children need help in understanding art. Their experience should not be limited to "self" expression through art.[6] Also, we are now learning more about individual differences in behavior in art. We are raising questions about the validity of any extreme method as adequate for all pupils. We are recognizing that some aspects of art are objective and intellectual and some are more subjective. The behavioral sciences have yet to develop the tools for identifying some of the more subjective and intuitive behaviors in art. We are recognizing the effects of living in different cultures on children's readiness for art experience. Cultural differences need to be considered in planning curriculum.[7]

The avenues for responding are more diversified in art than they are in some other school subjects. Children who grasp patterns and relationships through reason and cognition can use these means to respond to and through art. Children who are highly intuitive in their use of organization and expression can be encouraged to use this capacity. Learning can take place through manipulation, perception, cognition, and intuition, so children who are stronger in some of these areas than others can find means for the initial and continuing successes that are so important to progress. Furthermore, in art more diversity of response is acceptable.

"Flexible-Sequential" Programming

A "flexible-sequential" program allows for differences in readiness of individuals and groups of children, and it also gives structure and sequence to learning. It is devised so that one experience grows out of another. Concepts and understandings are built on what is already known. The development of one skill emerges out of the exploration of a prior one. In each case allowances are made for pupil variability in receptivity, capacity, and speed of response.

The need for such a program is based on the assumptions that:

1. Child *behavior* in art is a complex communication system which depends on the interaction of all the factors of the child's development—his inherited potentials, which in some degree are encouraged or inhibited by his experiences, his rewards, and his opportunities to learn.

2. A child's *art expression* will be unique because it will reflect the present development of his potential. His expression will depend in part upon his opportunities to learn, to perceive, to invent and express symbols, to organize, to design, and to use tools and materials. It will depend upon the particular subculture in which he was born and nurtured with the values, attitudes, habits, and art forms he has been exposed to since birth.

3. Through the school years there needs to be some sequential organization of learning that builds a body of appreciations and understandings needed by all youth. The nurturing of the child's unique potential needs some patterning so that it will have continuity for him and so that his prior learnings are reinforced.

4. There are some general tendencies or principles rooted both in aesthetics

and perceptual behavior that can help a pupil become aware of the dynamics of design and composition. There are experiences with tools and materials that can give a child confidence and increase his sensitivity to the diversity of expression that is possible for him. He can learn to increase his capacity to respond perceptually and aesthetically. A child can be helped to become aware of the roles of art in society, and his ability to appreciate art can be increased through experience and understanding.

Using Research in Art Education

One of the serious problems in the field of art education has been people's attitudes toward the relationship of the subject matter of art in art education and the uses of the behavioral sciences in making art teaching more effective. Many people feel that the arts and sciences are so far removed from each other that no relationship exists or can be made to exist. If one takes the extreme point of view that art as content can be learned by all students from all backgrounds and abilities in the same way, then one might assume than an understanding of individual and cultural differences is not needed in teaching.

If one is concerned with art in its broad social aspects, as it functions in the lives of people, and as a language that all people with very different attitudes and backgrounds need to understand, then one would need help from psychology, sociology, and anthropology, as well as art.

The artist works very closely with his own feelings and his responses to the world as he sees it. To become a teacher of art one has to go beyond one's own experience because people do not see, feel, or learn in the same ways. Many artists tend to be committed to a school or theory of art and to one segment of the broad arts we have identified. In public school art education, the teacher needs a broad understanding of the arts so that he can select the most appropriate goals for his students.

The purpose of this book is to give you a better basis for making decisions in teaching art. In the classroom, you are constantly asking yourself questions such as these:

1. What kinds of art experiences will have meaning for this particular group of children?

2. How can I motivate the children who appear to differ in many ways from the rest of the group? Why are they different?

3. What should I expect the children at this level to achieve? What experiences should come first? Which later?

4. Are the established objectives realistic for these children? How can the children be helped to reach their goals?

If the teacher has sound information about the kinds of individual differences he is likely to encounter, he can more easily make intelligent decisions. If he understands something about the nature of creativity and about the perceptual process, he is in a better position to evaluate possible activities for his class. He can decide whether the activities will encourage or inhibit the development of creativity, perceptual abilities, and aesthetic judgment, depending upon the children's background.

In order to help the teacher make such decisions, this book presents a foundation of research in experimental psychology and the behavioral sciences. The study of this research was done with the elementary teacher and the art consultant in mind. The research studies were selected for the soundness of their procedures and their applicability to children as well as adults. New directives for classroom procedures in art are always emerging. They should contribute to the teacher's effectiveness in the classroom.

A scientist, to be systematic, must test each change that he makes. This is a slow process. We teachers have our pupils to teach *now*, with all the problems of individual differences to solve *now* — we cannot wait.[8] To do the best job of teaching, we use as many scientific directives as we can. There is always a gap between what is tested and the problems we have to solve. The obligation of the teaching profession is to be aware of and to use the research that is already available.

The label "theory" can be attached to several kinds of ideas. Anyone who makes an observation and generalizes about its nature, source, or function can say he has a "theory," even though he does not test or analyze his assumption extensively. In scientific terminology, this kind of hunch is more a hypothesis than a theory. Although such a hypothesis can be useful, it must be distinguished from a theory which is developed from well-controlled experimental evidence or from extensive clinical or logical analysis.

One function of a theory is to help us organize numerous pieces of related evidence into a workable tool for dealing with problems. Scattered research that is not related to other research can do little to help us deal with complex problems like child behavior in art. Theory is necessary in understanding behavior that is complex, but the theory is always subject to change as new experiments are made.

A theory in the behavioral sciences is usually part of a larger body of theoretical study and research. The perception-delineation theory (P-D) presented in this book is eclectic. Many pertinent studies have contributed to its formation. Some of its roots are in Gestalt or "field" psychology.[9] The field (like the field in the physical sciences) means a whole situation, the parts of which are dynamically interdependent (the development of one influences the development of the others). More recent studies of personality and perception that contribute to the P-D theory utilize association theory (which stresses the relationships learned in past experience) and theories of personality in culture.[10] Recent studies on cognitive style, perception, cultural influences, and creativity are included.

The P-D theory is presented in the form of a diagram in Figure 1–2. Point One is the overall *readiness* of the child to respond cognitively, both perceptually and conceptually.

Point Two is the *psycho-cultural transaction within the classroom environment.* The child interacts with the values, attitudes, and new

Figure 1–2. The Perception-Delineation
Theory

1. Readiness

2. Psycho-Cultural Transaction within the Classroom

3. Visual-Physical Environment

4. Information Handling

5. Creative Delineation

6. Evaluation of Feedback and Transfer

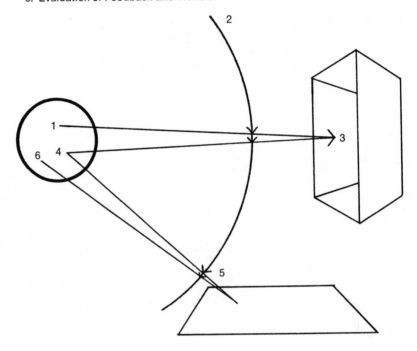

information presented in the classroom environment, which the teacher manipulates to foster more learning.

Point Three is the complex of things from the *visual-physical environment*—the man-made environment, including art, and the natural environment—that the teacher brings into the classroom environment to stimulate children. These include the affective, structural, symbolic, visual, and cultural qualities of the visual arts. Point Three includes those things from each child's past experiences in his home and community environment that he brings to the present through memory.

Point Four is the total of a child's habits of *information handling* and the teacher's efforts both to help him integrate new information into his established system and to expand his habits of information handling so that he can increase his concepts and percepts. His expanding capacities give him more alternatives for creative problem solving and more sensitive reactions to art.

Point Five is the *creative delineation* of his response. Through invention or borrowing of verbal or iconic symbols he communicates his perceptual and conceptual responses to his experience through a designed expression. If his response is to the art forms of others, his delineation involves his own unique analysis of the message, its affective qualities, its structure and its iconic meaning through the ideas he develops about the work of art.

Point Six is *the evaluation of feedback* the child gets from making his own responses that change his readiness and his ability to *transfer* his learnings to the next similar task.

As you read the book you will see how each part fits into this teaching model, showing the range of individual differences a teacher can expect to find as he assesses readiness, attempts to create an encouraging social environment; develops a stimulating physical environment; helps children handle visual information, memories, and impressions in creative, expressive ways; helps them to develop their expressions into art forms or respond to the art of others; and finally helps them to assess what they have learned.

The material in this book is based on the premise that, while scientific means are inadequate for completely explaining people's behavior, they will reveal certain patterns and consistencies from which a theoretical model of human behavior in art can be built that will be useful in teaching. From this study a teacher can develop a working method for dealing with likenesses and differences among students.

Chapter 9 contains an analysis of the theory in detail, using the implications from the research that is reviewed in the intervening chapters. We will study some of the social and psychological foundations of art education, art as it functions to communicate between men and groups of men, environmental experiences that influence children's readiness, and psychological and developmental differences that relate to behavior in art, particularly perception and creativity. Later in the book we will apply the implications from research to the classroom by establishing a basis for developing objectives, recognizing types of readiness for learning, and implementing appropriate learning experiences for primary, intermediate, and middle or junior high school students. The purpose of reviewing the research is to illustrate the variables in classroom practice needed to help children reach identifiable goals in and through art. Research studies do not prescribe how to teach but give the professional teacher more understanding upon which to base teaching decisions. Each school, drawing upon somewhat different segments of the population, and each teacher, with different aptitudes and effective ways of teaching, will need to work independently at the process of teaching, using some of the guidelines and general directives given.

Summary   In Chapter 1 we have set the stage for the whole book. Several positions have been taken which the reader will need to think about and evaluate as he reads. A teacher's attitudes influence the way he presents art to children. Often these attitudes and stereotypes are not recognized by the individual until he is involved in working in and learning about art. For this reason it is important for the teacher to consider the broad arts, not just some segment of art with which he may be familiar. He needs ample opportunity to explore varied media and processes to increase the alternatives he has to present to children.

The student of education is preparing to become a professional teacher who is interested in studying the variables in art and in children to prepare himself to make qualified, considered choices concerning why and how he will help children from varied backgrounds become more responsive to the broad language of art.

Art education is defined as an educational process to help diverse children and young people to (1) develop understanding of the language of art as it functions in society, (2) understand the range of art in the man-made environment, (3) develop the behaviors to produce creatively and respond to art, and (4) critically evaluate art through aesthetic judgment. The teacher's role in art education includes understanding this process, with emphasis on individual differences in readiness for art through the psychological and social study of human behavior in art, and curriculum development that will help diverse children achieve these abilities and understandings. Active problem solving in art needs to begin early and continue through the school years, particularly in the face of the learning from mass media.

Two extreme points of view about children and art are presented to help the teacher begin to identify some of his own assumptions. They center around the continuing controversy as to how much of behavior is based on heredity and how much on environment. One extreme point of view is that heredity is the main force in determining behavior, and that behavior evolves as the child grows old on a genetically determined growth pattern. The other extreme point of view is that heredity has little influence, and behavior can be changed by learning. Two leading biologists concur that it is the interaction of these factors that produces personality traits and behaviors, not one or the other. We suggest that the behaviors in art—perceiving, imagining, image-making, organizing or designing, manipulating, and judging aesthetically—are the result of the interplay of individual genetic potential with influences from the environment.

Extreme points of view about art range from "Art is so subjective it cannot be taught" to "Art is objective, with clearly defined principles that can be analyzed and taught." A middle position is that some of art and art experience can be analyzed and learned and presented so that almost any child can profit from the experience, yet some aspects of art are so subjective that they cannot be adequately analyzed with the present tools of the behavioral sciences.

A sequential yet flexible curriculum needs continual development to help diverse children learn through art.

Finally, a working model or theoretical structure (P-D theory) is presented to enable the teacher to organize the information of cultural and individual differences. Key points in which individuals respond to their experience in the environment and evolve or respond to an art form are used. Point One is a child's overall *readiness* to respond. Point Two is the *psycho-cultural transaction within the classroom environment*. Point Three is the complex of things from the *visual-physical environment* introduced by the teacher to stimulate learning. Point Four is the total of a child's habits of *handling information* and integrating it into what he already knows. Point Five is the *creative delineation* of his response through his own work or in the response to the art of others. Point Six is the *evaluation of feedback and transfer* gained from the art experience and the indication of a change in the child's readiness for the next art activity.

References

[1] June K. McFee, "Society, Art and Education," in *A Seminar in Art Education for Research and Curriculum Development*, ed. Edward L. Mattil (University Park: The Pennsylvania State University, 1966), p. 123.

[2] June K. McFee, "Sequential *vs.* Non-Sequential Art Programs," *Western Arts Association Bulletin*, 47 (April 1963), 10–13.

[3] From "The Role of Genetics in the Evolution of Man, Including His Future Evolution," Sir Gavin de Beer. Copyright © 1962 by Scientific American, Inc. All rights reserved.

[4] Theodosius Dobzhansky, *Mankind Evolving: The Evolution of the Human Species* (New Haven: Yale University Press, 1962), p. 100.

[5] David Krech and Richard S. Crutchfield, *Elements of Psychology* (New York: Alfred A. Knopf, 1958), p. 365.

[6] Manuel Barkan, "Curriculum Problems in Art Education," *A Seminar in Art Education for Research and Curriculum Development,* ed. Edward L. Mattil (University Park: The Pennsylvania State University, 1966), pp. 240–246.

[7] June K. McFee, "Art for the Economically and Socially Deprived," in the *64th National Society for the Study of Education Yearbook,* ed. Reid Hastie, 1965, pp. 135–175.

[8] J. W. Tilton, *An Educational Psychology of Learning* (New York: The Macmillan Company, 1951), p. 7.

[9] Kurt Lewin, *Dynamic Theory of Personality* (New York: McGraw-Hill Book Company, 1935).

[10] Jerome S. Bruner, "Personality Dynamics and the Process of Perceiving," in *Perception: An Approach to Personality,* eds. Robert R. Blake and Glen V. Ramsey (New York: The Ronald Press Company, 1951), pp. 121–147.

2

Art in Society and Culture

Child art is a part of man's art. Children use art as a means of learning about their society, symbolizing and organizing what they learn, and expressing their reactions to it. Art in society is the framework in which the perception-delineation theory operates. It identifies some of the processes of responding to art, the environment that stimulates art, and the ranges of children's individual differences in these processes. Teachers need to understand both the functions of art and the ranges of children's differences in art in order that *content* (the subject of art) and the *teaching method* (the ways used by a teacher to reach individual children) are synthesized in classroom practice.

Part of the process of education is to prepare children not only to learn through art but to deal with the complexities of art in adult life. It is then necessary for children as well as teachers to understand art in its broad communication functions. The purpose of this chapter is to help teachers understand more about art in society and to transmit their understanding to children.

Art is one of man's major language systems, a means of communication—of sharing his experience with others. In Figure 2–1 we can recognize symbols from different cultures in history. Each gives us information about the culture. Art can communicate qualities of experience that cannot be put into words. By sharing experience, through verbal language and through art, man develops and extends social groups and culture patterns. His records of what he does give man reference points from which to reflect and further develop and refine his experience. Communication through art is one important means of cultural development. It takes place as information is passed from one generation to another and as children learn from art how to respond to life patterns within their own culture. Their own individual expressions in art help them organize the symbols they are learning and give them bases for further learning. The amount and degree of symbolic creativity allowed children depends upon the values of the cultural group they live in.

What Is Culture?   Culture consists of the learned, shared, and socially transmitted forms of adaptation of human beings to the environment, which includes the habitat, other people, and their creations. A culture is the pattern of living among a given group of people. The pattern is developed by the group's shared values, beliefs, and opinions on acceptable behavior. Within the pattern people have roles to play and work to do. The culture in part directs how children are trained and how beliefs and values are maintained from generation to generation. Culture includes education, religion, science, art, folklore, and social organization.

The term *culture* is used some of the time to describe a very large society such as "Western culture." Among the nations of Western

**Figure 2–1. Transmitting Ideas through
Art Forms**

Europe and the Americas, and the peoples from these areas in other
parts of the world, there are traditionally shared beliefs and values

that differentiate them as a whole from other large cultural groups. *Culture* is also used to describe small, somewhat isolated or homogeneous groups where the similarities among the people are more evident. In talking about American culture, we refer to the *core* culture, meaning those values and beliefs shared in some degree by a majority of Americans. Different regional, ethnic, and religious groups within the whole are called subcultures. These people share the core culture in part but also have a nucleus of values and beliefs and ways of behaving that sets them apart.

Differences in values and beliefs are expressed through language and art forms such as dress, architecture, and decoration. Without verbal and visual means of sharing these ideas, cultures could not evolve. While there are nonliterate cultures (those without written language), there are no cultures that are without art forms, however primitive, for communicating ideas.[1]

Art is involved in most of the processes of transmitting what man has learned of his adaptation to his environment. The purpose of studying art in different cultures is to give teachers a somewhat broader basis for understanding how art functions in society generally, and how its functions are varied in meaning and style in any one specific society that has an identifiable culture pattern of values and attitudes. A society is a group of people who are organized for some political or social purpose. They do not necessarily have the same culture. A nation may contain several cultures and subcultures.

Within a single classroom there may be children who represent varied subcultures, who have been taught differing values, beliefs, and models of acceptable behavior. Though some people assume that art is a universal language, there are differences in symbolic meaning and style that do not communicate the same things to people who do not understand the culture in which the art was produced.

The rural economically deprived child who moves to the city may find little meaning in the beautifully illustrated children's book designed to appeal to metropolitan upper-middle-class children. The Kachina doll may appeal to many children with different cultural backgrounds, but only to a Hopi child will it go beyond the "little human" or doll symbol and represent an ancestral spirit.

What Is Art?

Art, like man, is a complex changing phenomenon, difficult to define. Anthropologist Melville Herskovits says art can be thought of as "any embellishment of ordinary living that is achieved with competence and has describable form."[2] The describable form may be very primitive or very complex, depending on the art tradition of the culture and the ability of the individual artist.

Thomas Munro has made a comprehensive study of art, combining the development of philosophical and anthropological concepts with theories in art history. Looking for trends and patterns, he summarizes art as " . . . man-made instruments for producing psychological effects on observers, individually and socially. These include perceptual, imaginative, rational, cognitive and emotional responses; also the formation of attitudes towards certain kinds of action and belief. Works of art are so used and always have been, even when not consciously intended."[3] Munro sees art as always expressing "something characteristic of its age in general. It also expresses only part of its age."[4] This means that art grows out of its past culture but has qualities of the present.

Using Munro's functional definition of art helps us see that art is a strong form of communication that operates as values, attitudes, and beliefs are shared and carried from generation to generation, from artist to artist, and from one cultural group to another.

Bohannon, an anthropologist, writes that " . . . art is a . . . mode of analyzing cultural images for better communication and more subtle appreciation. Language and art . . . are methods of communication and cultural statement—of capturing the image and transmitting it . . . of symbolizing the world of things and of sensations that create the image behind communication, social life and all culture. Symbolizing is the basic capacity of mankind that makes all culture and progress possible."[5]

Language (or art) is the mold into which perception must be fitted if it is to be communicated. Language is important for the individual in becoming Homo "sapiens"; learning to communicate one's perceptions is part of the growing up process.[6] Art is one of the primary means through which groups of people can examine their own images.

Julian Huxley links art with science and religion as one of the three main fields of man's creativity: "The essential function of the arts is one of bearing witness to the wonder and variety of the world and of human experience . . . it is to create vehicles for the effective expression and communication of complex emotionally charged experiences, which are of value in the process of human fulfilment."[7]

The following working definitions of art and child art may be useful:

Art   Art is that form of human behavior by which man purposefully interprets and enhances the quality or essence of experience through the things he produces — from the simple enhancement of a tool to the expression of his deepest feelings and profound projections in painting, sculpture, architecture, and city planning. Art is one of man's basic means of communication — sharing the essence of experience from man to man and from generation to generation.

Man's art enhances his experience, and his experience enhances his art. This reciprocal action may lead to aesthetic and cultural growth.

Child Art   The child uses art to communicate (to himself and to others) his interpretation of his interaction with his environment. His art enhances his experience, giving him opportunity to develop and relate his growing concepts and ideas. His experience enhances his art, giving him new ideas to express. When a child responds to and through art he uses his abilities to remember, to visualize, to symbolize, to see likenesses and differences. The use of the language of art is a major avenue for learning—a key tool in education.

Sources of Taste

Man's like-dislike behavior in response to art forms ranges from unqualified acceptance or rejection to the most complex analysis of art forms with many different criteria. Judgment may be made in terms of the object's (1) place in art history, (2) uniqueness or creative quality, (3) communicative function in society, (4) emotion-arousing impact, (5) design or compositon, or (6) technical quality.

Taste, with which a person makes judgments, develops within a given personality growing in a given cultural milieu. The individual's response is related to the personality structure he has developed, affected usually by the values and attitudes of his group. The commonly heard statement, "I know what I like, but I don't know why I like it," usually means that the individual has learned his preferences unconsciously. A person may prefer a ranch to a contemporary functional house without being able to analyze all the factors that determine his preference.

In addition to forming tastes uncritically, we often listen to other people's statements of what should be liked or disliked and accept their prejudices without questioning them. For example, an art education book published before 1930 made this statement: "The use of blue and green together is not good." No reason was given. The principle was only an expression of an attitude that was current at that time. Now blue and green are used together in profusion. They have always existed side by side in nature. If a teacher accepts the book's statement as true, he might limit the alternatives that he would provide children about blue and green. Lacking confidence in the field of art and assuming that such choices could be clearly "good" or "bad" taste, he tries to teach what he considers to be right.

The teacher is a "taste-maker." He reinforces or opposes the child's acquired attitudes or, by encouraging him to explore the dimensions of design and color, helps him to develop confidence in his own ability to make judgments. The child expands his aesthetic awareness by observing the taste of other people. The like-dislike behavior of individuals of the same local ethnic, religious, social, or economic status will probably be more alike than those of other backgrounds.

Your tastes are your "own." An exploration of the tastes of your contemporaries will show you which attitudes you have adopted without examination and which have grown as a result of your own observation. The darkened area in Figure 2–2 symbolizes an individual's taste. As a member of a national culture, he shares some kinds of experiences with all his fellow citizens. Certain experiences will be of importance only to a smaller group—social, economic, or other. The individual is more or less strongly influenced by training and experience within the subgroups of which he is a part. As part of a socioeconomic class he shares the tastes and values of that group. He also may belong to an ethnic or religious subculture that is varied from the whole class. As an individual growing up he has interacted somewhat differently from others with his subgroup or region, and so his experience has been unique.

The fine arts have sometimes been defined as expressive arts, and crafts or applied arts have been defined as enhancing arts. This dichotomy is losing its meaning. Expressive art products, such as paintings, sculptures, and prints, are not necessarily "finer" than ceramics, jewelry, and fabrics. Each individual product needs evaluation in terms of its relationships to other art forms with similar forms and functions. Many art objects are both expressive and enhancing; certainly some are higher in these qualities than are others.

Functions of Art in Culture   Though art products vary widely in style and content, their communicative functions have similarities. Gerbrands, a Dutch anthropologist, has made a detailed review of the functions of art in culture, of communicating the values, attitudes, and belief systems that evolve out

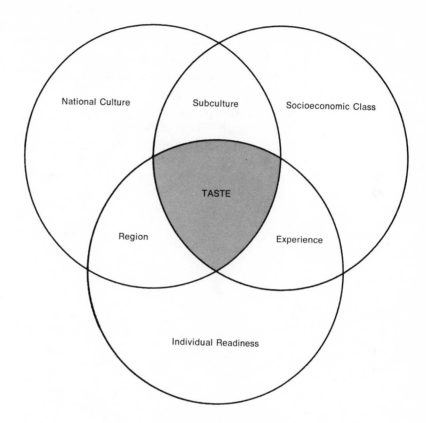

Figure 2–2. Sources of Taste

National Culture

Subculture

Socioeconomic Class

TASTE

Region

Experience

Individual Readiness

of the interactions of persons within a society. He ranks the functions according to the frequency of their appearance among world cultures.[8] First is the expression of the "supernatural" in visible and tangible forms; second is the identification of different kinds of social status; third is the maintenance of political institutions; fourth is a structure for play. We will examine these functions as identified by other anthropologists.

First is religion, or expressions of concepts of the supernatural.[9] In many cases the object of worship, a mask or carving, is considered to be animate—the thing worshiped, not just a symbol of it. The object's functions are to maintain the sense of reality shared by the members of the culture, to teach the religion to the young, and to hand it down from generation to generation.

Sand paintings show in visible form the Navahos' concepts of the nature of the world, its beginnings, the origins of man, and the whole complex myth system for maintaining their concepts of what is good and what is not good. The paintings are used as part of their ritual to help communicate the structure of their belief. In the healing ceremony, the

Figure 2–3. Navaho Sand Painting

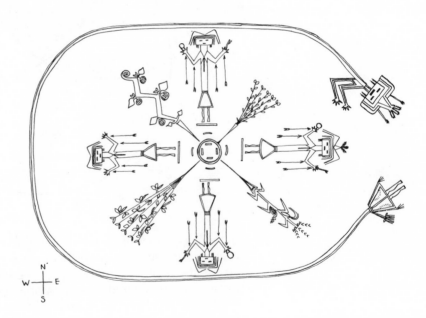

medicine man uses the sand painting to create a feeling of direct contact between the patient and the "holy people." Not only does the patient see the visual symbol, he sits on it and is rubbed with sand from it. The ritual is a dramatic art form, the sand painting a visual art form for maintaining their concepts of reality and training their children.[10]

Much art of the Romanesque, Gothic, and Renaissance periods was created to communicate religious concepts to the nonreading population. In our society a wide range of religious artistic symbolism exists. The churches that spread out from the Puritan tradition have had a standard of simple beauty. Often a single unadorned spire indicates a place of worship. By contrast, religions that use elaborate ceremonies have ornate churches with stained glass windows and altars rich in symbolic communication. With the advent of modern architecture the symbols of religious art have retained their meaning but changed their forms. All religions attempt to explain the nature of the universe — of reality.

The Kwoma people of New Guinea worship a *Marsalai,* a carved wooden idol. The artist who can make one has a position of prominence. The idol is used in secret societies, which in turn give continuity to the social organization of the group, give boys a means of achieving adult status through membership in the group, and separate the roles of the sexes. The men know that the Marsalai is only an idol, but women and small children live in fear of its power, though they never see it. The idol symbolizes an evil power that all the Kwoma fear. The fear holds the group together as a workable society. The abstract power becomes objective reality as an art form.[11]

These examples show how mankind uses art forms to give more meaning to interpretations of the nature of the universe. Language symbols alone are not enough, even for highly literate people. Nonliterate symbols are not stopped by the advent of written language. Physical scientists use models to illustrate their interpretations of the nature of the universe. The model is an ordered symbol used to communicate a structure of relationships representing time, space, size, and interaction in dimensions the layman can comprehend. Science and religion both use similar processes for communicating abstract concepts into symbols that can be looked at, manipulated, and touched.

The *second* most common function of art is to serve as an aid in identifying social position. The religious element may or not be present, but art objects can identify a priest or a medicine man. An art form may also identify a chieftain, a married woman, an unmarried woman, a believer, or a member of a clan, caste, or regional group. The art form may be a style of dress, jewelry, or body decoration with paint, feathers, furs, or fabrics. Status is identified both through variation in the art form and the symbolic status value of the material (see Figure 2–4). Women in Western civilization tend to prefer diamonds to shells

Figure 2–4. Social Position through Symbols of Dress

to communicate their intended marriage, but in nonliterate societies where diamonds have no known value shells may be much preferred.

The *third* function of art is maintenance of *political* stability. An art form may symbolize authority, show the boundaries of acceptable behavior, illustrate the results of law breaking, or induce fear of the supernatural to control behavior. In countries where the state dictates much of policy or a ruling class controls the art forms, art is used to teach doctrine, and the individual artist pursuing his own directions is suppressed.

The *fourth* function of art is play. Art contributes to entertainment and recreation. A costume may identify a play activity such as folk dancing, skiing, or swimming. Art may enhance objects used for play such as chessmen, playing cards, dolls, and toys. Satire, humor, and whimsy are found in art expression of the finest quality. Cartooning and illustration range from crude to elegant.

Identification of what is work and what is play is nebulous. A child may playfully manipulate paint for the fun of watching what happens; at another time the same child may use the same medium to communicate seriously an experience he has had. Is he playing or is he working?

In all its functions art provides aesthetic pleasure; its organization of forms elicits a sense of beauty. Art *enhances the experience of people* responding to or using the art form whether for religion, identification of social status, political maintenance, or play.

All of these functions help us learn about a culture through its art forms as well as through its written or spoken language. We use art to communicate who we are and how our culture works. So do all groups of people. We can then add a fifth main function of art in culture. When we look at all the functions of art in culture we find that art has an overall communication function. It is a form of cultural language.

Have you ever wondered why we decorate money? Why do we go to the great cost of minting coins and engraving currency? Apparently

Figure 2–5. Art as Enhancing Value of Money

decoration gives added meaning. From ancient times to the present we have enhanced the value of money by decorating it with symbolic forms (Figure 2–5). We use images of our cultural heroes, our mottoes of faith, and our national seal to authenticate the worth of a coin. The decoration of baskets, pottery, tools, and implements indicates a need of mankind to enhance the appearance of things he uses. Where the symbols used are part of the folklore, the enhancement has direct value in maintaining the culture.

The spoon designs in Figure 2–6 have their roots in different periods. In our culture, where we have borrowed the symbols and styles of so

Figure 2–6. Spoons Representing Many Cultures

many periods, the ideas in our ornamentation have often lost their original meanings. We have collected from all over the world, mixing and adapting decorations as fashions changed, at the same time inventing our own forms, as any culture does.

As forms of communication and historic record, the arts help maintain culture. Even after long periods of time we can learn much about another people by studying its art forms. The Egypt of the Pharaohs seems remote in space and time, yet we can see and touch the tools, the buildings, the jewelry, the calendars, the mummies, and the religious artifacts that have been so well preserved. Many museums throughout the world have objects from this ancient culture. We can achieve empathic understanding of those remote people by studying the ways they enhanced their lives. We share in some degree the quality of their experience as we respond to their art forms.

If we can do this with groups remote in time and space, think of the cultural impact of learning and experiencing from one generation to another in the same culture. A small child walking down a city street learns visually about his culture. The kinds of buildings mean different kinds of functions; libraries, post offices, and court houses are impressive in size and in importance to his life. What people wear tells what they are—policemen, big boys, dignified people, undignified people, soldiers, sailors, businessmen in tailored suits, and grocers in aprons. The three-year-old boy who said "Ladies wear dresses and mothers wear jeans" was observing that costume defines occupation and role. Displays in windows, billboards, signs on telephone poles, theater marquees, all teach him about his culture.

The homes, the implements, and the decorations children see are constructed in conformity with the social organization, the beliefs and traditions of their groups. Clothing and body decoration indicate status. The manner of dress, nearly always differing between the sexes, may change from childhood to adulthood. Wearing "make-up" is a sign of "growing up." In another culture, body painting of another kind, or tattooing, may indicate an adult role—social position, occupation (warrior or medicine man), or tribal affiliation.

Enculturation through Art

A child is learning about the cultural values of his society from his earliest years. The symbols of what is considered to be important, the interpretation of reality, the status and roles of people and institutions, and the symbols of the political system are learned through observing adults' attitudes and behaviors toward them. The art forms used in play are particularly important in the enculturation process, the way a child learns about his own culture.

A child is prepared for adult roles through the things he is given to play with. In some societies sex role learning is introduced early through differences in toys considered appropriate for boys or girls. Adults in other societies do not differentiate children's toys until middle or late childhood. Toys that imitate adult roles are found in many societies. The form and symbolism used to make or decorate them is often the key to the relationship, as the toys are limited in the degree they actually work.

Most of this learning is vicarious. The child is not aware of his learning, and so he is not in a position to evaluate what he learns or to realize that art is a language that he is responding to. These functions can be made more explicit in art education. By studying the functions of art in other cultures and the ways other children learn about their cultures, pupils in a classroom can become more aware of the things they are learning through art about their own culture.

One function, which educators and artists may consider important, has been left out of this study of art in culture. That is the role of the individual in society and the ways he uses art as a means of interpretation of or reaction to the culture of his society. Most of the study of art in society does not deal with the individual, the ways the child creates his own synthesis or reactions to what he is experiencing. By learning to compare the varied work of artists in the same culture, children can learn more of the role of the individual and the possibilities he has to use art to communicate. Wayne Dennis, a psychologist who has worked closely with cultural anthropologists, has studied children's art products and finds that they are good resource materials for studying the values of a culture.[12] By comparing the drawings of children from one society with one culture to those of children from another society with another culture, he has identified differences in values that are illustrated by differences in symbols and organization of drawings. Comparisons have also been made in studies of the differences in drawings among children from different cultures within the same society.

Functions of Art in Contemporary Society

Gerbrands made his study mainly in nontechnical societies. During this period of mass media, advertising, packaging of products, and intensive growth of cities, some new adaptations of the functions of art are developing.

Enculturation of Children Today

The children in today's world are bombarded with art forms that are used to increase the exchange of goods and services. All the cultural functions of art are brought into play. On television an artificial portrayal of the "good life" is given the appearance of *reality*. Advertisements present the assumption that everyone wants the same quality of life and that particular products will most quickly and pleasurably provide the feeling or essence of that life. Actors perform roles appropriate to the "good life," display objects used to achieve status, take part in acceptable forms of play. Commercial art is used to enhance the quality of experience by suggestion.

Through the design of packaging, coffee becomes the brew of kings, hair spray the magic potion to youth and beauty, and a package of detergent a man who helps in a lady's kitchen. Television sets the pace and suggests the values, which are reinforced on the shelves of supermarkets. Never before in the history of mankind have so few people, the selectors and dispensers of mass media, communicated to so many.

Before the advent of mass advertising, the development and maintenance of cultural values and attitudes were done by some kind of social leadership through government or religion. The main function of education was to teach values to the coming generations. In an ideal democracy the values of government would reflect the values of the people, as those values evolve through the democratic process. Ideal education contributes to the development and maintenance of values, representing the general agreement achieved by the interaction of all segments of society. One such value is freedom of choice for the individual. The role of the school in relation to this value is to enable children to explore the range of alternatives in choice making and to analyze qualitatively the consequences of possible decisions.

Now another form of cultural leadership has emerged to influence values and taste. The transmission of cultural reality becomes less the domain of government, religious systems, and the teachings of elder members of the community. Culture is dispersed by directors of mass media programming and advertising. They select content for the most extensive and penetrating communications known to man; they select values they assume will offend the smallest numbers and entice the largest numbers of people. A national mediocrity ensues as they educate by indoctrinating rather than by encouraging critical thinking; they teach by contributing to conformity rather than by encouraging critical evaluation of many alternatives, so necessary to a dynamic society. Never before have all segments of the population, all age groups, been exposed to one large general source of information. The enculturation of children into the dominant society begins when they are infants, on the same bill of fare as adults.

Contributors to the Visual Environment

Among other contributors to the national scene are building contractors and private citizens who may or may not be concerned with their contribution to the community, now or in the future. The long tradition of the rights of property seems to carry with it the assumption that people do not see beyond property lines, so that if a person wishes to create ugliness or monotony it is his right as long as he stays on his own land. As populations grow and the ugliness of cities becomes more intolerable, changes in cultural values will have to take place. Education is needed to help people take responsibility for their contributions.

While some builders use art in a superficial manner, other more humanistic architects, designers, planners, and landscape architects are attempting to bring order and fundamental meaning to the environment through the things they provide the public. Renewal and rebuilding are done with the range of life patterns and values of the people in mind. The quality of the experience of people who walk down a city street, turn a corner to view a new vista, or sit waiting for a bus is considered. The need for renewal and recreation is considered in the design of a few motels and resort areas.

On a smaller scale, some package designers conceive of the product as it functions in someone's home rather than how it will get a consumer's attention in a store. Some advertisers are concerned about their tremendous responsibility as they transmit values and attitudes to children and youth. Though there are significant beginnings in these directions, responsible commercial designers are a minority in the face of all the building and advertising that is going on.

Ethnic and Regional Contributions

In a modern cosmopolitan society like the United States, there are many ethnic, economic, and regional subcultures, and the range of art forms representing these different and overlapping cultures is extensive. The art work of people from many cultures contributes to the visual environment, with many different forms of ethnic symbolism giving richness and color. In architecture Greco-Roman and Gothic styles have come to us through the dominant core of American history and culture. The Spanish colonial influence is found in buildings in the Southwest, and has been borrowed in other parts of the country. Native materials were used by the American Southwest Indians long before the Spanish arrived, and adobe has been adapted to present-day use. Wherever Orientals have grouped together within larger cities, their own symbolism, religious artifacts, and social groups have developed and are still evident. The Scandinavian influence in what is called Sawn art or Carpenter's art flourished in the late nineteenth and early twentieth century in America. Many communities have a rich heritage of Scandinavian homes where a great deal of individuality has been expressed within a general style. America's own ranch house, which grew out of the simplest architectural form, still symbolizes the independent landowner to many people. Dutch and German influences in Pennsylvania, French influence in Louisiana, all contribute to the architectural diversity in the American environment.

One of the problems of the city today is confusion about symbols. The clusters of immigrants of the late nineteenth century could not change the architecture they found in the United States, but they soon produced symbols through the objects they sold in their community stores, in the ways the objects were displayed, and in the artifacts in their churches and homes that gave them a sense of identity. For many years homogeneous groups maintained environments in which ethnic symbols had meaning. Now many people have left the areas of their origins and have been absorbed into middle-class society, leaving their symbols behind. The present occupants of many of these older areas do not have the feeling of identity with the places that earlier residents had. The continued decay of old buildings and the lack of a distinct visual symbolic system on the part of the new inhabitants (except that which is given them by mass media) contribute to the decline of ethnically distinctive areas. In many cities such areas become slums.

We do not know whether the immigrants of the nineteenth century would have developed the sense of community they did if in every home there had been a television set telling them what symbols they had to have to live "the good life."

If we look at our cities and smaller communities from the standpoint of visual impact irrespective of the cultural history, we get a picture of what we in our haste for expansion, for progress, have produced. For some Americans the art forms of their community are decaying buildings, dark dreary streets, refuse. For others the art forms are gas stations, telephone poles, flashing neon signs, and billboards. Some Americans observe the harmonizing effect of shade trees in summer and the stark reality of unpainted disrepair of homes and bare trees in winter. Others live in monotonous but clean and neat housing areas. Some have inherited carefully planned villages whose quality may or may not be maintained. In areas of natural splendor the man-made hamlets are sometimes clusters of ugliness, as if the assumption were made that people look at nature, not the town.

**The Expressive Arts
in Contemporary Society**

Rapid communication affects painting and sculpture. The most exploratory artists search for "reality" in new dimensions of expression. A new trend or form of experimentation takes hold in art centers like New York or Los Angeles and it is quickly amplified and extended to other regions. Some university art departments are becoming regional art centers, bringing in artists-in-residence, and sending their own staff to other centers to increase the stimulation of creativity. In the artists' search for reality, styles change rapidly: "op" artists explored man's reactions to experimental perceptions; "pop" artists forced us to look at the ingredients of our society—hot dogs, soft-drink bottles, and comic strips; formal abstractionists and abstract expressionists continue their experiments, while other artists return to stark realism or to the basic structure of things as they construct abstractions of underlying parts of things. In psychedelic art the artist tries to reproduce the immediate reality of artificially induced states of consciousness. Kinetic art consists of constructions based on inner muscular feeling.

The speed of interchange of ideas does not change the function of the artist's search for reality, but interchange appears to accelerate changes in style and focus. In small cohesive societies and in large authoritarian systems the artist's function is to express the values of the controlling group. One of the great values of the individual exploratory artist in a democracy is that his work, as a form of free speech, provides yet another mirror for society to reflect upon itself. At the same time artists are not entirely separate from some segments of the culture of a complex society, and the art of a given period does give clues to the general values upheld.

The Subcultures of Artists

Among people who are concerned with some specific phase of the visual arts, there are subcultures and subgroups. All painters, all designers do not have the same values. It is important for the classroom teacher to recognize these groups so that he can understand the works that they produce and evaluate them in terms of the artists' value systems. Then a teacher can better evaluate his own goals for children in art. An artist may be working toward the values of some subculture among art groups and ignoring others, or toward some subculture of the society itself, which may or may not be appropriate for school children.

In almost every region there are groups of painters who organize themselves to preserve the naturalism of their area against the inroads of "modern" art on the one side and the art of products and commerce on the other. There are also weavers, potters, and other craftsmen who preserve regional traditions in fabrics, ceramics, glass, and leather goods. Examples are found in Appalachia, New England, and the Southwest. In many areas traditional crafts of needlework in varying degrees of quality are displayed at county and state fairs.

Craftsmen throughout the country who are experimental and creative in their work are developing national as well as regional qualities in their art. National and regional craft shows set new standards of excellence of design and establish new bases for uses of tools and materials. The craftsmen are as interested in the expressive impact and the design quality of their work as they are in the craftsmanship.

"Sunday painters" or nonprofessional artists have shows throughout the country. Sidewalk exhibits, art festivals, and community exhibits are organized for people who use their leisure for work in art. The work that is displayed ranges from copies of other paintings or photographs to work that is accepted in juried exhibitions.

The professional artist may work alone or he may be a member of a group of artists. He may be a teacher in an art school, a public school, a college, or a university art department. He may be working within some "school" of art—that is, a style of art or a philosophical framework. The quality of work among professionals varies widely. Though one school of art may be most popular at any given time, excellent artists within different schools maintain recognition in the art world.

There are many artists in industry — designers of fabrics, furniture, automobiles, appliances, printed matter, packages, products, interiors, costumes, and stage sets. In fields in which a few manufacturers control production the range of design is not great — particularly in automobiles and appliances. In furniture, fabrics, and publishing the range of quality is very great, from furniture built for quick turnover to furniture designed for gracious use and durability, from fabrics designed to catch attention to those that enhance the use of clothing or interiors, from pulp magazines to masterworks in graphic design. Awards for excellent design, exhibits of outstanding commercially produced products, and some excellent schools of design in art schools and universities are pace-setters. The great need is for a general public that is aware of the functions of design and that has developed some degree of discrimination.

Professional architects, landscape architects, urban designers, and city planners are found throughout the country. Some are conservative, preserving traditions; others break with tradition to establish new directions for environmental design. Still others try to achieve an environment that respects both the past and its contribution to the quality of the present and the accelerating demands for change. Designers must plan aesthetically and realistically for the burgeoning population and for the technical change that is upon us. They must create attractive spaces for the identifiable environment of the individual and small group as well as for the mass of society as people move within and without the structure of cities, traffic patterns, and rural areas.

The Need for Perceptual Education

One reason the language of art may be so suddenly complex for many students is that most of us were educated in terms of concepts. Few of us have learned adequately to look visually and, further, to look at art in its broad forms as language communicated through its visual qualities. We have learned what things are, how they relate to other things, and we have learned enough visual characteristics to identify objects. We have not been exposed to the study of the visual world as language, with its different cultural meanings, nor have we been taught its grammar, which is design. We have seen art as something apart from life rather than as an integral part of it. But even though we may not have been critically aware of art's functions, our visual environment has influenced the quality of our experience and in many cases our decisions. The artist and the designer are sometimes not recognized for their influence on the environment, nor are their services always utilized, because the public often has no conscious concern for the effect of the environment on the quality of existence. The rather sudden national anxiety about the visual quality of our cities and about our refuse-strewn natural environment has apparently risen because the situation has become so bad that it can no longer be ignored. Our perceptual world is now becoming part of our conceptual world.

A Clarification of Terms
A percept is an impression of an object obtained by use of the senses. A concept is an idea about an object, generalized from previous experiences with the object. To illustrate, let us assume that we are observing a late model automobile. If we depend upon concepts mainly we look for cues to identify the maker, the model, the color, and the key symbols the designer has used to identify this model and make from other models and makes of cars. If we have been trained to respond to the percepts presented by the automobile we see all the changing contours as we walk around the machine. We see many variations in the color as reflections, and lights change the visual image of the original pigment color that was sprayed on. What shape is a car? The more concept-oriented person tends to have a generalized stereotype of the form. The person who is visually sensitive realizes that there are as many different visual images of the form as there are positions from which he can view the automobile. In other words, perceptual reality and conceptual reality are not necessarily the same — but they can be combined when the concepts a person has cover all the variations in visual reality as well.

Our concepts come from what we know about things, our percepts from our ongoing scanning of things. Some persons observe within the limits of their concepts; others are open to new percepts which, by giving them more information, require them to increase the richness and variety of their concepts. As individuals attend to more visual information they develop more concepts for sorting and organizing the visual information. There is considerable evidence that learning is required in seeing, so one of the responsibilities of the teacher is helping children acquire more visual awarenesses and concepts with which to think about what they see.

Implications for Teachers

Where is the elementary school teacher to find himself in this vast world of art? Teachers usually have extensive backgrounds in the other language systems, beginning with their own training as children. The language of vision has not been stressed in schools, art has not been seen as a major form of communication at the same time that art forms have been overwhelmingly introduced into the mainstream of modern civilization. The discrepancy is between the accelerating intensity of the influences of visual communication, on the one hand, and the lack of ability to analyze and criticize either the message or the form through which it is projected, on the other.

A key purpose of this book is to help teachers bridge this gap, to help them see the so-called fine arts and children's art in the broader context of communication and culture. A second purpose is to help teachers to understand the grammar of vision, so that they may help children become more visually literate and sensitively aware, both to what is projected to them through the broad arts and to their own creations and contributions to society. To help children, teachers need more understanding of human behavior in art, design in art products, and factors that influence choices. A third purpose is to help teachers understand the ranges of readiness that children in different socio-economic, ethnic, and geographic areas may have for perceiving, for becoming aware, for solving problems creatively, and for expressing their ideas.

Summary

Art is a major language system of society. Through art man can share his experience with other men, and groups of men can communicate their shared values and attitudes, their culture, with other groups of men.

A society can be made up of one culture or many, with each subculture developing art forms that are somewhat different from the others. Some societies have a core culture that is shared in part by the subcultures of the society.

There are many definitions of art, but most include the points that art interprets, enhances, and communicates man's experience. The child uses art to interpret and enhance his experience to himself and others. It gives him a tool for symbolizing and learning.

An individual's taste or aesthetic judgment is learned in his national culture, his own particular subculture, and his unique experience as a developing individual.

The major functions of art in society are to maintain the sense of reality of the culture's belief system, to identify the status and roles of people and institutions, to maintain political institutions, and to enhance and structure aspects of play.

Children learn about their culture through art, and by being exposed to adults' reactions to art forms. Art is also a way for them to respond individually to society.

In today's society, much of children's learning about culture comes to them screened through television and other mass media; the transmission of cultural values to the young has shifted more to media specialists, rather than the family and other social organizations. A sameness about culture is learned.

Our cities and towns reflect the various cultures that have contributed art forms to our society. But neglect and decay are turning our cities into dark and dreary places. Styles in the expressive arts change with great rapidity as society changes. Artists have many roles in this society, but their contributions are not generally recognized.

All of these forces in society point up the need for perceptual as well as conceptual literacy and emphasize the challenge to teachers to help children cope with the complexity of change in society through understanding the functions of art.

References

[1] Ralph L. Beals and Harry Hoijer, *An Introduction to Anthropology* (New York: The Macmillan Company, 1953), p. 538.

[2] Melville Herskovits, *Cultural Anthropology* (New York: Alfred A. Knopf, Inc., 1955), p. 235. Reprinted by permission.

[3] Thomas Munro, *Evolution in the Arts* (Cleveland: The Cleveland Museum of Art, 1963), p. 419.

[4] *Ibid.,* p. 492.

[5] From Chapter Three, from SOCIAL ANTHROPOLOGY by Paul Bohannon. Copyright © 1963 by Holt, Rinehart and Winston, Inc. Reprinted by permission of Holt, Rinehart and Winston, Inc.

[6] *Ibid.,* p. 48.

[7] Julian Huxley, "Evolutionary Humanism," in *New Bottles for Old Wine* (London: Chatto and Windus, 1957), p. 306.

[8] A. A. Gerbrands, *Art as an Element of Culture, Especially in Negro Africa* (Leiden: E. J. Brill, 1957).

[9] *Ibid.,* p. 131.

[10] Clyde Kluckholn and Dorothea Leighton, *The Navaho* (Cambridge: Harvard University Press, 1956), p. 151.

[11] John W. M. Whiting, *Becoming a Kwoma* (New Haven: Yale University Press, 1941), pp. 215–216.

[12] Wayne Dennis, *Group Values through Children's Drawings* (New York: John Wiley & Sons, Inc., 1966), p. 210.

3

Perceptual Readiness for Art

The range of art is broad, and basic assumptions about the nature of art and the nature of children differ widely. Cultural communication takes place in all environments. Yet not all members of a society see their environment in the same way.

Several different kinds of behaviors are related to the way a person responds to his surroundings. A sorting process is basic to response—a sorting of the visual qualities of things by size, shape, color, and texture. A second type of behavior is the integration of the visual qualities with the cultural values one has learned. A third type of behavior is the process of being consciously aware of what one is seeing. These behaviors are influenced by personality traits, cognitive habits, and attitudes.

Response takes place in a present environment. The behaviors of responding precede and interact with the process of drawing or painting symbols and of responding to the art of others.

In this chapter we will explore the perceptual processes with which we sort visual information and some of the cultural factors that influence what is attended to and how it is interpreted. In the following chapters we will study other environmental influences on perception and personality traits and habits that also influence the ways children and adults interact with their environment.

Sorting Visual Information

Every time we respond to even the simplest visual object we use only part of the information reflected upon the retinas of our eyes. Select an object from your desk or table, pick it up and put it out of your sight. Now make a list of the attributes that you noticed while selecting, picking up, and handling the object, or that you remember from past experience with it. Draw a picture of the object. Now bring the object back into view and look at it again. You may find that you missed many details such as the variation of the same color in different lights, variation of texture, and proportion of form. Move the object around and look at its form from different angles. Your drawing was probably a *one-position*, stereotyped symbol of the object. You may have learned a stereotyped symbol in the past or possibly you initiated one for this task.

This simple exercise illustrates the complexity of even the simplest task. The first two acts, choosing and drawing the object, depended upon your *readiness* to see and draw; the third act, bringing the object back and looking again for details, was the beginning of a learning process in which you attended to more details and analyzed more relations between you and the object in space and light.

Much of formal education has been focused on the recognition of objects to sort them into concepts, rather than analysis of their visual qualities. As a result many people grow up without learning to see beyond conceptual recognition. They classify an object according to their past categorizing experience. If an individual has had rich visual experience, then his processes of recognition will bring many visual aspects into memory. If not, his experience may be limited and stereotyped. He will miss much of the beauty around him and be more likely to ignore the ugliness he and others may create.

Teachers need to be aware of perceptual processes—particularly to help children respond to the richness of their visual environment and to increase the depth and variety of their own expressiveness. Furthermore, without this awareness children are ill prepared to evaluate and contribute to their homes and communities.

Attneave has introduced some of the concepts of information theory into an analysis of the perceptual process. He deals with perception as an *information-handling process*. Much more visual information is available than we use. Attneave refers to Polyak's estimate that the retina contains not less than 4 million cones, saying, "At any given instant each of these cones may be in either of two states: firing or not firing."[1] The possible kinds of different configurations of visual information that the eyes can handle would reach $2^{4,000,000}$. Attneave has identified three major processes with which we sort out, reject, or use and classify all this information.

1. We Classify Similar Things as Units. We do not respond cognitively to all the leaves of a tree or to all the blades in a plot of grass. We deal with green trees and grass unless we purposefully look for small details and variations.

2. We Classify the Random by Averages. When we drive in fast-moving traffic, we do not have time to recognize cognitively each kind of car we pass even though our eyes may be receiving enough visual information for us to do so. We have to average out the visual qualities of all the cars in terms of their movements in relation to our own car. We select and use those averages of movement and direction that are necessary to us in the act of driving, and we constantly change our behavior on the basis of these averages.

3. We Classify According to Wholes or Completions.   If we see part of a face we tend to envisage the rest of the face; we see part of a circle as belonging to the whole circle.

Arnheim proposes that we see in wholes most of the time, noting only as much detail as is necessary or as our learning and experience have prepared us to see.[2] We may see something moving at a distance and classify it first as a small animal; getting closer we see enough detail to know that it is a dog. Looking longer we get enough visual cues to see what kind of dog it is, and finally we see that it is our dog. Certain visual cues are enough to help us decide whether it is ours or not without our having to see all the visual details. In other words, we do not use more visual cues than necessary to decide how we should behave in terms of the thing at which we are looking.

Research findings related to the Gestalt theories are at present in a state of flux. Evidence suggests that the effects of past experience and perceptual training make some differences in how a person sees. When past associations or learned relations do not interfere with perception, a person uses *proximity, similarity,* and *continuity* to make order out of chaotic visual information.

The following figures based on Gestalt psychology show how this relating is done.[3] Figure 3–1 illustrates the principle of *proximity*. The dots in *A* are closer together in the horizontal, so we get the visual effect of horizontal lines. In *B* the dots are closer together in the vertical, and we get the impression of vertical lines. The line effect is achieved by our grouping of the visual information according to the principle of proximity. No actual lines are present, only dots. We make the lines by grouping.

Figure 3–1

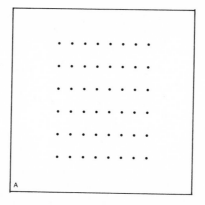

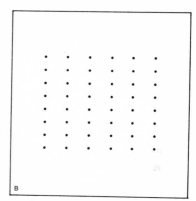

In Figure 3–2 we tend to see three narrow columns with a line left over at the right, rather than three wider columns with a line left over on the left. Notice how hard it is to make yourself see the wide columns. Again we organize our perceptions by the principle of proximity.

Figure 3–2

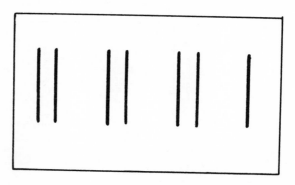

In Figure 3–3 the principle of *similarity* rather than proximity is in operation. The dots are all equidistant. But, because we tend to group

Figure 3–3

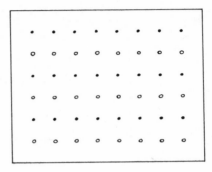

similarities, we see horizontal lines of the two sizes of dots. In the same way we relate similar shapes, lines, colors, and textures that are farther apart, as we will see when we put these principles to use.

Figure 3–4

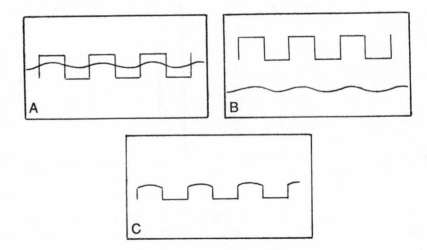

Another Gestalt principle is that of *continuity*. We tend to follow a line in its most easily perceived direction. Figure 3–4 has three parts. *A* shows a combination of lines; *B* and *C* show two ways of following the lines. It is much easier for us to follow the lines in *B* than in *C* because the lines in *B* are continuous rather than shifting from rounded to square lines. In Figure 3–5, why is line *A* more restful than line *B*?

Figure 3–5

Which handwriting is easier to read in C? Our eye can follow the flow of line in the lower example much more easily.

Another form of continuity is *closure*—recognizing the whole from a suggested part (see Figure 3–6). We use this system in much of our

Figure 3–6

process of perceiving, attending to enough visual information to know what is available for us to see. By the time we have formed a concept we have gone on to other processes.

To recognize a visual pattern we divide the visual impressions into "figure" and "ground"—that is, "subject" and "background." Have you ever watched in a crowd for someone you know and seen only the crowd? The instant you see your friend, the crowd becomes background and your friend stands out. Forms, to be seen clearly, need space around them to create a sense of edge that defines their shape. Sometimes a line will suggest figure or ground on either side of it. Figure 3–7 can represent two faces or a lamp base, depending on what areas you see as figure and what areas as ground.

Figure 3–7

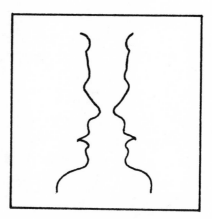

These sorting, organizing processes are more apparent when the objects we observe have little conceptual meaning to us. If we are given a jumbled mass of unsorted abstract forms, of different shapes, colors, sizes, and textures, and are asked to do something with them, we try to find some order in the disorder, grouping similar shapes, colors, sizes, or textures. We are ordering by visual qualities. But if the objects are "things" that we have names for we might organize them according to what we already know about them. This latter method would be ordering by concepts. The visual ordering goes on even while we order things conceptually. For example, two rooms may contain objects having the same functions—chairs, tables, lamps, rugs—but be visually very different. In one room each object might be a different color; the chairs, tables, lamps, and rug might be unusually large or small; the grouping of the objects might be disorderly as in Figure 3–8. Most of us would find such a room chaotic. Another room by contrast might

Figure 3–8. Disorder

have all the objects the same color, all the same size, and all placed in neat orderly rows. This room would have visually ordered objects as in Figure 3–9. Most people would find the disordered room

Figure 3–9. Complete Order

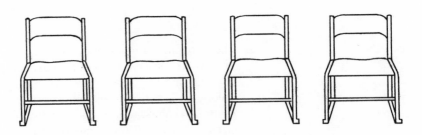

confusing and the well-ordered room monotonous. In Figure 3–10 there are order *and* variety.

Design is based on the principles of perceptual ordering. Designing is a complex form of problem solving, in which shape, line, color, texture, size, and space are ordered and varied through proximity, similarity, and continuity.

Figure 3–10. Varied Order

A designer could use the same kinds of objects as were used in the two extreme examples of rooms, and create a room with interest and harmony by arranging the objects into *proximities* (that is, clustering in groups); he could repeat sizes and colors without becoming monotonous by using *similarities,* and create *continuities* by picking up lines made by the edges of objects and relating them to lines made by the edges of other things. The task of the designer, whether he be a painter organizing symbols on a canvas, an architect planning spaces that lead the flow of people in and out of areas, or a craftsman in fabrics designing patterns that will enhance the appearance of people wearing the fabric, is to create order with some degree of variety to stimulate interest.

The ordering in art appears to be a direct outcome of the ordering in perceptions. Many artists and some children appear to design intuitively. Perhaps they use their perceptual organizing processes without conscious analysis when they design. In a complex society, where people live in close association, the ability to design cannot be left to only those persons who can design intuitively. Understanding of the functions of design helps many students become more discriminating about design and become more aware of their contributions to the visual environment. This is the reason that the processes of perceptual ordering are important for elementary classroom teachers to understand, as a basis for helping more children use them.

Conceptual and Visual Learning

Try to imagine a child who lives in an Arctic region and has never seen a tree. His teacher has told him about the jungle. Books have shown him pictures of tropical trees and told him their uses. He has a concept of a tree. His concept of trees is different from that of a child who has experienced trees as something to climb and to build tree houses in. A third child, who has been encouraged to develop an awareness of the visual qualities of trees, their forms, the effects of light and shade on color, and the way they change shape in the wind, will have still another kind of preparation for seeing. Each of these children, introduced to the idea of tropical trees, will utilize his individual past experience as he imagines what the tree is like. These same factors will function in his responses to trees in his own environment. The child who has had all three types of training—conceptual, tactile, and visual—has the greatest potential for responding.

There is a tendency for us to identify things by their functions or known physical characteristics rather than by their visual qualities. For example, a child learns the *thinglike* quality of the ball—its functions, such as rolling and bouncing. Adults teach him about balls through manipulation—learning to roll, catch, and bounce a ball. Rarely are the visual qualities of a ball in light and space introduced to him; nor is he encouraged to respond to a ball visually except for simple recognition of size and color and possible decoration. For this reason he learns to recognize the ball as being the same ball twenty feet away as in his hand, the same color in bright light as in shade. Similarly, he does not see that a building block changes in shape or appearance when he views it from left or right or from above or below his line of vision. The tendencies to depend on what is known are called constancies.[4] The constancies are needed to make the cognitive nature of things clear. We need to *know* what a thing *is,* regardless of its distance or angle from us. But use of the constancies alone obscures the *visual* qualities of things.

The Perceptual Constancies

1. *Brightness and color constancy* is a tendency to see objects as having the same color and the same brightness, regardless of the particular color of light or shade they are seen in at a given time. Observe carefully the color you actually see when you place a brightly colored object first in direct sun and then in shade. You will find that the light or color in the surrounding area will change the appearance of a colored object. Most of us operate visually without taking color and brightness change into consideration. A photographer knows how important a light meter is to find out just how much brightness or light is reflected from an object.

2. *Size constancy* is a tendency to see objects as being the same size or as having compromised size rather than as the actual comparative size, depending on the distance between the object and the viewer. When an artist holds up a pencil with his arm outstretched, he is helping himself to overcome what he knows about size relationships by measuring the relationship between something close and something far away, as it appears visually. Try this method of the artist. Stand at the corner of a building and, holding a pencil vertically, measure the difference in height of the nearest and farthest windows of the same actual size and on the same floor. Although you have been aware that the visual size gets smaller as an object recedes, you may be surprised by how *much* smaller it becomes.

Hilgard indicates that there are three ways we can see perspective: (a) ". . . according to the geometry of perspective, seeing it as smaller the farther away it is. . . . The retinal projection of an object at 20 feet is half the retinal projection at 10 feet''; (b) by considering the object to be the size we know it to be; (c) by making a compromise between what we know and what we see.[5] Most people see distance by some degree of compromise. Teachers have found people who apparently have not considered perspective at all and who appear to be almost entirely dependent on knowledge. Arnheim describes the reaction of a young woman who hid her face in terror the first time she saw that lines converge in space.[6] Drawing students have become quite upset when they learned that they were responding so inadequately to what they saw. Suddenly to see the visual world in perspective when it has always appeared flat is quite a change for some people.

3. *Shape constancy* is a tendency to see things as being the same shape regardless of the angle from which they are viewed. For example, those windows you just looked at are all rectangles, and even though you discovered a difference in visual size you may not have recognized a difference in shape. Look again. When you are parallel to the building and the windows right in front of you are at eye level, they are rectangular. As you walk toward one corner they gradually become more trapezoidal and just before you go around the corner they become straight lines. (See Figure 3–11.) Many of us have not

Figure 3–11. What Shape *is* a Window?

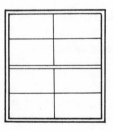 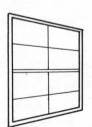  

been trained to take these changes into consideration. Some art students and many children draw all windows as rectangles, even when two sides of a house are shown in a drawing.

Try another visual experiment. Take a round bottle or glass with a top large enough to be seen clearly as a circle. Hold it with the top above your eye level and gradually lower it. What happens to the circle? Is it always a circle? If you do not have a suitable object, make a circle of your thumb and forefinger and watch it change shape as you lower it below your eye level. Study a transparent tube. At any given position are the "circles" at top and bottom identical in shape? Can

Figure 3–12. Circles Appear as Ellipses

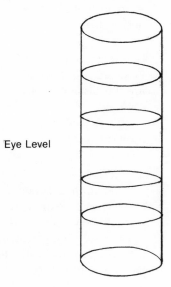

Eye Level

one be an ellipse and, at the same time, the other be a line? The two circles become the same shape only when the center of the tube is nearest your eye level—half of it above the horizon line and half below it as shown in Figure 3–12.

Children do not make the same compromises in size or space relations that trained adults do. X-ray drawing, showing the inside and outside of objects, and unusual size relationships often found in children's drawings may be caused by differences between children and adults in the way they adjust *what they see* to *what they know*. Wide individual differences among both children and adults are found because *the learning factor is always present;* we do not all learn the same things in the same way and to the same degree.

Experiences such as seeing the way colors change in bright light and shadow, observing things grow "smaller" with distance, and watching the way objects change their perceived shapes in space will help children to develop a keener responsiveness to their world. Encouraging children to explore their visual world is better than introducing them to formal perspective systems before they have learned to *see* perspective.

Variations in the Constancies

Learning to see in space requires several different kinds of tasks. These tasks are (1) judging the size of a thing that is in the distance, (2) judging the distance between the viewer and the object, (3) making an estimate of the size of the object in relation to what the viewer expects to see, and (4) estimating the angle of the object in relation to the position of the viewer.

Individuals respond differently in their dependency on the constancies. McNamara and Solley showed that dependency can be modified by differences in experience with things. In form constancy things are seen as being the same irrespective of the viewing angle. The researchers gave an angular nonsense form, cut out of plastic, similar to that in Figure 3–13 to Group one of their study. Group two received the form printed in a booklet. Each group received examples of the

Figure 3–13. Nonsense Form

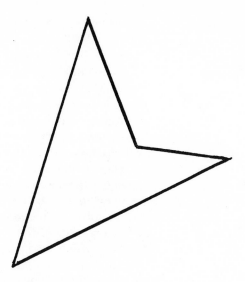

form as a reward for work and used them to play games. They could exchange them for goods at the college bookstore. After two weeks the subjects were tested to see how consistent they were in reproducing the angles in the form when they saw the form reproduced at each of the four 90-degree angles. It was reported that though some of the subjects were more nearly correct in reproducing the angles and many of the subjects were less nearly correct, all of them tended to be *consistent* in their estimates no matter how they were viewing the form. Group one, which had the most varied use of the form, was the most consistent in their estimates even though the estimates were incorrect. Group two was less consistent, and a control group was the poorest. This study gives us some clues that using an object in various ways and giving value to the uses without specific perceptual training does not necessarily lead to more awareness of visual reality but may lead to more stereotyped vision.[7]

A delightful description of an individual whose whole perceptual experience had been in one environment and who suddenly faced a new situation where old habits did not work was given by the anthropologist Turnbull.[8]

After working some time with the BaMbuti, Pigmies in the Ituri Forest of the Congo, the anthropologist took his good friend Kengi out of the dense forest in which his people had lived for thousands of years onto the rolling, grassy hills of the Ishago National Park. Many things the Pigmy saw for the first time — distant vistas, mountains with snow, grass with no trees, a lake. They caught his attention and aroused his curiosity. He had hunted for the purpose of survival all his life, yet at first he ignored elephants, antelope, and buffalo that were clearly seen by the people who lived on the plain. Finally the buffalo caught his attention and he asked "What *insects* are those?" The anthropologist could not at first understand. Then he realized that here was a man whose prior world of vision for judging size and distance was so limited by the density of the forest that he could not function where he had no basis for comparison. When told the insects were buffalo he roared with laughter and told his friend not to tell such lies. Looking at the lake, he identified a boat full of people as a floating piece of wood. As he came closer to the buffalo he stared without speaking. When he was facing them, he refused to accept them as real and said he was not going to get out of the car until they left the area.

Many university students have learned to see inadequately. They make compromises between an object's front-face form and its visual form as seen from other viewpoints, and, as a result, they have inaccurate perceptions.

For example, a "straight A" physics major in his senior year was fearful of receiving a lesser grade in a drawing course. He worked very hard. He had learned to overcome the constancies and to see how forms, colors, and sizes do change according to light and viewer-object distance. He had studied the circle visually to see it become various elliptical shapes. Then he was asked, along with the class, to select an object. He selected a ceramic bottle. From his viewpoint it looked somewhat like Figure 3–14A, the ellipsis becoming propor-

Figure 3–14. A Conflict of Concepts
and Percepts

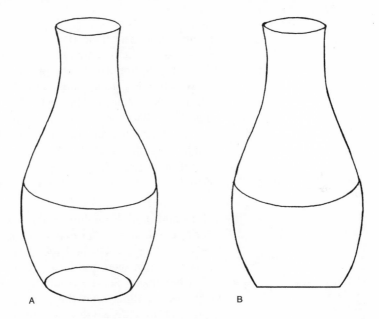

A   B

tionately wider on the front-back axis as the object was placed farther down from his eyes. He produced what he considered to be a perfect drawing, which looked like Figure 3–14B. When told it was a very careful drawing and well done but that one key point had been overlooked, he appeared quite puzzled and he blushed. Only when the instructor pointed to the bottom line did he recognize his mistake and blurt out, "Yes, but I knew the table was flat. The bottom of the bottle was flat so I drew it flat!"

This intelligent young man was frustrated because what he *knew* about things got in the way of his seeing visual reality, even when he had learned to draw the circle from different viewpoints and had overcome the constancy of form. When he had to apply his perceptual training to a three-dimensional object, what he knew about the object was a stronger influence than what he saw. He had dealt with circles all his life, analyzed their properties mathematically, but had never learned to see them adequately in space. This man's lack of perceptual education had imposed limitations on his responses to his environment in a way that is glaringly apparent when contrasted with the research of Braine and Shanks, who were able to teach five-year-olds to recognize the difference between phenomenal and real shapes. In this case the children were trained to recognize the differences between straight rods that looked bent in water and bent rods that looked straight in water. They learned to respond correctly to the questions "Which looks bent?" and "Which is really bent?"[9]

Values and attitudes influence the perception of size. Children judge a jar of candy as heavier than an equally heavy jar of sand.[10] Favorite foods were reported to be larger than less favored foods,[11] and Santa Claus drawings were found to appear bigger before Christmas than after Christmas.[12] Similar results were found with collegiate students in nurses' training, who drew pictures of a director and instructor larger than they drew fellow students.[13]

Dorfman and Zajonc studied children from different economic backgrounds and compared their reactions to differences in the visual background in which coins and similar size discs were presented to children for them to judge which was larger.[14] In this experiment children from both economic groups estimated both coins and equal-sized discs as larger against a black background than a white one. A key difference not recognized in similar studies was the visual context in which the coins were given children.[15] Several factors—economic status, size of coin, and context of the coin—affect in some degree the perception of the size of the coin.

Categorizing Perceptions with Language

Much of the sorting of visual information apparently takes place before the viewer conceptualizes or puts into word categories what he sees. Only the concepts he has available are used to categorize visual information. For example, if he knows only the colors red, blue, yellow, and green, he tends to lump all redness to red—light red, dark red,

red-violet, red-orange; all blueness to blue, from blue-green to purple; all yellowness to yellow; and all greenness to green.

Man uses symbolic language to mediate between his input of information and his response to it. Language is not only used to communicate ideas, it is also a *means of categorizing experience.* A Navaho has three words for our word *rough*—dighol, dichiizh, and digóón (rough road, rough rock, and the rough surface of a file). By contrast, for our three words *knife, metal,* and *flint,* they have one word, béésh. Metals and knives were introduced into their experience at the same time to replace the stone flints they used for tools and arrowheads.[16] This is only a small example of the myriad ways language systems provide a categorizing system with which to organize the complexities of visual perceptions.

This example helps us see how important it is that the language of vision and the language of words be reciprocally developed with children, so that words will bring rich visual memory into play and a child's response to his visual world will not be limited because he has no mediating language with which to handle it. Art activity without perceptual and conceptual emphasis does not necessarily lead to visual sensitivity and appreciation. Wilson compared the language used by fifth, seventh, ninth, and eleventh grade students in responding to paintings. The responses were identical for all the grade levels. Verbal responses were mainly concerned with literal description of the content of the paintings, but there was little response about the qualities, the form, line, color, and texture interaction, and the composition. Yet the eleventh grade students had had studio art experience for three years in the sixth, seventh and eighth grades, and in some cases three years of high school.[17]

Apparently "self-expression" through art does not necessarily lead pupils to see or understand the form, design, or aesthetic qualities of art.

There are still conflicting theories and research on the relationships of concepts to percepts and the processes of cognition or knowing through which learning takes place. Harris reviews some of these differences in relation to children's art.[18] More recent studies relate the processes more closely. Helson theorizes that perception is an adaptive process in which the cues from the things viewed in focus and things in the background are integrated with past experience, what one already knows about the subject.[19] This process involves both percepts and the conceptual categories in which one stores the visual information. Forgus places cognition and perception as parts of the same process.[20] Hochberg stresses the effects of the stimulus in influencing what one sees, but is also concerned with the ways cultural and social learnings influence what one learns from what he sees.[21]

The following relationship may be particularly useful for the art teacher. Percepts are information that is derived from sensory input. This information does not have to be put into concepts or words in order to be used in cognitive processes. For example, perceptually trained persons can know and use many subtle variations in color that do not have color names, and such persons can cognitively compare, relate, and discriminate with the concepts they have. They can reorganize and refine designs without having to have words to process the decisions. In other words, perception is a cognitive process that is not dependent upon words. Conception, on the other hand, is a process of using words to categorize and relate experiences, which may be direct sensory experiences or responses to the language of others. Both conception and perception are cognitive processes.

According to Harris, concepts change as new discriminations (percepts) divide old concepts into more discrete concepts.[22] For example, a child has a first experience with an apple. He learns words for the tactile-visual-gustatory percepts he experiences. These concepts might be smooth, red, and sweet. If his second experience with an apple is different, both his ability to learn perceptually and conceptually are increased, provided he has the opportunity to learn concepts in which to categorize his perceptual information. Without conceptual learning he might categorize the second apple as "bad" because it was different from the first. But if the child's perceptual information is categorized into concepts of rough, green, and sour, he has a better basis for discriminating between the two apples. Both his perceptual and conceptual discrimination are increased.

We cannot assume that the sensory learning is direct and does not need to be taught. A child must have many experiences to differentiate among gradations of smooth and rough, red and green, sweet and sour. Conceptual and perceptual knowing reinforce each other, and they help the viewer in the discriminating and comparing process.

A child's subsequent learning is dependent on his prior learnings and on the opportunities he has to learn, to relate concepts to percepts, and to discriminate in detail. Two children the same age with different past learning opportunities will approach the same discrimination problem with very different readiness to learn from it. Much of what children learn is not as specific as our example with the apple. In later chapters we will see how the child's experiences in his environment affect the ways he learns percepts and concepts.

Implications for Art Education

Art teachers have often been concerned with a holistic approach to art, identifying children as more or less "artistic." The materials in this chapter indicate that a child's behavior may appear to be artistic, realistic, or creative according to the particular kind of perceptual processes he has been encouraged to develop.

Increased opportunity to experiment consciously, to sort and design shapes, colors, textures, and lines, may help nonintuitive children respond to more design in their environment. Design can be learned analytically as well as intuitively. Both analysis and intuition need encouragement in the classroom, so that children who are more developed in one capacity than in another can increase their perceptual and designing abilities.

Conceptual and perceptual learning can reinforce each other so that both are enriched in the learning process. Learning about objects as they move in space and light can go along with learning what objects *are* irrespective of visual changes. But if most learning is in terms of static descriptions, then visual qualities of size, color, value, and shape in light and space tend to be ignored. These are the qualities that are in the environment and in art. To respond to and to evaluate art and the environment, children need to develop perceptual sensitivity as well as categorizing skills. They need to understand the world of vision as it is perceptually ordered and designed and as it changes in light. They need to see that their spatial relation to things causes the things to change in visual size and visual shape. Requiring children to learn a perspective system before they have learned to see three-dimensionally may only confuse them.

A teacher should realize that all children in his classroom will not sort and organize as he does. The teacher and the children are more or less dependent on the perceptual constancies and the degree to which they are aware of their designing of the visual environment intellectually or intuitively. Furthermore, the teacher and students of diverse cultural backgrounds have learned to organize information in different situations, and so they have different interpretations of the same sensory data. Differences in values apparently influence size relations and the choice of what will be seen as figure and what as background in a complex visual field. In Chapters 4 and 5 we will discuss the relationships of cognitive styles to art behavior as affected by culture and social class.

Summary

This chapter concerned ways in which we sort and organize visual information so that we can make responses to what we see.

Our primary perceptual processes, according to Attneave, are to sort things that are similar as units, things that are random by making averages, and things partially seen as wholes. According to Gestalt theory, things that are in proximity are related; things that are similar are seen as a group; things that have similar and continuing lines produce continuity. We also separate figure from ground.

Design is based on the principles of perceptual ordering. When designing is intuitive, the principles are used without conscious analysis; but the principles can be learned by less intuitive people who will then design more effectively.

Perceptual constancies are the tendencies to depend upon what is known about objects rather than upon the direct sensory data received about them. People tend to "see" things in terms of the color, size, and shape they know them to be, irrespective of visual images that result from differences in light, distance from the object, or the viewing angle of the object.

Past experience varies the ways individuals respond to the constancies. People who live in areas where objects are always in close proximity have not learned to recognize the same objects as the same size when they appear much smaller at a distance. The more ways objects are used, the more people tend to see them in a constant way, irrespective of how they view them at a given time. Values and attitudes also influence the way objects are seen in space.

The language a person uses also affects the way he categorizes visual information. There is much to be resolved concerning the reciprocal relationship of concepts to percepts. Cognitive processing includes both the use of percepts and concepts. Percepts are information that is derived from sensory input which may or may not be put into conceptual categories to be used cognitively. Concepts are the verbal symbols that stand for things and processes in our experience.

Art teachers need to recognize the perceptual and conceptual variations among their students in order to help them learn to see more discriminately and to design more effectively.

References

[1] Fred Attneave, "Some Informational Aspects of Visual Perception," *Psychological Review*, 61 (1954), 183.

[2] Rudolph Arnheim, *Art and Visual Perception* (Berkeley: University of California Press, 1954), p. 130.

[3] Ernest R. Hilgard, *Introduction to Psychology*, 2nd ed. (New York: Harcourt, Brace & World, Inc., 1957), p. 371.

[4] *Ibid.*, pp. 363–370.

[5] *Ibid.*, p. 368.

[6] Arnheim, *Art and Visual Perception*, p. 131.

[7] H. J. McNamara and C. M. Solley, "Influence of Experience upon Form Constancy," *Perceptual and Motor Skills*, 16 (1963), 31–37.

[8] Colin N. Turnbull, *The Forest People* (New York: Doubleday and Company, The American Museum of Natural History, 1962), pp. 260–265.

[9] M. D. S. Braine and B. L. Shanks, "The Conservation of a Shape Property and a Proposal about the Origin of the Conservations," *Canadian Journal of Psychology/Rev. Canad. Psychol.*, 19 (1965), 197–207.

[10] W. F. Dukes and W. Bevan, "Accentuation and Response Variability in the Perception of Personally Relevant Objects," *Journal of Personality*, 20 (1952), 457–465.

[11] H. L. Beams, "Affectivity as a Factor in the Apparent Size of Pictured Food Objects," *Journal of Experimental Psychology*, 47 (1954), 197–200.

[12] C. M. Solley and G. Haigh, "How Children Perceive Santa Claus," *Menninger Quarterly*, 12 (1958), 23–24.

[13] W. D. Dannenmaier and F. J. Thumin, "Authority Status as a Factor in Perceptual Distortion of Size," *Journal of Social Psychology*, 63 (1964), 361–365.

[14] D. D. Dorfman and R. B. Zajonc, "Some Effects of Sound, Background Brightness, and Economic Status on the Perceived Size of Coins and Discs," *Journal of Abnormal and Social Psychology*, 66 (1963), 87–90.

[15] H. Taifel and S. D. Cawasjee, "Value and the Accentuation of Judged Differences: A Confirmation," *Journal of Abnormal and Social Psychology*, 59 (1959), 436–439.

[16] Clyde Kluckhohn and Dorothea Leighton, "By Their Speech Ye Shall Know Them," in *Readings in Anthropology*, eds. Jesse Jennings and E. Adamson Hoebel (New York: McGraw-Hill Book Company, Inc., 1966), pp. 280–281.

[17] Brent G. Wilson, "An Experimental Study Designed to Alter Fifth and Sixth Grade Students' Perception of Paintings," *Studies in Art Education*, 8 (1966), 33–42.

[18] Dale B. Harris, *Children's Drawings as Measures of Intellectual Maturity* (New York: Harcourt, Brace, & World, Inc., 1963), pp. 230–233.

[19] H. Helson, "Current Trends and Issues in Adaptation-Level Theory," *American Psychologist*, 19 (1964), 26–38.

[20] R. H. Forgus, *Perception, The Basic Process in Cognitive Development* (New York: McGraw-Hill Book Company, Inc., 1966).

[21] J. Hochberg, *Perception* (Englewood Cliffs, N.J.: Prentice-Hall, Inc., 1964).

[22] Harris, *Children's Drawings*, p. 231.

4

Children's Individual Differences in Readiness for Art

One of the most rewarding acts of teaching is finding ways to help individual children learn how to express their ideas. One of the most frustrating experiences is failure to reach them. The purpose of this chapter is to help you as a teacher understand and reach more children. We will focus on children's differences in art-related processes that are facets of their personality. As unique individuals, they have learned patterns of response as they interact in their environment—their orientation to space, their habits of handling information, their psycho-social behavior, and their learned response sets.

Orientation to Space

An extensive body of research has been gathered on ways in which children and adults orient themselves to their environment. The art educator Viktor Lowenfeld identified children who depended more on how they perceived their world than on how they felt about it, and compared them with children who reacted to their world according to how they felt about it. He called the former "visuals" and the latter "haptics." Lowenfeld described "visual" and "haptic" people as having certain inborn tendencies. He defined the extreme haptic as a person who is "normal-sighted and uses his eyes only when compelled to do so; otherwise he reacts as would a blind person who is entirely dependent upon touch and kinesthesis." A visually-minded person he defined as one who "is entirely lost in the dark and depends completely on his visual experiences of the outside world." Lowenfeld believed that individuals tend to group toward the extremes in distribution of these traits. However, the process of space orientation is much more complicated than just the use of touch versus the use of vision. Recent research indicates that other important influences on space orientation can be found. It must be recognized that Lowenfeld made a major contribution to thinking in art education but that the haptic-visual concept cannot account for all the variations among people in perceptual orientation behavior.

The psychologist Witkin has been studying perception for more than twenty-five years. At first he believed that people could be divided into two groups: those who depended more on information from their visual field and those who depended more on information they received from bodily cues.

In an experiment, he had each of several subjects seated in a chair that could be tilted by the use of levers to the left or right (see Figure 4–1). The chair was in a small room that could also be tilted to the left or right, either with the chair or in the opposite direction, and to different degrees. Both chair and room could be manipulated by the subject or the experimenter. Sitting in the chair in a normal position, the subjects were blindfolded, then moved to a position where neither the field nor the chair was at the true upright. Then, after the blindfold was removed, they were given the task of righting themselves.

Figure 4–1. Test for Use of Visual or
Postural Cues[1]

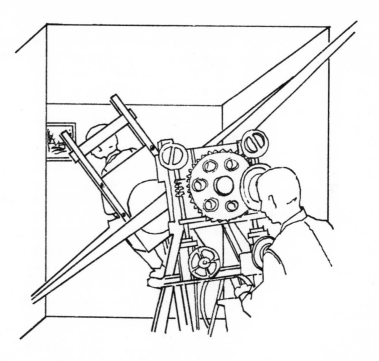

Some of the people who used their bodily feelings of uprightness were able to right themselves regardless of the slant of the room. They could recognize that the room was not upright, separate themselves from the field—the room around them—and achieve the true upright. At the other extreme were people who would align the chair according to the tilt of the room, sometimes even pulling themselves through the true upright to achieve the alignment. A large majority made a compromise between the cues from the field and the cues of their bodies and said they were right side up when they were at a point between the field and the true upright. People who depend on cues from their bodies are said to be "posturally oriented." Those who depend on cues from the field are "visually oriented."[2]

A cue is a stimulus that gives us information we need in order to respond. When we are hungry we get feeling cues that it is time to eat. With our eyes we receive cues from our environment. The kind of information we get depends on which kinds of receptors (senses) we are using. Usually we are using more than one set of receptors. When we are hungry we usually start looking for something to eat. If we are in a kitchen, we have three sets of receptors working, giving us hunger cues, visual cues, and olfactory cues. If we *hear* someone working in the kitchen as well, even more cues are available to us. In the study of space orientation, researchers are finding that people tend to differ in which sets of receptors they use to get cues about their uprightness and their relation to space.

In another experiment Witkin used the same tests with children aged eight to seventeen. Although he found wide variation among children at these ages, he found a tendency for the group as a whole to be more visually oriented in their younger years and to become more posturally oriented as they grew older. Averaging the responses of the boys and girls separately, Witkin found significant sex differences appearing by age fifteen. At that age the boys became more posturally oriented and the girls more visually oriented. In each group there were wide differences. Also, he found that even the most visually-oriented children were able to use postural cues very successfully when blindfolded.[4]

Harriet Linton retested much of Witkin's work and found similar results. She further tested the relationship between the ability to use bodily cues and the ability to separate figure from ground in a complex visual task. In the embedded figure test she used a drawing of an object (the figure) surrounded by a number of lines or colors (the ground) that tended to hide the form of the object. She found a strong tendency for posturally-oriented people to find the embedded figure much faster than people who depended on the visual field.[5]

Witkin, curious about why people learn different ways of orienting themselves, did further research to find out how child-rearing practice is related to space orientation. He studied a group of ten-year-old boys. They were given the battery of space orientation tests. Then interviewers, who did not know the boys' test scores, interviewed their mothers. The mothers were evaluated in terms of whether they were "growth-constricting" or "growth-fostering." Those mothers who appeared more fearful for their sons, who restricted their range of activities, and who did more for them than is usual were identified as "growth-constricting." Those mothers who were "growth-fostering" were not especially protective. It was found that those boys whose mothers gave them more freedom were able to separate themselves more from the field and were able to use postural cues in orienting themselves to space. Those whose mothers restricted their growth were more dependent on the field.[6]

In another experiment Linton identified an additional factor in perception: the influence of authority figures on people's perceptual skills. Subjects in a darkened room were asked to estimate the distance a moving light traveled. After several trials an average was made of their estimates. Before the second set of trials was made, an authority figure (in this case, one recognized to know more about psychology than the subjects) gave his estimate of the distance the light moved. His estimate to each subject was 5 inches longer than that subject's average in the first trials. Most subjects changed their estimates to be like that of the authority figure. Only thirteen per cent of the subjects were uninfluenced by the authority figure and performed in the second set of trials as they had in the first. These same subjects were also most successful in separating figure from ground, and in using postural cues.[7]

This study indicates that ability to resist the visual field is related to ability to resist authority figures as well. It also supports the hypothesis that people's space-orientation tendencies are related to their approach to their environment and experience as a whole. Space-orientation tendencies appear to be in a large part learned and developed at an early age. The sex differences Witkin found at age fifteen may be due to the culturally defined dependency role for women.

Later studies led Witkin and his associates to enlarge the field-indepen-dence–field-dependence concept. They now believe it is more a general characteristic of the way individuals function *cognitively*. Children who were field independent were found to have a cognitive style of being more generally analytical and better able to differentiate themselves and objects from the environment than others. Children who were field dependent had a style that was more global; they were less able to separate themselves or objects from the larger field.

Witkin adheres to the point of view that environment and genetic potential interact. He shows, for example, that a given mother's pat-tern of behavior with an active child will be different from her behavior with a lethargic child. The child-and-mother relationship "involves a complex continuous interaction between characteristics of each." Because mother and child share part of the same environment, they modify each other through their interaction with each other.[8]

Witkin's concern for the environmental causes of differences in re-sponse can be very useful to us as teachers, both in understanding student differences and in seeing how we may be encouraging or dis-couraging more or less analytical responses.

Witkin made a comparison of children's scores on his perceptual and space-orientation tests and their behavior while taking the Thematic Apperception Test. The TAT requires that the child tell the interviewer what is going on in a set of pictures. The child's verbal response was not recorded but his behavior was. Some children sought help from the adult, showed lack of confidence in their responses, showed signs of being anxious, and seldom used the first person singular. Other children with stronger self-direction and confidence evidenced no anxiety and referred to themselves as "I." As expected, the first group of children were the more global, the latter the more analytical children.

Later studies with children responding to Rorschach inkblot tests showed that the analytical children structured the ambiguous figure much more highly than did the more global children. The first group defined their responses to the inkblot with clear language and definite descriptions; the latter were vague.[9]

Witkin and his associates then interviewed ten-year-old boys. Their responses to questions about their own experience were rated in a five-point scale of cognitive clarity and were compared to their scores on the Witkin perceptual index (their perceptual test scores). The more field-independent children were found to be more cognitively clear in describing their personal experiences than were the more field-dependent.[10]

Figure drawings by ten-year-olds followed similar patterns. The more global children drew more primitive features than did the more analytical children on a Body Sophistication Scale, as summarized in Table 4–1.

Table 4–1. The Features of Children's Figure Drawings[11]

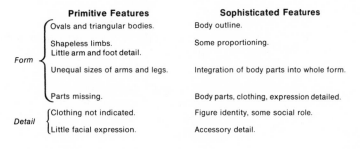

	Primitive Features	Sophisticated Features
Form	Ovals and triangular bodies.	Body outline.
	Shapeless limbs. Little arm and foot detail.	Some proportioning.
	Unequal sizes of arms and legs.	Integration of body parts into whole form.
	Parts missing.	Body parts, clothing, expression detailed.
Detail	Clothing not indicated.	Figure identity, some social role.
	Little facial expression.	Accessory detail.

This study would indicate that children's drawings might give clues to their general orientation, but such information should be used with caution because it is but one index of a complicated relationship.

An average score was obtained for the ten-year-olds on each of these tests and compared to their field-dependence–field-independence scores. Clearly, the range of scores of the field-independent children was different (differentiated, clear, and analytical) from the field-dependent (global), with only one overlapping score. Intermediate children were clearly clustered in the middle.

Extensive interviewing and testing of mothers of these children indicate that the more global field-approach mothers interact with their children in ways that inhibit children from becoming more differentiated and analytical, while analytic, highly differentiating mothers tend to rear children who also differentiate, through the kind of interaction "climate" they create. But many personality variables modify the interaction.

In general, mothers who gave approval for compliant, undemanding, "good" behavior in their children and disapproval for "bad" behavior had children who were global in their reactions to their environment. Mothers who rewarded creative, self-actualizing behavior and encouraged the assumption of responsibility by their children tended to have children who were analytical and able to differentiate clearly in their environment.[12]

A later study by Dyk and Witkin supported the earlier findings. Field-independent boys, who had highly developed cognitive capacities to differentiate between things, were also those boys who were early encouraged to be independent of their mothers, but who were cared for with a degree of freedom appropriate for their development. The boys who scored the highest had fathers that they described as supportive.[13]

Konstadt and Forman found that field-dependent children were much more affected by adults' disapproval of their work than were field-independent children. The studies suggest that children who are more dependent on parents and whose parents are more authoritarian need careful help from a teacher who encourages them to evaluate their own work or who attempts to get them to try new ways of seeing, expressing, or manipulating in art. The teacher's efforts to be encouraging may be interpreted as criticism by such children.[14]

In summary it would seem from these reports that a child's style of interacting with his environment is consistent, whether he is relating to his outside world, to pictures, or to his own symbolic expression. Further, the kind of interacting environment the child has experienced tends to direct his development of his interaction style.

Implications for Teachers

This body of research brings up three questions: (1) How can teachers identify differences among children? (2) How can teachers motivate children and plan curriculum for them? (3) How does the action of the primary grade teacher, in his role as an extension of the mother, continue to reinforce or contradict what the child has already learned?

Identification of children's characteristics is always tentative. We identify characteristics that we can work with. But we must retain an openness to changes in the child and to new evidence that may change our concept of him. When we categorize children according to IQ scores, we may fail to take into account the fact that the tests were a sample of behavior on *one* day, that abilities *can* change, and that responses may be influenced by test-taking skills, anxieties, and alertness. The tendencies identified by Witkin can have tremendous influence on children's behavior, but we must use our information flexibly and we must continuously be open to cues that tell us that our assessment was wrong or that the child is changing.

Developing curriculum for individual and cultural differences will be analyzed in Chapter 10. At this point we can point out that the same activities will probably have very different meanings for different children.

The Witkin studies can give teachers insight into their own reactions to children. Are you a growth-fostering teacher who encourages analysis? Can you tolerate a diversity of activity by the more involved children at the same time you structure activities for the more dependent children as long as they need it? Or are you much more comfortable when all the children are doing as they are told and are seeking your help to do so rather than exploring other possibilities?

Information Handling

Information handling is a fundamental part of problem solving in art as in mathematics. It requires (1) attending to a situation, (2) sorting the information into some kind of categories, and (3) mediating—analyzing the material so that some kind of response or solution to the relationships can be made. Children's art activities involve many problem-solving situations as they respond to experience, sort and organize their information, and mediate it into an art expression or respond to art forms in their environment. Understanding individual differences will help teachers modify art experiences so that they will be more appropriate for the learning processes of different types of children.

In art activities we have long assumed that children have likes and dislikes about media and about organizations of art forms, but we have not explored different ways in which children process the information they are getting in different kinds of art-related tasks. Psychologists have not been much concerned with individual differences in information handling but rather have tried to understand the general process. The extensive research of Witkin and later Kagan[15] gives us useful ways of identifying possible differences in cognitive styles among children.

Kagan and his associates gave children their Conceptual Style Test. They showed children three black-and-white drawings of familiar objects and asked them to identify two of the three pictures that were "alike or go together in some way." Each child was then asked why he grouped as he did.[16]

An *analytic response* was made when the child responded to parts of the objects that were related. In the drawings of a watch, a man, and a ruler, an analytic response would refer to numbers on the watch and on the ruler. A *functional response* to the same pictures would be that the man wears the watch. A *categorical response* would relate the watch and ruler as both inanimate compared to the symbol of an animate man.

In further tests, analytic children responded to inkblots with detailed descriptions ("butterfly with wings and feet"). Nonanalytic children responded with more single concepts like "mud, cloud, or paint." The analytic made more new verbal responses to geometric designs rather than just describing the more obvious features.

A mean trend toward more analysis comes with age but individual differences are extensive at all ages tested. Individual children were found to be about the same over a year's period.

To extend the understanding of these relationships, extensive testing of elementary school children was done in tasks where their more analytical or more impulsive behavior was compared in tasks of separating figure from ground, analyzing subtle differences in pictures, recalling abstract design configurations, matching familiar pictures, and matching tactile and visual images. Impulsive responses were made quickly, without evidence of reflection or analysis.

If a child was able to be analytical in one kind of task he was generally analytical in others. If he was impulsive in one he tended to be more impulsive in others. First and second grade boys who were analytical in their responses to the Conceptual Style Test had high scores on the Wechsler Individual Score for Children Picture Arrangement Test and gave highly articulate responses to inkblots.[17]

Kagan's tests were given under different time situations. The Conceptual Style Test, the Design Recall Test, and the Embedded Figure Test were given to two groups of second grade children. The first group was encouraged to work quickly, but the second was encouraged to work slowly and think about the answers. The slow-working children were more analytical in their selection of related pictures and made fewer errors on the Design Recall Test, in which they see a design and then have to pick it out from a series of related designs. They were given more time and encouraged to reflect on what they did.[18]

Fourth grade boys were compared on their ability to analyze conceptually and to analyze geometric forms into distinct figure and ground. Boys who scored high conceptually tended to be high in separating figure from ground.[19]

Kagan suggests that the accumulated information shows that the abilities to reflect on (take time to think about) alternative solution possibilities and to analyze visually are fundamental to cognitive processes and perceptual recognition.

The tendency to analyze conceptually is related to the ability to analyze visually. In the original Conceptual Style Test the most obvious cognitive relationship was thinking of the man as wearing the watch or using the ruler. A more analytic response was to suppress the more obvious response and see that both watch and ruler had numbers.

Students who were strong in this analytic style could sustain concentration on intellectual tasks, showed little irrelevant gross motor action, and inhibited impulsive solutions to problems.

A tendency to reflect *before* completing the various perception tasks was one of the most consistent and stable behaviors found. Children whose pattern it was to take time to reflect did so more consistently in the different activities when many alternatives were open to them. By contrast an impulsive child faced with many alternatives would quickly choose one and more often be incorrect.

Recognition errors, mistakes in seeing the pattern and finding its match in the Design Recall Test and the Familiar Figures Test were positively related to verbal skills. This might suggest that success in verbal interaction might decrease the child's need for developing perceptual skills. Since verbal skills are more rewarded in education, these children have little need or opportunity to develop the analytical mode of information handling.

This finding is somewhat in contrast with the study of fourth grade boys in which high conceptual skills were found to be related to high ability to separate figure and ground. In this study, *errors* in pattern recognition and recall were related to high abilities in verbal activity. This suggests that the ability to separate figure and ground is not necessarily related to ability to work well with pattern and design materials.

A person's ability to analyze visually and his tendency to be more reflective or more impulsive influence how he classifies information, how he will respond to it, and how he will solve problems. He will establish his own strategies for solving problems. Kagan illustrates with the impulsive child who quickly chooses a wrong cue, fails in his solution, becomes anxious on recognizing his failure, and is handicapped by his anxiety when he must make his next choice. This maladaptive behavior can lead him to reject problem situations and become either apathetic or openly hostile when in problem-solving situations. Another child whose success in art has always been through impulsive expression may not have learned to reflect on what he does. Helping him to reflect and to think about his work could help him develop reflective habits as well.[20]

Another important finding was that boys who evidence gross motor behavior and who are easily distracted are less able to make analytic responses.

We do not know how much the characteristics of being impulsive and being more global relate. An impulsive response would tend to be more global because less time would be taken to respond in more detail. Both Witkin and Kagan have identified what seems to be one consistent cognitive style—analytical, reflective, and differentiating.

The experimenters state that they do not want to give the impression that one style of behavior is "better" than the others; they believe analysis and reflection are needed in the sciences but that a very strong reflective orientation could be a hindrance in the arts and the humanities.[21] By contrast, in art education impulsive expression has sometimes been stressed at the expense of analytic expression. Since

the time of the strong reaction to classic realism and disciplined drawing and the emergence of the child-centered curriculum, teachers
have focused on "self-expression" at the expense of much reflective
problem solving.

Reflective behavior and visual analysis are more needed in some
phases of art, impulsiveness more needed in others. This research
would indicate that some children will succeed more readily in one
mode than in another, so teachers should make provisions for both
kinds of interaction. But the clues that these are in large part learned
behaviors would suggest that more children could develop both
kinds of response.

Lovano[22] has studied children's behavior on tests used by both Witkin
and Kagan, the Children's Embedded Figure Test,[23] the Kagan Conceptual Style Test, and the Witkin Sophistication of Body Concept.[24]
The first of these measures ability to separate figure and ground and the
last two measure the analytical-global dimension. She tested boys in
grades two through six. Only at grade four did she find a significant
(.02) correlation (.56) between the CEFT and the CST. When all the
grades were pooled the correlation was very low (.099) and not significant. She postulates that one reason for this result may be that the
behavior needed to respond in the CEFT is reflective problem solving,
while the behavior needed to respond to the CST is to make and record
a first response, which would tend to be impulsive. But on the other
analytical-global test, Witkin's SBC, a drawing test, the subject has
time to be more reflective and to add details. In this case she found
that there was a correlation (.351) which was significant (.001) when
all the grades' scores were pooled and particularly so at second grade
(correlation .491, significance .02).

Implications for Teachers

As more research is done with these studies more discrete differences
and testing instruments will probably be found. It is important for
teachers to recognize that differences in cognitive style among their
students may account for inadequate learning, even though this particular field of inquiry is in its early stages of development.

Perceptual development is fundamental to analysis in design and to the cognitive processes of evaluation in art. The behaviors used in making iconic symbols (images of things) are apparently similar cognitive processes to the behaviors used in making word symbols (ideas of things). Information is responded to, sorted, organized, and then expressed through symbols. A child's cognitive style may or may not be similar in both uses of symbols. His style depends upon his degree of perceptual and/or conceptual development and his experience, reward, and/or punishment in using icons and words. When a teacher finds a child who is highly analytical in one behavior and highly global in another, he should investigate the child's readiness and prior experiences to see what may be limiting the child's development in the particular use of symbols. When a child is global in both, the teacher can investigate the classroom situation to see if this child is given enough time and encouragement to respond more analytically and if he has been encouraged to be more reflective.

The art teacher will need to provide a wide range of complexity in the tasks he sets for children because the children will have a wide range of differences in ability to separate figure and ground, analyze pattern and detail, and respond to art as a whole.

Highly verbal children may be so lacking in perceptual skills, such as the ability to analyze visually, that they need particular help in learning to discriminate before they can become interested in symbolizing through drawing or responding to art.

Highly active children, who may be reached through rhythmic motor activities, may eventually become aware of rhythm in visual information. Experimentation is needed with both these groups to discover ways to help them develop the visual avenue for information handling.

Perceptual training has not been emphasized either in education generally or in child art experience. It is of particular importance that such training identifies *visual analysis* as fundamental to conceptual analysis when this aspect of education has been so neglected. Further, it is important to realize that strengths or weaknesses in analytical ability are important differences as they relate to a child's overall cognitive style.

Visual analysis and conceptual analysis are processes that are used in problem solving, in design, and in evaluating art forms. As was stated in Chapter 3, many people do not design intuitively and need to learn to design conceptually and analytically.

Psycho-Social Behavior
A third area of research in psychology, with implications for art, relates personality as it is developing in the child to his ability to respond to his environment through art. It is impossible to separate the development of personality from influences in the environment. But for the sake of analysis we separate the study of that research which comes from the field of psychology and that which comes from anthropology and sociology. We separate them to see their implications, but in practice in the classroom we cannot separate a developing child from the environment that is modifying his behavior or his influence on the class.

Wallach and Thomas asked the following questions: (1) Does the nature of an individual's environment, being isolated or interacting with others, change the expansiveness or constriction of his drawings? (2) Do individuals with some types of personality traits react through their drawings more strongly to one type of experience than another?[25]

The first question is asked about the environment as a whole, the second about individual differences within groups. Teachers must ask both kinds of questions because some of the time they need to make decisions based on what would be the best probable teaching strategy for the whole group. At other times they can be more concerned about subgroups or individuals.

Eighty freshman college girls served as subjects in an experiment. The girls listened to music, wrote stories related to the music, and drew pictures related to the stories. Then they doodled to the same music. Three samples of doodles were obtained from each girl. Then the girls were randomly assigned to two groups. Group one girls were isolated in an almost bare sound-resistant room, without a timepiece, for one hour. There they repeated the doodling-to-music sequence. Group two spent the hour in smaller groups of six discussing rules in their dormitories; then they repeated the doodling test. Later the girls were tested on the Maudsley Personality Inventory[26] to see how they scored on extroversion-introversion and on their degree of anxiety. These two dimensions have little relation to each other; one finds both high- and low-anxiety introverts and high- and low-anxiety extroverts.

A comparison showed that Group two had twice as much expansiveness (amount of space used) in their drawings *after* the social interaction situation.

When the scores on the anxiety scale were compared to the two social situations, isolation and interaction, quite different results were shown. Low-anxiety girls showed little or no increase in expansiveness after isolation, but low-anxiety girls who were in the social interaction situation increased seven times in expansiveness. By contrast, high-anxiety girls showed almost as much expansiveness after isolation as after interaction, but much less than the low-anxiety girls. This indicates that expansive behavior of low-anxiety people is more affected by the immediate environment than is the expansive behavior of highly anxious persons. One suggested reason may be that anxious people's anxiety is operating so strongly that their expansive behavior is little affected by these particular variations in the environment.

When the more extroversive and the more introversive girls' graphic responses were compared, strong differences appeared. The extroverts were almost two and one half times as expansive after being in the interaction situation than after being in isolation. The introverts were only slightly more expansive in their drawings after being in the interacting situation than after being in isolation. This indicates that introverts were less affected by the environment.

There has been an assumption among art educators that an art room where pupils are allowed freedom to talk and move about is more conducive to creativity than a room where everyone works alone and does not talk. If we believe that more expansive expression usually tends to be more creative than restrictive expression and that all our pupils are extroversive, this assumption might be valid. This study leads us to question whether one kind of environment is best for everyone. When the groups of girls as a whole were compared in the two situations the socialization was more effective in modifying them toward more expansive drawing. But the introversive girls were the least affected. A teacher should not be surprised if his efforts to motivate introversive pupils through social interaction are not effective.

Another assumption among art teachers is that it is "good" for children to work big. They should have large sheets of paper and be encouraged to fill all the space. Whether this kind of expansiveness leads to any specific aesthetic or educational goal needs investigation. But if a teacher has such a goal, then the teacher would need to use different motivations for the high-anxiety children. Further, a teacher may think a low-anxiety child is developing very fast in art because he is working bigger and bigger—when actually it is the social situation that is changing and is influencing the child's behavior. Put the same child on his own, working by himself, and he might again make smaller art products.

Understanding some of the effects of anxiety on art-related behaviors can help teachers find more effective ways of encouraging the anxious children who are little affected by changes in the classroom environment.

There is a considerable body of research that indicates that people use fewer cues in situations where anxiety is aroused.[27] In a study of children's anxiety and ability to discriminate, Knights gave a test of anxiety to 197 eight- and nine-year-old third grade boys from three elementary schools. He selected 66 boys representing the extremes and the middle of each test. His purpose was to find out whether the highly anxious boys would be less accurate in visual discrimination because of test situations or because of the content of what is presented. The boys were shown four slides: three had social scenes, one representing aggression (a boy kicking a man), another nurture (a man hugging a boy), and another neutrality (a man and a boy walking); the fourth slide showed geometric shapes. After each showing of a slide the boys were briefly shown four slides simultaneously, in four degrees of variation from the original. The task was to select the one most like the original. Scores were determined by whether the response was correct, or, if incorrect, how far from the original slide picture the error was. High-anxiety children were *much less accurate* and *made larger errors* than either the average-anxiety or low-anxiety children. When they made errors they tended to pick the pictures *most unlike the original.* The nature of the picture made little difference to accuracy of performance, whether it was aggression, nurture, neutrality, or the geometric shapes.

When a longer or shorter period was given for the testing, the highly anxious children made more mistakes under the *longer situation* while the less anxious children improved their scores with more time.

McCoy tested 28 high-anxiety and 28 low-anxiety fourth grade boys on two hypotheses: (1) that highly anxious children tend to see all tasks more as test situations, and (2) that fear of failure is basic to the anxiety aroused by test situations.[28]

On the first test, the boys were given simple tracing tasks. One half of each group received the instructions as if the task was a game to play; the other half was told that it was a test of their ability. The low-anxiety boys made fewer mistakes when they thought it was a test than when they thought it was a game. *No difference between situations was found for the high-anxiety students,* supporting the first hypothesis.

In the second test, a two-part drawing assignment, the children were asked to make a "picture" and draw a "poskon," a nonsense title for an ambiguous task. Again, half the group was told that the task was a game, the other half that it was a test. No differences were found between the game and test situations for the "picture" task for the high-anxiety students. But in the "poskon" task they drew much smaller drawings and did less talking. In the test situation of the ambiguous task they switched colors and materials more than in the game situation. The low-anxiety children used more colors and materials in the game situation. This study supports the second hypothesis in part: when the task is ambiguous and the students are high anxiety, fear of failure is greater.

Implications for Teachers

Penny compared fourth, fifth, and sixth grade children's scores on tests of reactive curiosity (the seeking of varied stimulation in a variety of experiences) with anxiety. He found that children who seek novelty of experience in many situations are generally less anxious. The trend was particularly evident at fourth grade, though the direction was similar at grades five and six.[29]

Several tendencies are important here for teachers. High-anxiety children's multiple use of colors and materials may be a more desperate attempt to solve a problem by *changing those things available* while low-anxiety children's similar behavior may be a more playful creative expression. If we were to judge children's drawings we would need to know the nature of the situation in which they performed them as well as their *anxiety level* before we could even begin to find out what the drawings meant in terms of creative or artistic ability.

How a person with an identifiable trait performs depends on the situation and his other traits as well. Anxiety may be a temporary response in a strange environment that changes as the environment becomes familiar, or it may be the result of long experience in anxiety-producing situations and may have become a habitual mode of response. Here is a place where the teacher should delay his categorization of a child until he has ample information.

McCoy's study would indicate that a play situation does not motivate low-anxiety boys as much as does a test situation. This finding may explain the lack of growth in art by boys who are not challenged in a classroom where art is considered "play."

These three studies with school-age children indicate that highly anxious children who have learned that school situations are threatening or who bring their anxieties with them from situations in the home or outside the school are not performing as well as less anxious children. Not only do they get less visual information from their environment, but what they do get is less likely to be correct. Further, their errors are greater in degree than are those of low-anxiety children. Whether school tasks are presented as tests or as play, these children see them as threatening.

Learned Response Sets

Up to this point in this chapter we have discussed differences in cognitive styles that can influence the ways children respond in art activities. Now we consider learned response sets, ways a child's learning in the past operates to direct the way he learns in the present.

What we know about a thing operates in some degree as a control over the way we can see it. This body of knowledge has built a response set. The way we perceive the qualities of an object, its usefulness, is affected by the "set" of prior training. Two research studies demonstrate this.

Birch and Rabinowitz directed experiments on functional fixedness, comparing two groups of students in their use of a switch and a relay. A switch and a relay have practically the same function (to make, break, or change the connections in an electrical circuit) although they look somewhat different. They are about the same size. In this training one group examined a *switch,* learned what it would do, and learned to recognize it as an object having a definite use. The other group did the same with the *relay.* After this initial training the students were tested individually with the two-string problem—tying together two strings, hanging from the ceiling, too far apart to be reached at the same time. The purpose was not to see how they would solve the problem, but rather which of the two objects on the table, the switch or the relay, they would use. (The solution is to tie an object on one string and swing it like a pendulum so that both strings can be brought together.) Most of the students used as a weight the piece of equipment they *had not* learned about. If they knew a thing was a switch, it *was* a switch, not a weight. A third group, all engineering students who had used both kinds of equipment, were almost equally divided in their choice of switch or relay. After the test the students were asked why they had chosen one piece or the other. They gave many rationalizations, and some students were vehement about the correctness of their solutions.[30] This type of response set is called "functional fixedness."

In another experiment students were asked to match the colors of cut-out shapes with colors on a color wheel. The subjects watched as the shapes were cut out of the *same sheet of orange paper*. When presented with the paper figure of a banana and then asked to turn away and select the matching color on the wheel, the students tended to choose the yellowish hues. With other objects, including figures of a carrot and a tomato, they selected a color on the wheel near the color of the real object as learned from past experience—even though the task was to match the exact color of the shape which they had seen cut from the same orange paper. In this case the immediate prior learning (that all the paper shapes were the same color) was not as cogent as was the lifelong learning about the objects.[31]

The two studies indicate that, when prior learnings conflict, the stronger habitual learning tends to prevail. With the switch and the relay, all the students had the same visual image of the two instruments reflected in the retinas of their eyes. Point One of the P-D process was in operation in their choice of qualities to respond to. Their preparation for the task was different. Knowledge of the mechanical parts identified (and limited) the uses students could see in one object. Size and weight (qualities needed to construct a pendulum) were easier to identify with the object that was unfamiliar, whose specific qualities and functions were less well known.

In the second experiment the well-known shapes of familiar objects appeared to be the most important factor in identifying them, even when the color was the visual quality to be matched. Point Four was in operation when the students grouped the visual information into the categories they knew best.

Another learned habit is assuming that a certain pattern of lines means a certain shape. At the Hanover Institute there is a wall with three peepholes. People who look through the holes see cubes, and all the cubes look alike. Yet when they go around to the back of the wall they see that they have been looking at (1) a wire cube-shape, (2) a drawing of a cube on a board, and (3) a construction of wires and strings that does not resemble a cube from any viewpoint except that of the peephole.[32] The revelation that their perceptions are not always adequate is disturbing to some of these observers; they have always depended on their perceptions to tell them how to respond or to behave, and here they discover that their perceptions can be unreliable.

Implications for Teachers

As teachers, we can recognize several major implications from these experiments: (1) children handle differently the visual information they receive in the classroom; (2) since these differences appear to be in large part learned, more adequate means of handling visual information can be taught; and (3) teachers can prepare children for more complex visual tasks by helping them to understand the nature of new things in terms of what they already know.

If a teacher should ask children to respond through art to an object that is new to them, they might respond in the same way that the students trained to use the switch responded to the relay. They might ignore many of its properties. If they had explored the functions of the object, learned a great deal about it, they would tend to be prepared to look for more details in it. Also, if they learn to look for many possible uses of things, they will not be so likely to experience functional fixedness (being limited to the uses one has learned).

To make an African mask more meaningful to children, so they can respond more fully to its visual qualities, the teacher could read aloud the story of symbolic meaning behind the mask, its functions in the lives of the people who made it, its part in tribal ritualistic life. The class could learn how it was made, the tools used, and the role of the artist who made it. To understand the structure and possible forms of masks they should view it in many lights to see its contours and design, the textures and colors. All of these understandings increase the children's preparation for observing the object. *This is an example of reciprocal action between conceptual understanding and visual perception.* Knowing the nature of the mask increases the number of things one will look for. Being able to look at the mask in terms of its visual qualities enriches the concepts the children are developing about African masks. To give them less restricted learning about the mask, they could be encouraged to improvise on it by making masks of their own. More advanced children might like to design masks for our own culture or for another group of people they are learning about.

Our learned habits of perception are necessary to us in order to deal efficiently with what we see, but they do not tell us the exact nature of our environment. The important concept for teachers to understand is that children, depending on their background of experience, develop different cues for interpreting their environment.

Response sets can be used constructively by the teacher. If an art task is quite complex of if something to be observed has many parts, the teacher can encourage children to look for one aspect and then another. Or the teacher can stress the functions of art to help children understand how art forms tend to make them feel certain ways. But the teacher must also be aware of the variations in cognitive styles and in learned response sets that may keep a child from becoming aware of the art of others or expressing himself through art as fully as he might.

Summary

In this chapter we have focused on those individual differences that appear most influential in modifying children's responses in and through art: (1) orientation to space, (2) information handling, and (3) psycho-social behavior.

The way children are raised tends to encourage them to develop habits of orientation to space, either independent of the visual field, with strongly developed use of bodily cues, or dependent on the field, with less developed discriminatory cues. Research by Witkin relates these differences to cognitive style, with field independents being more analytical, field dependents more global. Independent analytical children drew figures with more detail than did dependent global children.

To examine the patterns of information handling, Kagan and his associates tested children on many processes used in creating art or responding to art, relating objects, separating figure and ground, analyzing subtle differences, recalling designs, matching familiar forms, and matching tactile with visual images. Boys who could easily separate figure from ground tended to be high in conceptual ability. By contrast, those who made the most errors in remembering details in design, seeing patterns, and remembering design qualities were also high in verbal skills. This would suggest that separating figure and ground is not necessarily related to seeing and remembering a designed pattern.

If a child tends to be strong in a behavioral trait he will tend to show this trait in most tasks. Four such traits are those of being analytical, being global, being impulsive, and being reflective.

In the matter of psycho-social behavior, only the psychological aspect is discussed in this chapter. Research on the effects of social interaction compared to social isolation indicates that low-anxiety students produce larger drawings after social interaction, while high-anxiety students produce drawings of about the same size, whether they have been alone or with a group. High anxiety may also lead to mistakes in perception of detail. Low-anxiety students tend to make more correct responses in test situations than in play situations.

All the studies indicate that a teacher can well assume considerable diversity among his pupils in their capacity to respond to almost any art-related task. More complex motivation is needed to get more children involved in art. Children whose drawings lack detail, richness of information, or integration of parts may be lacking in the discrimination needed to learn from their environment. Children who are difficult to involve in the emotional qualities of art may not be getting enough meaningful information from a work of art to respond to it. Anxious children may need classroom experiences that will reduce their anxiety so that they can become capable of making a response.

In Figure 4–2 the key differences in pupils discussed in this chapter are illustrated with four of the many possible combinations of tendencies a child may have developed. These are not distinct categories. A given child can be much stronger in one aspect than another, but these abilities along with the particular situation he is in and his prior learnings all contribute to his ability to respond at a given time.

Figure 4–2. Sample Variations of Traits among Subjects

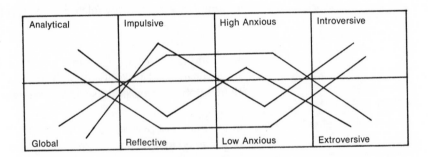

References

[1] Viktor Lowenfeld, *Creative and Mental Growth,* 3rd ed. (New York: The Macmillan Company, 1957), pp. 262–263. Reprinted by permission of the Macmillan Company.

[2] H. A. Witkin, H. B. Lewis, M. Hertzman, K. Machover, P. Bretnall Meissner, and S. Wapner, *Personality Through Perception: An Experimental and Clinical Study* (New York: Harper & Row, Publishers, Inc., 1954), Ch. 2–8.

[3] *Ibid.,* p. 52.

[4] *Ibid.,* pp. 120–152.

[5] Harriet B. Linton, "Dependence on External Influence: Correlates in Perception, Attitudes, and Judgment," *Journal of Abnormal and Social Psychology,* 51 (1955), 502–507.

[6] Herman A. Witkin, "Perception of the Upright," *Scientific American,* 200 (February 1959), 50–56.

[7] Harriet B. Linton, "Autokinetic Judgments as a Measure of Influence," *Journal of Abnormal and Social Psychology,* 49 (1954), 464–466.

[8] H. A. Witkin, R. B. Dyk, H. F. Faterson, D. R. Goodenough, and S. A. Karp, *Psychological Differentiation* (New York: John Wiley & Sons, Inc., 1962), pp. 271–272.

[9] *Ibid.,* pp. 82–93.

[10] *Ibid.,* pp. 103–113.

[11] *Ibid.,* pp. 119–120.

[12] *Ibid.,* pp. 311–312.

[13] R. B. Dyk and H. A. Witkin, "Family Experiences Related to Development of Differentiation in Children," *Child Development,* 36 (1965), 21–56.

[14] N. Konstadt and E. Forman, "Field Dependence and External Directedness," *Journal of Personality and Social Psychology,* 1 (1965), 490–493.

[15] J. Kagan, B. L. Rosman, D. Day, J. Albert, and W. Phillips, "Information Processing in the Child: Significance of Analytic and Reflective Attitudes," *Psychological Monographs,* No. 578, 77, No. 1 (1964), 1–37.

[16] *Ibid.,* p. 3.

[17] *Ibid.,* p. 9.

[18] *Ibid.,* p. 19.

[19] *Ibid.,* p. 35.

[20] *Ibid.,* p. 37.

[21] *Ibid.,* p. 25.

[22] Jessie J. Lovano, "The Relation of Cognitive Style and Modes of Perception and Graphic Expression." Unpublished Ph.D. dissertation, University of Oregon, 1969.

[23] Stephen A. Karp and Norma L. Konstadt, Manual for *Children's Embedded Figure Test* (Palo Alto, Calif.: Consulting Psychologists Press, 1963).

[24] Witkin, et al., *Psychological Differentiation* (1962), pp. 119–120.

[25] Michael A. Wallach and Helen L. Thomas, "Graphic Constriction and Expansiveness as a Function of Induced Social Isolation and Social Interaction: Experimental Manipulations and Personality Effects," *Journal of Personality,* 31 (1963), 491–509.

[26] A. R. Jensen, "The Maudsley Personality Inventory," *Acta Psychol.,* 14 (1958), 314–325.

[27] Robert M. Knights, "Test Anxiety and Visual Discrimination of Social Scenes," *Child Development,* 36 (1965), 1083–1090.

[28] Norma McCoy, "Effects of Test Anxiety on Children's Performance as a Function of Instructions and Type of Task," *Journal of Personality and Social Psychology,* 2 (1965), 634–641.

[29] Ronald K. Penny, "Reactive Curiosity and Manifest Anxiety in Children," *Child Development,* 36 (1965), 697–702.

[30] Herbert G. Birch and Herbert S. Rabinowitz, "The Negative Effect of Previous Experience on Productive Thinking," *Journal of Experimental Psychology,* 41 (1951), 121–125.

[31] J. S. Bruner, L. J. Postman, and J. Rodrigues, "Expectation and the Perception of Color," *American Journal of Psychology,* 64 (1951), 216–227.

[32] Merle Lawrence, *Studies in Human Behavior* (Princeton: Princeton University Press, 1949), pp. 67–69.

5

Environmental Influences on Children's Readiness for Art

In the previous chapters we have seen the wide ranges of individual differences among children and adults in their modes of becoming aware, of sorting and organizing information, and of making creative responses. These behaviors are central to behavior in art. Now we will turn our attention to those things in the environment that inhibit or encourage children in channeling their learnings in different patterns. The subculture in which a child is raised, his immediate interaction with his close relatives and his peers, and his secondary interaction with teachers and his school environment also direct the development of his patterns of cognitive behavior and his perceptual and conceptual development. These are his tools for interpreting and responding to his environment, and they become his bases for responding to and creating art.

Our society has many more subcultures than are generally recognized. Milton M. Gordon's extensive analysis of the persistence of subcultures in perpetuating themselves shows that child-rearing practices, values and attitudes about reality, and ideas about education are not "melting" into the social "pot" to the degree we assume.[1] Gordon introduces the concept of "ethclass" because he found, for example, that middle-class Americans have similarities in culture whether they are Negro, Jewish, Anglo-Saxon, Oriental, or of any other ethnic group. In other words, the melting pot of common goals and education has made diverse people more alike. But at the same time, each of these groups has ethnic-related differences.

Social-class groups also have life-styles that vary, as we will see in later studies. People who live in slums or ghettos are usually stereotyped as lower class, but they will vary widely in cultural pattern depending upon their particular experience and ethnic background. Blue-collar workers, often making as much money as middle-class people, have somewhat different life styles, and these vary with industry, region, and ethnic background.

Thus Gordon believes that knowing an individual's ethclass—his ethnic background and his social class—will give us a better basis for understanding his behavior and the environment in which he has learned to respond through interaction.

To gain perspective on the roles of culture on art behavior we will first look at cultures more remote from our own and then return to look at the immediate situation in which we are teaching. We will be concerned with the ways in which a child's subculture affects the development of his abilities and habits of responding.

Culture as a Factor in Children's Art

In the anthropological sense, culture means the attitudes, values, the patterns of roles and acceptable behavior, and the concepts of reality shared by a group of people. The particular culture that a child lives in affects his perceptual development and the nature of his art. The culture influences the direction of his perceptual training by giving him many more opportunities and rewards for observing the things important to his group than for observing those that are not stressed. In order to see the differences among children who have experienced different cultures, we will examine nonliterate cultures. The purpose here is to give us better insight into our own culture and its many subcultures.

Among the Zia Indians of New Mexico a marked difference in the drawing ability of boys and girls has been observed. The differences become apparent in the first grade and continue throughout life. In this culture boys are expected to be able to paint animal pictures on the walls to encourage animal fertility. A requirement for attaining manhood is the ability to paint the ceremonial masks and other religious objects. Parents and siblings encourage the boys and praise their progress. Girls, on the other hand, are not given representational art goals to work toward; their art work is limited to geometric designs on pottery. Boys, who are encouraged to observe and draw many things, draw pictures that show greater detail than do the girls' pictures. The difference in sex roles in this culture has a strong relationship to the perceiving and drawing behavior of the children.[2]

The Orotchens are a nomadic tribe of Northern Siberia who live by herding reindeer. In a climate of long winters, short springs, and rainy colorless summers, the Orotchen is dependent on reindeer for his food, clothing, and shelter. At the time of this study the only apparatus these people had from the outside world consisted of a few pots and sewing equipment. The group had few visible art forms. Their tents were undecorated; clothing and shelter were their major productions. A few members of the group had been in the outside world, and some of these had learned to read and write. Literacy was estimated at two or three per cent. The children had never been to school and, except for a few wrappers on packages, were not familiar with symbols that have meaning on a page.

An anthropologist, studying the tribe for a summer, ran a school for the children. There were a few primers that included simple pictures. The teacher also provided sketch pads and pencils. Not being an artist himself, he did not attempt to teach the children to draw. These children had received no drawing training, but all their drawings showed the influence of sharpened visual perception and keen observation. One drawing of a reindeer by a ten-year-old boy has foreshortening in the antlers and legs indicating the forward motion of the animal (Figure 5–1A). The general size and proportions are lifelike. The eyes and the antlers show fine detail. (A man in the same picture is a stick figure with little detail except he has a head, a body, two arms, and two legs.) A drawing by a thirteen-year-old (Figure 5–1B) shows sensitivity to the essence and feeling of the reindeer through the use of beautiful line and form.[3]

Figure 5–1. Orotchen Children's Drawings A. A Ten-Year-Old B. A Thirteen-Year-Old (from A. Schubert)

The objects that are important to the child and the values he has learned direct him to observe some things more closely than others. The importance of value as a director of perceptual training is clearly evident. Among the Orotchens the reindeer is the central factor in the culture, and observations of the reindeer are reinforced again and again throughout the life of the child.

A study of the perceptual tendencies of children on Saipan was made by two psychiatrists who are highly skilled in the use of the Rorschach Inkblot Test. Part of their purpose was to determine whether these children responded to fine detail or to large detail in responding to the ink blots. Fifty boys and fifty girls in each of the two tribes, the Chamorros and the Carolinians, were selected. They ranged in age from five to seventeen. The researchers found that whole responses and large-detail responses occurred twice as frequently in the records of the Carolinian children as in the records of the Chamorros. This is an example of an island having two cultures which differ to the point that their children's perceptual responses are measurably different.[4]

In each of these groups, differences in culture roles or in values tend to vary the perceptual experience, practice, and in some cases the art activity of the children. We can assume that such differences would be found among children in Western cultures as well. Anastasi and Foley, differential psychologists, carefully analyzed the drawings at an international exhibition of children's drawings, held at Rockefeller Center in 1934. Children between six and twelve from forty-one countries were represented. Differences in emphasis in detail in the same painting, comparable to those of the Orotchen children's, were found. Wide differences in the amount of detail and in the kind of subject matter appeared among the children of the same age in Western culture countries.[5] In the drawing of vegetation, European children tended to show only the general features while children in tropical areas drew plants in such detail that varieties could be identified. Children in societies where ceremonial dress is elaborate, such as Hungarian, Czechoslovakian, Balinese, and American Indian, often showed the costumes in great detail but neglected detail in other objects.

Culture as a Director of Drawing Development

In cultures where a strong system of symbolic communication has been developed (such as the Kwakiutl) the children's drawings tend to approach the "symbolic realism" of the culture. In the case of the Orotchen tribe, there was no apparent system of communicating through symbols in the culture. Yet the children's perceptions of the highly valued reindeer were so acute that they were able, without instruction, to draw them in detail. In drawing objects like the human figure they tended to use the crudest form of symbolism. The cultural values acted as directors that increased their ability to draw some objects. By contrast, in those cultures where a strong pictorial art form exists, the children tend to develop their drawings in terms of the accepted culture symbols.

Psychologists Anastasi and Foley studied the drawings of children of the Indian cultures from the Kwakiutl, Nass River, Bella Bella, Haida, Tsimshian, and Bella Coola tribes. The children, 90 boys and 69 girls attending a government school at Alert Bay, ranged in age from five to eighteen.[6]

The drawings had been collected in 1931 by anthropologist Franz Boas, who had asked each child to draw an animal. These children had been affected by Western culture to some degree at the school, but the influence of their own culture and experience was clearly evident. Individual differences were found at all age levels. The psychologists found that many of the children from age nine up were drawing "stylized" symbols of animals as found in adult art of their own tribes. These included the culture symbols of the killer whale, the sea lion, the mythical thunderbird and double-headed serpent. The drawings were similar to those of adults, not only in subject matter but in technique. Another group of drawings by children in both the younger and older groups were outline symbols but had little detail. Some of the children made realistic drawings of animals in their immediate environment, the boys of animals to be hunted and the girls of the smaller domestic animals.[7] Anastasi and Foley summarize their analysis of these drawings:

Both the subject matter and the technique of the drawings reflect specific cultural and experimental factors rather than age differences or developmental stages. Any attempt to employ specific features of the child's drawing as an index of developmental level independently of the child's experiential background is doomed to failure. An Indian child of the north Pacific coast . . . may produce a symbolic representation rich in stylized details that it would be futile to evaluate in terms of norms established elsewhere.[8]

The "Draw-a-Man Test" developed by Goodenough in 1924 has had
extensive use and development as a nonverbal IQ test.[9] It is important
in studying behavior in art because it measures the child's cognitive
development as modified by culture and experience, his memory of
past perceptions, and his ability to sort visual information into ideas
which are then symbolized in a drawing. Drawings are analyzed to
see how well the child discriminates within a class of objects such as
details of the human figure, the parts and details of hands and feet, or

details of clothing. It was first assumed to be "culture fair," usable in any culture because it did not employ words. In his 1963 work, Harris recommends that points of the scale be restandardized for every group having distinct dress forms, educational opportunities, and life style.[10] His recent studies also indicate that culture change affects scores and that present-day children score higher than did the children of 1924. Sex differences are closely related to child-rearing practices and to the different motivations given boys and girls. Among groups of American Indians boys usually excel girls in drawing, but the reverse was found among American Negro and Puerto Rican children.[11]

The psychologist Dennis has studied responses to the "Draw-a-Man Test" for some years; recently he compiled a cross-cultural analysis of six-year-olds' drawings from three continents and eleven countries. Six-year-olds were chosen because they were least influenced by schooling. In each school all the six-year-olds present on a given day were tested.[12]

Dennis found wide differences in mean IQ scores ranging from 53 to 125. An analysis of the places where mean scores were above 110 indicated that these children lived in cultures where art forms were highly developed, as in Japan, or where the children had many visual stimuli of pictures, books, magazines, art objects, crayons, pencils, and visual play materials, as in a predominantly middle-class Midwestern town in the United States.[13] Navaho and Hopi Indian boys scored high, probably because art is central to their society and is related to male status and religious ritual.

Brooklyn Jewish boys in Yeshiva schools also scored above 110. But in another study, Brooklyn Jewish boys nine to eleven years old in the ultraconservative Hassidic group, who are not allowed to observe the mass media nor to draw the human figure, had a mean IQ score (as measured by the Goodenough test) of 79, a score that did not correlate highly with other measurements of this group's intelligence.[14]

In a study of children in the Middle East, Dennis found Moslem children's mean IQ score (as measured by the Goodenough test) decreasing as children in successively older grades were measured, a change which indicated that the more they learned their culture value against drawing the human figure, the less able they were to draw it in detail.[15]

Dennis also found that sex differences seem to be related more to culture—environmental influence—than to biological factors. For example, in Rockville, Maryland, white girls had a mean score of 119 while boys had a mean score of 109; but on several Navaho Indian reservations, girls had a mean score of 91 while boys had a mean score of 115.[16]

Dennis interprets his data to indicate that modernization and/or an artistic or pictorially stimulating environment contribute to children's scores before the children are much exposed to schooling (first grade).[17] These data strongly support the idea that perceptual experiences with pictures are important variables in children's readiness to respond to their environment and then symbolize it. All these children *see men*; the variable is apparently exposure to iconic or photographic representations, including pictures of men. The differences were not just urban-rural either; low-scoring and high-scoring groups could be found in both large cities and small towns. Early exposure to iconic information—pictures and other art forms—appears to affect a child's ability to handle information, to differentiate, to observe, and to symbolize his knowledge. These abilities, as measured by the Goodenough tests, are important contributors to cognitive growth and readiness for art activity.

These abilities are also important for the development of complex civilizations. Bohannon, who has analyzed art and communication, considers art a major means for communicating cultural images. He says that an important part of the maturation of human beings is learning to communicate what they perceive.[18] The art developed by a group of people is an outgrowth of their shared perceptions and their shared expressions, as these are modified by their values and belief systems and the variations in individual interpretation. Art then is a major communication system. Art experiences, both in producing and responding to art, are means for developing both conceptual and perceptual cognition and cultural understanding.

Cognitive Growth in Different Cultures

The effects of the environment on the development of cognitive styles has also been shown with studies of problem solving.

One of the most extensive studies of the effects of different environments on the direction of cognitive growth has been done by Bruner and his associates.[19] They have studied problem-solving processes of children and adults in different parts of the world so that comparisons could be made of the effects that the environment has on the ways people handle visual information and solve problems. They are concerned with the use of percepts and concepts in the sorting and organizing habits of people who have different cultural and educational experience.

Among the studies reported by the Bruner group, Greenfield analyzed the ways in which enriched or impoverished environment affects cognitive growth—as contrasted to Piaget's theories based on studies of middle-class European and American children.[20]

Greenfield studied nine groups of Senegalese Wolof children. Three degrees of urbanization and three age levels were tested. The ages studied were six to seven, eight to nine, and eleven to thirteen. Group I children, rural unschooled, lived in extended family compounds of several small thatched huts. Group II children lived in similar compounds but were attending school. Group III children were exposed to Western culture, living in urban Dakar and attending first, third, and sixth grade in French style schools. The minutely detailed curriculum was the same for both bush and city schools.

The children were given the *conservation of quantity* test, which was

Figure 5–3. The Water Jar Test

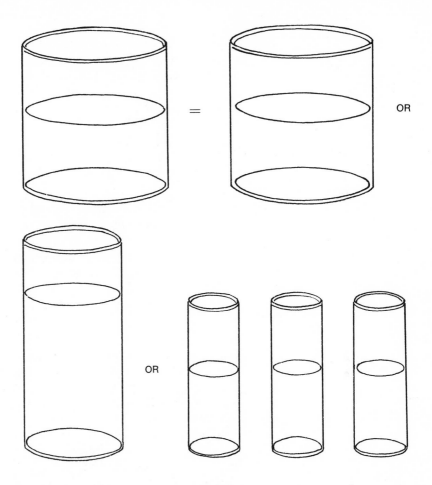

also used by Piaget. In the test the subject judges whether the amount of water is the same or different in varied shaped beakers (see Figure 5–3). A child has achieved conservation when he sees that the amount of water is the same irrespective of the size or shape of the containers.

About 50% of American children achieve conservation (they see the amount of water as the same even though it looks different) by first grade, 75% by third grade. In the Greenfield study, 52% of bush school children achieved conservation by first grade (but they were older) and 80% by third grade. Dakar children were much poorer on performance, but they appeared to try to reason more in making their decisions. Less than 20% of them succeeded after six months in first grade, less than 40% at third; but they, like the bush school children, achieved close to 100% by the sixth grade. The bush unschooled children did not achieve the average third grade level of correct responses even by sixth grade.

Tests with adults in Senegalese and other cultures indicate that persons who have no schooling do not improve their ability to achieve conservation after the age of nine. The influence of the environment through schooling made the cognitive development of some bush children much more like that of American children than like that of unschooled bush children raised in the same or similar villages. There was ample evidence that the unschooled were as bright as the schooled; they were all tested with instructions in their native language.

Maccoby and Modiano made studies comparing urban and rural American children with urban and rural Mexican children in a test of their abilities in grouping pictures of objects.[21] They found that six-year-old American and Mexican children were similar in their use of *perceptual qualities*. Older Mexican children had increased sensitivity to perceptual subtleties of color and form. The older American middle-class suburban children were more abstract in their thinking processes. For example, they grouped pictures of things by ways the things functioned or by large categories which contained all the things, such as all the things that could be eaten.

When rural and urban Mexican children were compared at ages eight to ten and twelve to thirteen, other differences also were found.

Twelve-year-old rural Mexican children were found to be sensitive to the differences between things, to perceptual characteristics of the objects and also to their extrinsic functions, what one can do to things. The older urban Mexican children showed more abstract thinking, using names of things for grouping. Their classifications were highly functional, concerned with what things can do. The urban children were also more sensitive to likenesses than to differences.

Maccoby and Modiano propose that "if the peasant child is not dulled by village life, he will experience the uniqueness of events, objects and people. But as the city child grows older, he may end by exchanging a spontaneous, less alienated relationship to the world for a more sophisticated outlook which concentrates on using, exchanging, or cataloging. What industrialized, urban man gains in an increased ability to formulate, to reason and to code the ever more numerous bits of complex information he acquires, he may lose in a decreased sensitivity to people and events."[22] This intense education in "using, exchanging, and cataloging" leads urban children to alienate themselves from the qualities of their visual environment.

Education is a major force for enculturating children into a society. As Dennis found that the older children who were exposed to enculturation processes in Moslem society decreased in ability to draw the man because of cultural prohibitions against such drawing, so we find evidence that increased conceptual emphasis in American education decreases children's use of perceptual cues.

The effects of extended schooling on middle-class children were shown in picture-relating tasks done by children ages six through twelve in a study by Olver and Hornsby.[23]

Forty-two watercolor drawings (Figure 5–4) were shown to boys ages six to twelve in suburban Boston. They were asked to sort the pictures into similar groups and tell why they grouped them as they did. Each of 90 children repeated the task ten times, sorting by perceptual attributes. Grouping by "how things look" was the largest category at age six (47%), but decreased to 27% at age eight, and to 20% at age

eleven. Functional attributes (how things work) increased from 30% at age six to 48–47% at ages eight and eleven. Nominal grouping (by name classification) was only 6% at age six, 23% at age eight, and 32% at age eleven.[24] This study suggests that these children tend to rely less on perceptual characteristics and more on functions and name categories. Studies seem to indicate that schooling, in general, emphasizes the conceptual tools and leaves children's perceptual development to chance. There is nothing in the data that suggests that one type of learning precludes the other. Adults can be highly developed in both. Male commercial art students and female fine arts students are among the upper third of the intellectual population yet are highly perceptual.[25]

Art programs can provide consistent and continuing perceptual experience to help children develop cognitive styles which include both conceptual and perceptual development. But art education which stresses projective "self-expression" may only be helping children to express their concepts and may not be helping them increase their perceptual awarenesses. Children can develop both perceptual and conceptual awareness when they are encouraged to explore visual phenomena; to observe changes in shape, line, color, and texture as these elements interact in space and light; to solve problems involving the interactions produced as these same elements are ordered and varied in designed space; and to study varied affective responses—different emotional feelings—stimulated by differences in iconic symbolism and design.

In these studies we have seen that educational processes in Western civilization tend to channel learnings through conceptual abstractions of visual reality rather than through visual reality itself. Sorting and organizing of information is done more in terms of what things *do* rather than how they look.

Some degree of perceptual development does take place in all people. Apparently not only the school but also the larger cultural environment affects how children learn to interact. At the same time that school children are becoming generally more conceptually abstract and are using fewer perceptual cues in their cognitive process, school experience is modifying their uses of some of their perceptual abilities. In a study in South Africa, Hudson compared children who attended school and children who did not attend school, both Negro and white, on the kind of responses they gave to a black-and-white photograph and to outline drawings.[26] Learning to "read" three-dimensional qualities in two-dimensional pictures is apparently a learned behavior. The children in school gave more frequent correct responses, indicating they saw the photograph as representing three dimensions. The school children had learned to see better in photographs than in outline drawings. The school children also responded more often to outline drawings that contained size differences according to depth and overlapping than they did to drawings showing linear perspective (see Figure 5–5 A, B, and C).

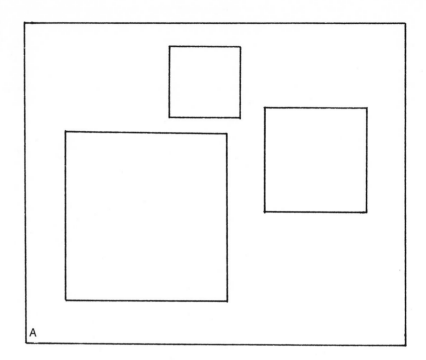

Among the children who did not attend school, not one saw the photograph as having three-dimensional qualities. They also were less able than the school-attending children to see depth in two-dimensional drawings representing three-dimensional space.

Since those children in segregated schools in South Africa are all trained in Western traditions, we would assume that they also would use conceptual cues more than perceptual cues to solve problems; the nonliterate would use perceptual cues more. Yet these non-literate children facing drawings and a photograph lacked the ability to respond to cues of three-dimensional space. These materials indicate that seeing is a complex behavior.

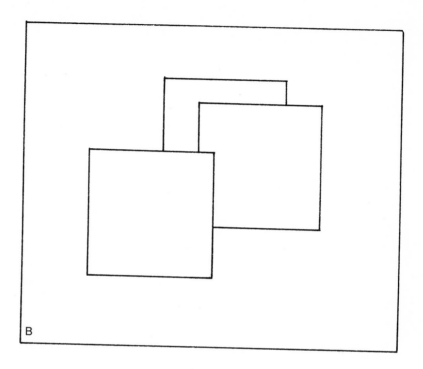

Segall, Campbell, and Herskovits have made an extensive survey of their own and other studies relating perception to culture.[27] They have found that perception, like other human behaviors, is strongly influenced by culture; that perception is in large part learned behavior; that people in a given culture tend to show the same perceptual behavior; that living in a carpentered right-angled world produces different perceptual habits than living in a simple rural environment — that is, one brings to bear on new situations the information one has learned in the past. As the rain forest Pigmy Kengi discovered, past experience in a close-range environment is inadequate when one is taken to the open plains; Kengi had to respond to familiar objects at a greater distance than he had ever before perceived.

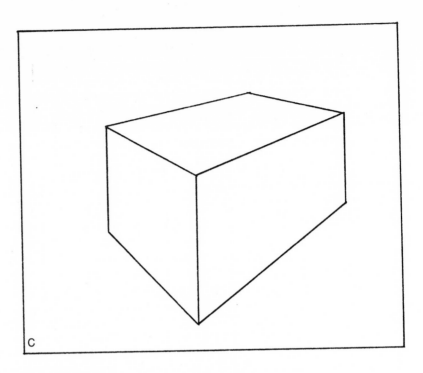

C

Art Behavior and Subcultural Differences

The studies we have already reviewed indicate that middle-class children are probably more concept-oriented than percept-oriented in their learnings. Yet, considering the diversity of ethnic subcultures in Western society and the differences in experience of children in different socio-economic groups or ethclasses, teachers in every classroom have pupils of widely different degrees of readiness to respond to art forms and to nature and wide differences in ability to symbolize or make images.

Lesser, Fifer, and Clark studied four mental abilities (verbal, reasoning, quantitative, and spatial conceptualization) among four ethnic groups of first grade children (Chinese, Negro, Jewish, and Puerto Rican) of both middle-class and lower-class families.[28] They found that each ethnic group fit a unique pattern in relation to the other groups but that within this pattern social class made a difference. When the scores of ethnic groups as a whole were analyzed there were distinctly different patterns. Jewish children were first in verbal and quantitative skills, second in reasoning and spatial conceptualizing. Chinese children were third in verbal abilities, first in reasoning and spatial conceptualization, and second in quantitative skills. Negro children were second in verbal ability but fourth in the other three abilities; Puerto Ricans were fourth in verbal ability but third in reasoning, quantitative skills, and spatial conceptualization. But when the middle-class children in all these groups were compared they were more like each other than were the lower-class ethnic groups when they were compared. Apparently, learning to be middle class involves learning those skills which enable one to do better on these kinds of tests. Irrespective of the class likenesses, the ethnic pattern persists; for example, the middle-class Negro children were higher in verbal skills than in the other three abilities, and the Chinese were better than the Jewish in reasoning but not in verbal skills. Lower-class children as measured in this sample also were in the pattern of their ethnic group, but in all cases their mean scores were lower than scores of middle-class children of the same ethnic group. The authors point out that these differences are due to living among people who share the same culture and are not due to factors of race.

In a cross-class study of drawing ability, Eisner found that disadvantaged children did less well than advantaged children when they had to translate their experience and memory of three-dimensional space on a flat two-dimensional plane.[29] Children in grades one, three, five and seven from Negro and white families in both slum and upper-middle-class communities were given a standardized drawing test. Independent judges rated the drawings on fourteen categories of spatial organization, including the use of the base line, overlapping, floating objects, and combinations of these organizations from most simple to most complex.

Several interesting findings resulted. *One,* there were no significant sex differences at any grade level. *Two,* there was little difference between the mean at grade one and the mean at grade three for either boys or girls, but between grades three and five and then five and seven, mean scores were found to be higher at each higher grade level. Though no test of significance was reported, it would appear that these differences would approach significance; that is, they could not have happened just by chance. *Three,* when the children were compared by social class very significant differences were found at all levels, with the advantaged children being much more adept in depicting space according to typical childhood techniques such as the drawing of images on the base line. The use of the base line is probably associated with Western-style education in which children learn to put symbols on lines. Advantaged children who have more experience with books are more often exposed to the base line orientation.

At the seventh grade the differences between the two groups are still in evidence but the difference is much smaller. Eisner suggests that neither group of students has been given much training in use of technical perspective for depicting space. Eisner's study relates to that of Hudson; middle-class children could respond to overlapping cues better than they could to formal perspective space cues.

In terms of what we know of the space constancies and of the increased dependence of school children on conceptual rather than perceptual information, we may interpret the Eisner data as evidence that both groups of children have learned stereotyped concepts for viewing space. The advantaged group has learned to use more complex forms. Neither group has learned to analyze form in space, although perhaps they would be able to learn to do so. Yet our cross-cultural data show that Orotchen children and Japanese children who score highly on the Draw-a-Man test also evidence three-dimensional detail in their drawings. This comparison indicates that when a culture stresses acute perceptual development, children draw perspective without first having to learn a perspective system. This occurrence does not mean that perspective should not be taught, but rather that teaching a formal perspective system without helping children learn to *see* forms change in size and shape can be frustrating to both teacher and pupils.

Though there is strong evidence of the persistence of culture in the various ethclasses of society, we have found that middle-class people are in many ways similar to each other. There also are common traits that can be found among the different ethnic groups that are economically deprived. A teacher such as the art specialist, who moves from classroom to classroom, may have large numbers of students. He cannot plan so much for individual differences as he can for cultural differences among schools or classrooms. He must plan a curriculum that is appropriate for the largest number of pupils.

One of the most critical problems in the world today is the education of great masses of children whose backgrounds do not prepare them to operate effectively in the dominant cultures of their countries. School values usually reflect the dominant or core culture. There are economically and socially deprived children in the United States who live close to the most affluent of the world's cultures yet are separated by many social, economic, and psychological barriers from participation in it, except vicariously through mass media.

Many studies have been made of their problems. Comparisons have been made of the behavior of deprived children with that of middle-class white children, and the difference has been considered a deficit on the part of the lower-class children. Actually, if behaviors were judged according to what a child has learned in coping with his *own environment*, the middle class in his and the lower class in his, the meanings of the findings on ability to learn might be quite different.

If information about the child's learned relation to his environment were used as a means of structuring a more meaningful educational experience for him, then perhaps more learning would take place. Unfortunately, studies of the many cultures of people who are not in the mainstream of American life are few.

Kluckhohn and Strodtbeck have made extensive contrast studies of the cultures of different Southwest peoples, some of whom are advantaged by being part of the dominant white culture and others who are deprived by being part of low-income groups as well as being members of numerically smaller ethnic groups.[30] A Mormon group and a rural Texas group were considered as part of the dominant culture; Zuñi, Navaho, and Spanish-American groups were considered deprived. The first two groups follow the pattern of dominant American society; they are future oriented, they believe that man has power over nature, they stress individualism over family organization, and they have strong values on doing over being.

The Spanish-American, Zuñi, and Navaho groups are concerned with the present, they work with nature rather than trying to control nature, and they are more concerned with the family than with individualism. The Zuñi and the Navaho are more involved with doing, an attitude which is reflected in their many crafts. The Spanish-Americans tested were more concerned with the qualities of being.

Schneiderman studied the contrasting values of middle-class school teachers and social workers with a group of white people who had long histories of being on relief.[31] The teachers and social workers had values similar to those of the Mormons and the rural Texas group. The people on relief, who had learned to adapt to different life conditions, were more concerned for the present, were less concerned with individuality, and were much more concerned with being than doing. When being for today is contrasted with doing for the future we see how much in conflict teachers' values and pupils' values may be.

In a study of impoverished children from various subcultures in the Southwest, a group of teachers and I found that the children had had little experience with *doing* anything with their hands — using tools, repairing, cleaning, or polishing. Most of their activities were passive. Their most important value was being happy. Only 25% reported that getting ahead of others or working alone was important.[32]

A teacher working with such children needs to make some important value judgments. He needs to ask himself, "Can I help these children to become more self-directive, to succeed in art, and to learn to cope with life in the dominant culture without destroying their sense of belonging in their family group? Can I encourage them to be concerned about the future without destroying their concern for the present? Does learning the dominant culture mean leaving the subculture?"

McFee has identified what he calls "the 150% man" among Blackfeet Indians. He found Indian-oriented individuals who also understood and could operate successfully in the rural Montana culture. They were leaders among their own people as well as being effective in their dealings with the dominant culture both on and off the reservation.[33]

One of the problems most teachers have is that they either were reared in the dominant middle class or have learned its values. People tend to be ethno- and class-centric, seeing other ethnic groups and other classes as variations from their own culture. To help children from the many subcultures, the teacher must try to understand the workings of other value systems in order to understand the children's behavior. For example, a Spanish-American child may appear to be uncreative because he is lacking in self-direction and motivation to do things that will affect his future. Actually he may be a frightened child, because the culture and the rewards at school are so different from those at home. Encouragement to express "himself," what he feels and thinks, could be meaningless when he has been trained to feel and think like his extended family group, to enjoy passively rather than to manipulate or to change things.

While middle-class children are advantaged in cognitive development, they may be disadvantaged in terms of their motivation to engage in free use of materials that suggest a value conflict with "keeping clean." In a study of nursery school children of different socio-economic backgrounds, Alper compared finger-painting behavior to toilet training practice. As a group, the eighteen middle-class children had an average of 11.2 months longer toilet training than did the eighteen lower-class children. The middle-class standards of cleanliness were also much more exacting. Each child was asked individually to paint, and his behavior was reported by trained observers. Seventeen lower-class but only five middle-class children began to paint immediately. Seventeen lower-class and only eight middle-class children used both hands. Ten lower-class children and only one middle-class child used warm colors.

In another study with two similar groups, crayons were used instead of finger paints. The differences in response between the two groups were slight.[34]

A teacher might misinterpret a lack of creativity in a child as due to the child's lack of potential. The child's behavior may instead be a reticence to use the particular medium being offered. Understanding of the values in a child's subculture would probably lead the teacher to introduce other media of expression.

In such a case the teacher would need to recognize the child's learned values and see how the child might be encouraged to work creatively within the context of his own subculture. A group of children working together on a task related to their own subculture, a task that uses their ability to reflect on the present, could be a beginning of a teacher's experimental efforts to find avenues for the development of the children's creative potential. Each situation needs to be handled somewhat differently. Not all Spanish-American children have the same values. Some are from predominantly Mexican-Indian background, some are mainly Spanish, some have a mixture of heritages. Some are from closely knit extended families, others are neither strongly Mexican nor strongly Anglo. Holland found many children in Arizona who spoke neither Spanish nor English very well and who knew little of either Mexican or American culture. Some of these children appeared eager to become Anglos; others wanted to retain their own Mexican culture.[35]

The teacher in a large city has the responsibility of helping children learn to live in different kinds of environments during urban renewal and to develop responsibilities for their contribution to the shared environment of the city. He should also help the children find avenues for maintaining their own subculture through art.

In a review of others' research and his own research with deprived children Jensen notes that the child's early environment affects his capacity to learn, to see, to select from the visual information he receives, and to interpret its meaning. His early perceptual learning experience becomes the foundation upon which subsequent perceptions are learned.

The nature of one's early learning is a strong determinant of the rate and kind of information handling one will have in the future. Experimentation with rats indicates that visually deprived rats can learn and make up for their earlier experience by later experience with a more stimulating visual environment. Jensen assumes that visually deprived children can also improve their ability to handle information if they are placed in a more stimulating visual environment.[36] Bruner has shown that children who are deprived in sensory development are handicapped in their ability to construct models of their environment.[37]

The relationship of mother-child interaction and learning differs between middle-class and lower-class children. Hess and Shipman have studied the ways mothers in these groups use language (global or differentiated) and encourage learning styles (rote or problem-solving) as they help their children learn. The researchers tested 163 Negro mothers and their four-year-old children from middle-class, blue-collar, and lower-class socio-economic groups.[38]

All the mothers were taught three simple tasks that are related to art behavior:

1. To arrange a group of plastic toys, by color and by function.

2. To sort eight children's blocks by two visual characteristics simultaneously.

3. To copy five designs.

Each mother then taught the tasks to her child, with some concern for the elements of size, shape, color, and/or form as appropriate. Each mother-child session was evaluated by the experimenters.

Generally speaking, middle-class children learned better than lower-class children. No differences were evident between the socio-economic groups in the affective attitudes of mothers. Middle-class mothers did use more descriptive detailed language, while the other mothers were more global. Lower-class mothers were more insistent that their child perform correctly and that he respond impulsively. Blue-collar-class mothers expected their children to learn passively; middle-class mothers encouraged more active reflective and problem-solving learning.

In a summary of art in compensatory education, Hess, Hess, and Rosen interpret this study and other studies with implications for art education.[39] They point out that a child's visual mode or style is the result of the way he learns to give meaning to what he sees through his interaction with adults in the same situation.

For example, a mother with highly differentiated concepts might describe a child's toy train by saying, "This little train is just like the big train that we rode into the city. Both have powerful engines run by electricity; both have cars for people to ride in as they go to work and return home at night. Your little train, like the real one, has a light which is very bright to alert people at crossings down the track."

A mother with highly developed percepts as well as concepts would also describe how the train looks, "See the shining red engine, the pattern of the cars as they go along the track, the shadows the train casts as it goes alongside buildings and trees and open country. See the way the cars change shapes as they go around corners, the color of the lights." Such a mother might then ask the child to imagine the changing view that a passenger would see from the window.

A mother whose percepts and concepts were less well developed might tell her child that this was a toy train, it runs by electricity, and has cars for dolls to ride in.

The first mother was relating functions with uses, the second was adding visual qualities to functions and uses and was encouraging her child to develop active visualization and imagination, while the third was only categorizing things about the train without showing relationships or giving her child a more complex pattern for learning and retaining new information about the trains, relating percepts and concepts. In our example, each mother was stressing the development of a somewhat different cognitive style, more conceptual or more perceptual, with different degrees of differentiation or detail.

The Hesses suggest that teachers should help children increase discrimination through observation and then give them opportunities to express their perceptions imaginatively. They suggest that such visual and tactile experiences can help the child whose language is meager. He can become aware of spatial elements, of likenesses and differences in his visual world, and then develop conceptual tools to increase his verbal communication of what he sees. They believe that many of the programs for the disadvantaged that include many trips to new places are beyond the children's readiness to see. They strongly recommend giving these children direct experience in observing their own environment. The Hesses believe that art will actively help passive, deprived children assert themselves in interaction processes necessary to learning.

Edmund Gordon, in a review of research on deprived children, indicates that such children must understand the differences between their subcultures and the dominant cultures in order to move upward socially.[40] But he questions whether it is *necessary* to demean all a child has learned in his own social environment. Gordon points to the great cultural variety among deprived children. As Milton Gordon pointed out (see page 112), great cultural variety exists at all class levels of society.

Discontinuity

Each culture develops a system of right-and-wrong behavior. Much of the conventional behavior within a culture is known by all the members and is adhered to by most of them, because a system of rewards and punishments has been set up to compel members to conform. In Western culture, if a person does "right," he is rewarded with money, praise, security, and various pleasures. If he does "wrong," he is punished with ridicule, imprisonment, fines, or even death. While the rules are not always clearly defined, nor the rewards and punishments always consistent, most adults have a fairly good idea of what is expected of them and can take responsibility for their degree of conformity.

Not so the child. He is not born with the knowledge that to say "thank you" is right and to break windows is wrong. He learns item by item what behavior is expected of him. Adults reward and punish him according to *their* values. Not all adults have the same values. The two parents may differ; and when the child goes to school and is in a new subculture, he may find still a different value system, a system that he must learn to conform to by experience. He may find that what he was rewarded for at home brings no reward here, and that what he was punished for at home is not punished here. He is experiencing a *discontinuity.*[41]

Discontinuity and Culture Change

The child must continually deal with discontinuities, because not only is he moving about in several subcultures, he is also living in a rapidly changing larger culture. The core culture and the subcultures are never static. They are acted upon by various forces. *Cultural maintenance* is the force that, to some degree, attempts to perpetuate the customs and values that are accepted by the group. Parents and schools and other institutions give each succeeding generation the means by which they can maintain the culture.

Cultural reaction is the force of those groups who want to return to earlier ways of life, generally resisting all other kinds of change. In a school this force may appear as suggestions to bring back the "old hickory stick."

Cultural change is caused by happenings within the group and throughout the world. Basic inventions that lead to many new inventions influence the whole world. They result in *innovations*. Whenever people of different cultures have contact with each other, *cultural confluence* takes place. People who meet change each other. Cultural confluence has been accelerated by the ease of travel and the widespread distribution of books, art forms, and almost immediate communication. Wars, threats of war, and catastrophes also change the way of life of a people. Civil-rights developments, racial conflicts, differing attitudes about sex, and counterreactions to all these forces contribute to cultural change. (See Figure 5–6.)

Figure 5–6. Cultural Dynamics in a Complex Society

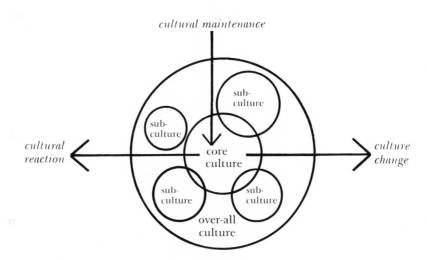

Each child in school represents a particular family variation of the core, or of a subculture group or ethclass within the larger society. He is influenced by cultural reaction, cultural maintenance, and cultural change as his group is influenced. Also the child, being unique, has received his family's culture in a way somewhat different from other children in the same family.

Each teacher in a school represents a similar family and subculture group at some point of change. He is operating in a regional and a particular socio-economic society, of which the school is a unit. The teacher is a cultural mediator; he selects those values, patterns of behavior, and concepts of reality that have most meaning for him. He needs to be aware of his own values in order to appraise what he is transmitting to children.

What the child learns from the teacher depends on his cultural preparation to learn. The teaching in one classroom may be the same—with one teacher—but the learning will differ according to the individual children. They represent varied phases of culture change or reaction.

Enculturation

Enculturation is the process by which children learn their culture. Much of this learning takes place before children come to school; it continues through much of their face-to-face group experience and through mass media. Enculturation, a major factor in personality development, contributes to the psychological environment in which children are learning habits and attitudes. Harsh and Schrickel[42] state: "The earlier view of personality as a kind of substance with inhering properties or traits is giving way to a dynamic conception wherein personality is viewed not as a thing . . . but as a complex of functions of interactive forces. . . ." Today a major force in the interaction process comes from mass media. We do not fully understand the effects of the value conflicts a child may be learning through the differences in face-to-face and face-to-media learning.

The actions of parents encourage children to learn the habits of their subculture. Adults are often unaware of how apparently ordinary conversation implants basic values in the young. The following is a transcribed tape recording of a few minutes of conversation in a middle-class American family at dinner time. It will give you some idea of how values are taught over and over to children. The family includes father, mother, and three sons: Ronnie, four; Mark, three; and Jimmie, two.[43]

MOTHER: Ronnie, get your coat off and come get ready for supper.
RONNIE: No. (*no force—sounds more like an automatic acknowledgment.*)
MOTHER: Please? You take your coat off while you're watching the cartoon and then come get ready for supper.

JIMMIE (*in high chair near mother in kitchen*): Ah-ya-ya-ya-ya-ya-ay- (*pounds loudly on his plate.*)
MOTHER: Hey! Sh-h-h.
JIMMIE: Dadadadadadada.
MOTHER: No, you be quiet. We are going to get ready for supper now.
Jimmie continues pounding.
MOTHER: No!
Jimmie pauses, then pounds more.
MOTHER: Stop pounding *now!*
JIMMIE (*pauses, then pounds some more*): Eat. Eat. (*pounds.*)
MOTHER: Don't you do that any more. Come on.
Jimmie pounds intermittently.
MOTHER: What do you want—milk?
JIMMIE: Mmmmyah—
MOTHER: No, you can't have it, Jimmie.
MARK: No.
MOTHER: No.
RONNIE: No.
MOTHER: Don't put your hands in your milk.
MARK: Why?
MOTHER (*loud, exasperated*): Oh, Jimmie! Now don't spill your milk in your plate like that. That's not *nice* to do that!
MARK: No.
RONNIE: No.
MOTHER: *Eat* your fish. Your're supposed to *drink* your milk.

The values stressed in this short time are (1) being ready and punctual, (2) keeping clean and not making messes, and (3) being quiet. Over and over the mother stresses these points. The two older children help by repeating what she says. In further recordings it was found that the two younger children, Mark and Jimmie, resisted the mother much longer than did the older child. Jimmie would continue saying "No," but each time with less emphasis and finally after much encouragement would say "awright." The oldest child's experience with the family interaction was different from the experience of the two younger children—possibly because the mother's influence is stronger when she has one child than it is when her attention is divided among three children. The older child, before the others were born, missed this interaction with the larger group. Different regional, ethnic, religious, and social-class groups will vary considerably, not only in values but in the ways values are taught to children.

Differences in values influence children's behavior in art. From the information we have about Jimmie, Mark, and Ronnie, we can anticipate some problems they might have in art activities.

The first two values being taught—punctuality and cleanliness—if overstressed, might inhibit a child's work in finger paint, clay, papier-mâché, or any material he might interpret as "messy." If he has to keep clean at all times and be on a strict time schedule, his freedom to explore and play with these media is likely to be curtailed. These three children, in an art activity, are likely to react to a teacher's suggestion quite differently. The two younger children may be much more self-directive and may need less encouragement to become motivated than would the older, more passive child.

A teacher motivates children by trying to get them interested and involved in reaching goals. Sometimes he encourages children to set their own goals. A child's motivated behavior is usually an interaction of his own needs and drives with his interpretation of the situation in which he finds himself. The teacher, by various methods, tries to arouse the child's curiosity, encourages him to try, and introduces things into the environment that may stimulate his interest. Sometimes threat of punishment is used to motivate the children to learn or perform. Whether the child is motivated or not depends on what the teacher does, how the child interprets it, and the way the child's past experience has prepared him for the situation. The teacher sets up the stimuli and contributes to the child's psychological environment. The way the child responds depends in part on his readiness, the values he has learned, the way he was taught them, and sometimes his place in the family.

When people are faced with value standards that are unfamiliar to them—when they are rewarded for a behavior in one situation and not in another or, conversely, punished for a behavior in one situation and not in another—because of differences in values among the persons in authority, they are experiencing discontinuity. For example, children who have always been rewarded for being obedient and doing just what they are told may have a difficult time in an art situation where they are asked to experiment with materials and are *not* told what to do. If they become anxious and afraid because they do not know what kind of performance will be rewarded, they may show the behavior of people under stress. They may (1) withdraw from the situation, (2) overcompensate by working extremely hard to achieve a "right" result, or (3) insist on doing something for which they know they will be rewarded.[44]

Value differences in the subcultures of the home, the school, the church, mass media, and the peer group create the discontinuities children and adults experience. Part of our job as teachers is to help pupils to learn to deal with discontinuity, to learn that the rewards or punishments will not always be the same in every situation. Some adaptation is necessary in a large complex society, especially in a period of rapid culture change, with underprivileged people and their children having more opportunity to enter or influence the mainstream of society. At the same time greater discontinuity between different aspects of the society in different stages of change will be faced both by teachers and children. Changing values on television, the varying intensity of children's involvement with it, and the amount of discontinuity between their subculture, the school, and mass media values all contribute.

Changing Values and Discontinuity

In a study of changing values during a ten-year period (1952–1961) Spindler found that graduate education students continued to express the same ideal values: the equality of man, the value of the individual, the belief that work leads to success, the importance of action rather than talk, honesty, and the high value of time.[45]

During this period there were particularly strong changes in values concerning artists and intellectuals (see Table 5–1). In 1952 Spindler's sample of students considered artists in a strongly negative way, in 1958 they were strongly positive, but by 1961 the cycle had reverted to 1952. The attitudes toward intellectuals, though not as extreme, followed the same pattern.

Table 5–1. Changing Values of Students

	Attitudes toward Artists			Attitudes toward Intellectuals		
Year	Negative	Neutral	Positive	Negative	Neutral	Positive
1952	43%	32%	20%	32%	30%	30%
1958	12	25	60	0	60	30
1961	40	30	15	36	50	10

Spindler suggests that "being an artist or an intellectual is a form of deviation in the framework of . . . conservative-traditional middle-class culture. To them the artist does not do 'work' and produces 'goods' of questionable value, and is rarely a financial success. If he looks like the artist stereotype 'he is by definition a deviant' in these people's minds. The intellectual's work also is suspect as it isn't 'at' anything tangible to their standards. Being 'smarter' than most people, he is suspected of being dangerous."[46]

In a sample of college undergraduates in 1968 in the same school, Spindler found some of the key values of honesty and individualism still standing, but among these students there was a shift not seen before. "Concern for others" was dramatically increased over any other year. Also among these students, artists were acceptable.

No matter what grade level we teach, changing value patterns of students will continue. The gaps between teachers and students will be greater or lesser, depending upon the teachers' own orientation. But the teacher who understands that values do change and who is aware of the many forces that affect the ways values are learned will keep an open attitude toward possibilities for value conflict and will continue to try to find ways to communicate with students.

In recent years large numbers of young people have openly questioned the validity of many of the core values. The middle-class reaction to the "hippie" and subsequent movements suggests that the core of values has not changed much. As early as 1955 in a study of artistic adolescents Stewart found the effects of the dominant culture's values reflected in the reactions of one student subculture.[47] Self-portraits of forty boys and forty girls of high school age were judged according to selected criteria in drawing, such as complexity, integration, naturalistic representation, symbolism, use of line versus use of shading, aesthetic quality, technical skill, vividness of styles, vitality, etc. Three judges evaluated each picture on each criterion.

Those portraits that showed the strongest "artistic ability" according to the criteria were given further analysis. Because these students had been the subjects of intensive study by the institute since they were in fifth grade, considerable information on their personality structures was available.

The experimenter found that the overall pattern for boys in this group was "strongly suggestive of neurotic introversion, with symptoms of anxiety, low self-esteem, lack of social skills, and isolation from peers." For the girls the pattern suggested "creative and introversive tendencies, which, although accompanied by lack of interest in social contacts, are not related to anxiety, tension, or maladjustment."

Stewart interprets the findings for boys as indications of cultural value conflicts. He stresses the deviation of the stereotyped idea of the artist from the average male in American society. Certainly the description of these boys is different from "the ideal American boy" reported the same year by Spindler. The traits of the "ideal" boy were sociability, average IQ, clean-minded morality, and consideration for others.[48] Stewart feels that many artistic boys do not see a means of attaining adult male status and still continuing their artistic work. These boys may be experiencing discontinuity between their personal rewards from achievement in art and the lack of opportunity for reward from society. The full-time painter or sculptor is generally pictured as living in poverty. Master craftsmen, potters, weavers rarely support themselves from their artistic work alone. The economic anxiety, Stewart feels, is closely related to the boys' adjustment problems. Today this study has relevance for many other young people as well as for art students.

When society is in a state of rapid change, the action and reaction between the forces of change and forces of resistance to change become more intense, and the conflict between people who seek to resist change and those who want to implement change becomes more aggravated. Core institutions, such as education, which are shared by most people, become centers of controversy. Each group of people strains to define the roles of these institutions to fit its own viewpoint.

For example, one of the key value conflicts in American life today is between the agrarian value of strong independence and individual control over property and the reality of the urban situation where interdependence is necessary for cities to survive. In the agrarian situation self-dependence was necessary to survive. Part of the conflict is that many people assume that these two values are mutually exclusive, that the use of one destroys the other. The present state of urban decay in large areas of our cities and the resultant social unrest indicate that the agrarian value of individual control is an inadequate base for solving the overall problems of the city.

The challenge is to preserve the rights and responsibilities of individuals, which are basic to a democratic civilization, and still create the machinery for cooperation and planning necessary to make the cities comfortable places for everyone to live. Citizens are needed who understand how their city works as well as how it looks and how both appearance and operation influence the quality of urban living. Each citizen should be able to create and maintain his own private environment so that it fills the needs of his own life style without interfering with the quality of life of others. He needs to understand the interdependence of urban people and to value cooperative problem solving in determining the character and quality of private and public places, spaces, and structures that contribute to the public environment.

The value conflict of responsibility in the city is reflected in education. If each individual were completely free to control what he owned in the environment, then there would be no need for public school education to prepare children to understand the shared environment and to be able to evaluate their contributions to the city. If cooperation is interpreted to mean that some agency of government does the planning, then decisions about the environment will be left to specialists. But if cooperation is developed by participating individuals in a democratic society, then concern for the environment, aesthetically, socially, and structurally, should be a part of every citizen's education.

To prepare children and youth to function effectively in the urban environment, educators must face the task of understanding and communicating with *one*, the increasing number of children of families migrating from rural to urban centers and, *two*, the ghetto children, whose expectations for the possibilities of a better way to live have been awakened by the social revolution, as deprived peoples press for the right to participate in the core society.

Some people react to changes such as these by withdrawing their support of urban education, because their value systems are not geared to dealing with either the need for understanding the shared environment, or the need for educating children who have developed little readiness for achieving in middle-class schools.

Another change that is causing a sharpening of value conflicts in society is the increased immediacy with which some aspects of social conflict are projected through mass media. When problems face the nation they make instant news. On the television screen a new kind of realism is developing. Events are seen as they happen, and an overall coverage is achieved that no one person in any one part of a situation could experience. Bits and pieces of violence, turmoil, and reactions as well as serious and penetrating reviews of social problems are projected to millions of viewers of television. Each person viewing a scene is faced with forming some kind of reaction, some kind of value judgment. Isolation from confrontation with national problems is increasingly difficult for adults.

As educators we must be concerned with the enculturating effect that television has on children and youth. How are they learning to evaluate what they see? What is the culture pattern they are learning? How do they relate the violence in news to the violence in entertainment? Can they separate the fictional from the television version of the real? What is the relationship of what they learn through mass media to what they learn in school? How does television affect their readiness for learning in school?

What are the feelings of the children who directly experience urban poverty, social rejection, environmental decay, and social explosions? How are they being socialized to participate in our society? Are we, as teachers of art, exploring all the alternatives for helping these children learn that they can modify their environment, work together to improve their situation, and develop the skills and understandings to live in the city?

Summary and Implications for Teaching

In this chapter we have explored some of the enviromental factors such as cultural patterns, economic status, and life styles that influence the ways in which groups of children from the same subculture and class tend to be trained alike. When a classroom is made up of children from many subcultures their differences will be more individual but the reasons for some of these differences are environmental.

Teaching is a cross-cultural experience whenever the children differ in values and attitudes from the teacher. We have seen that both socio-economic class and ethnic background create differences in subcultures. The school itself is a force for maintaining what is shared in the total culture, but the teacher must be sure to provide educational opportunity for children of all subcultures.

Interpreting what we have learned about anxiety and discontinuity, we can assume that children whose main experience in school is learning how inadequate they are in coping with the school environment would tend to become even more socially immobile.

We have found that culture affects the kinds of things children are directed to attend to, the objects in the environment that are valued, and by whom they are valued. Some things will be learned visually in greater or lesser detail because of one's sex and one's role in the culture. Cultures also encourage not only perception but the drawing of perceptions. Sometimes children draw according to visual reality; at other times they draw the visual symbols the culture uses to symbolize certain experiences. In this latter case the child learns to read his culture's iconic or image history or his religion.

We have seen that the amount of iconic information, the art that is used in a culture, apparently influences children's ability to organize and remember visual detail such as that used in completing the Draw-a-Man Test. Anthropologists indicate that the depiction of perceptions into culturally meaningful symbols or icons is the way individuals and cultures grow.

Western education systems apparently tend to develop children's conceptual cognitive processes but leave their perceptual processes to chance. Some perceptual processes, such as reading three-dimensional cues in two-dimensional material, are helped by education. Where village life is not monotonous, peasant children sometimes have richer, more immediate visual experiences than do urban children.

The evidence indicates that perception is in large part influenced by culture, which means it is in large part learned. The sorting and organizing processes may be similar in different cultures, but the material that is attended to and the cognitive and perceptual styles for handling the material are modified by both personality and culture.

Cross-class studies of perception and cognition indicate that mothers' cognitive and perceptual discriminations influence the information-handling processes of children. Mothers who lack perceptual and conceptual discrimination skills raise children who are less able to respond to their environment because they do not early develop a differentiated cognitive framework for responding to new learnings. The importance of early visual experience as a preparation for further learning is most critical.

Some common traits were found in the life styles of deprived peoples: concern for the present, little self-direction or independence from the family, adapting to nature or to the environment rather than controlling it. At the same time other differences among subcultures are still strong: in child-rearing practices, in art forms that have meaning, in religion, in degree of desire to assimilate or stay separate from the dominant middle-class society.

We find evidence that it is possible for people to operate effectively in more than one culture, provided they understand each culture. This evidence indicates that the school does not have to force children to reject their subcultures in order for them to operate effectively in the dominant culture. The art teacher should provide opportunities for children to work and be rewarded for working in the art forms of both groups. Discontinuity can be overcome if the child is helped to recognize the appropriate rewards in a given situation.

Each teacher needs information on the cultural backgrounds of the children in his classroom. The Draw-a-Man Test would give him considerable evidence as to the degree to which the child can differentiate parts or wholes of figures. Using Harris scoring scales will help generally. If a child is from a very different culture then the tests can be used to see how much detail of his own culture he uses, but his IQ cannot be adequately assessed by criteria established in the core culture of the United States.

Interviews with parents concerning children's art work will help the teacher see what kind of conceptual-perceptual base the child may have developed by the mother's speech patterns as well as the parents' attitudes toward art. Children's art work and their verbal descriptions of their work will also tell how much they have learned to discriminate.

Such information will help a teacher decide which of his students most need visual stimulation and visual comparisons. Understanding their background and culture will help the teacher select familiar material with which to begin perceptual training. As perceptions develop, concepts need expansion to categorize the new information.

Most important, understanding cultural diversity gives the teacher a more flexible basis for solving problems about curriculum. Such a teacher will be more ready to experiment with ways of presenting both the content of art and processes of art in the search for more appropriate learning experiences.

During periods of intense change teachers have the increased responsibility of observing such change and the particular ways the children or adolescents in their classes are being enculturated by the impact of television or direct experience with change. Children who come from homes where values are different from the values of the schools or from one or the other extreme of reaction to change may be suffering more discontinuity between home and school than other children and youth. Urban children are caught up in the value conflicts of the larger society, while rural children's real experience and vicarious experience through mass media may be in strong conflict.

References

[1] Milton Gordon, *Assimilation in American Life* (New York: Oxford University Press, 1964).

[2] Robert J. Havighurst and Bernice L. Neugarter, *American Indian and White Children* (Chicago: University of Chicago Press, 1955), p. 171.

[3] Anna Schubert, "Drawings of Orotchen Children and Young People," *Journal of Genetic Psychology,* 37 (1930), 232–234. Used with permission.

[4] Alice Joseph and Veronica G. Murray, *Chamorros and Carolinians of Saipan* (Cambridge: Harvard University Press, 1951).

[5] Anne Anastasi and John P. Foley, Jr., "An Analysis of Spontaneous Drawings by Children in Different Cultures," *Journal of Applied Psychology,* 20 (1936), 689–726.

[6] Anne Anastasi and John P. Foley, Jr., "A Study of Animal Drawings of Indian Children of the North Pacific Coast," *Journal of Social Psychology,* 9 (1938), 363–374.

[7] *Ibid.,* pp. 363–374.

[8] *Ibid.,* p. 374. Reprinted with permission.

[9] Florence Goodenough, "The Intellectual Factor in Children's Drawings." Doctoral dissertation, Stanford University, 1924.

[10] Dale B. Harris, *Children's Drawings as Measures of Intellectual Maturity* (New York: Harcourt, Brace & World, Inc., 1963), pp. 133–134.

[11] *Ibid.,* p. 129.

[12] Wayne Dennis, "Goodenough Scores, Art Experience, and Modernization," *Journal of Social Psychology,* 68 (1966), 213–215.

[13] *Ibid.,* pp. 219–220.

[14] *Ibid.,* p. 223.

[15] Wayne Dennis, "The Human Figure Drawings of Bedouins," *Journal of Social Psychology,* 52 (1960), 209–219.

[16] Dennis, "Goodenough Scores," p. 221.

[17] *Ibid.,* p. 228.

[18] Paul Bohannon, *Social Anthropology* (New York: Holt, Rinehart and Winston, Inc., 1963), pp. 32–34.

[19] Jerome S. Bruner, Rose R. Olver, Patricia M. Greenfield, *et al., Studies in Cognitive Growth* (New York: John Wiley & Sons, Inc., 1966).

[20] Patricia M. Greenfield, "On Culture and Conservation," in Bruner *et al., Studies in Cognitive Growth,* pp. 225–256.

[21] Michael Maccoby and Nancy Modiano, "On Culture and Equivalence," in Bruner *et al., Studies in Cognitive Growth,* pp. 257–269.

[22] *Ibid.,* p. 269.

[23] Rose R. Olver and Joan Rigney Hornsby, "On Equivalence," in Bruner *et al., Studies in Cognitive Growth,* pp. 79–85.

[24] *Ibid.,* p. 80.

[25] J. W. Getzels and M. Csikszentmihalyi, *Creative Thinking in Art Students* (Cooperative Research Project E-008, University of Chicago, Chicago, Ill., 1964).

[26] W. Hudson, "Pictorial Depth Perception in Subcultural Groups in Africa," *Journal of Social Psychology*, 52 (1960), 183–208.

[27] Marshall H. Segall, Donald T. Campbell, and Melville J. Herskovits, *The Influence of Culture on Visual Perception* (Indianapolis: Bobbs-Merrill Co., Inc., 1966).

[28] Gerald Lesser, Gordon Fifer, and Donald H. Clark, "Mental Abilities of Children from Different Social Class and Cultural Groups," Society for Research in Child Development, *Monograph* 30 (4), Serial No. 102 (1965), 81–84.

[29] Elliot W. Eisner, "The Qualitative Aspects of Children's Cognitive Development." Paper presented as an address at the National Art Education Association Convention, Philadelphia (1965).

[30] Florence R. Kluckhohn and Fred L. Strodtbeck, *Variations in Value Orientations* (New York: Harper & Row, Publishers, Inc., 1961).

[31] Leonard Schneiderman, "Social Class, Diagnosis and Treatment," *American Journal of Orthopsychiatry*, 35 (1965), 99–105.

[32] June K. McFee, "Art for the Economically and Socially Deprived," in the *64th National Society for the Study of Education Yearbook*, ed. Reid Hastie, 1965, pp. 135–175.

[33] Malcolm McFee, "The 150% Man in Blackfeet Acculturation," *American Anthropologist*, 70 (February 1969), 1096–1107.

[34] Thelma Alper, Howard Blane, and Barbara Adams, "Reactions of Middle and Lower Class Children to Finger Paints as a Function of Class Differences in Child-Training Practice," *Journal of Abnormal and Social Psychology*, 51 (1955), 439–448.

[35] William R. Holland, "Language Barrier as an Educational Problem of Spanish Speaking Children," *Exceptional Children*, 27 (September 1960), 47.

[36] Arthur R. Jensen, "Social Class and Perceptual Learning," *Mental Hygiene* (1966), 231–233.

[37] Jerome S. Bruner, "An Overview" in Bruner *et al.*, *Studies in Cognitive Growth*, pp. 319–321.

[38] Robert D. Hess and Virginia Shipman, "Early Blocks to Children's Learning," *Children*, 12, No. 5 (September–October 1965) 189–194.

[39] Robert D. Hess, Betsy N. Hess and A. Abbot Rosen, *The Use of Art in Compensatory Education Projects: An Inventory* (Chicago: University of Chicago Press, 1966).

[40] Edmund W. Gordon, "Characteristics of Socially Disadvantaged Children," *Review of Educational Research*, 35 (1965), 377–388.

[41] Ruth Benedict, "Continuities and Discontinuities in Cultural Conditioning," in *A Study of Interpersonal Relations,* ed. Patrick Mullahy (New York: Hermitage Press, Inc., 1959), pp. 297–308.

[42] Charles M. Harsh and H. G. Schrickel, *Personality—Development and Assessment,* 2nd ed. (New York: The Ronald Press Company, 1959), p. 375.

[43] Malcolm McFee, unpublished ethnographic material. Used with permission.

[44] G. G. Thompson, "Multiple Responses to Frustration," in Jerome M. Seidman, *Readings in Educational Psychology* (Boston: Houghton Mifflin Company, 1955), pp. 305–310.

[45] George D. Spindler, unpublished material. Used with permission.

[46] *Ibid.*

[47] Louis H. Stewart, "The Expression of Personality in Drawings and Paintings," *Genetic Psychology Monographs,* 51 (1955), 45–103.

[48] George D. Spindler, "Education in a Transforming American Culture," *Harvard Educational Review,* 25 (1955), 145–156.

6

The Creative Process

What is "creativity?" What is a person doing when he is being "creative"? Philosophers have been asking these questions for centuries. Experimental psychologists are currently exploring creativity and giving us some information about man's capacity for achieving it.

One of the major objectives of art education is the development of the creative potential of children. To pursue this objective, art teachers need to gain much more understanding of the creative process. They need to try to discover what kinds of experiences encourage students to develop habits and attitudes that can lead to creative work. This chapter explores some of the current research in order to find directives for encouraging creativity in the elementary classroom.

"Creativity," as used in this book, refers to the behavior of a person when he is doing such things as (1) inventing a new pattern, form, or idea; (2) rearranging already established objects, patterns, or ideas, or (3) integrating a new or borrowed factor into an already established organization. A child is being creative when he delineates a different but recognizable symbol for an object. He is being creative when he takes another child's construction of building blocks and rearranges them to represent something new. A group of children painting a mural may discover that an important idea has been left out. If they find a way to incorporate this idea into what they have already painted, they are solving their problem in a creative manner.

The four paintings in Figure 6–1 are by sixth grade children. The art teacher had introduced an interesting bicycle for them to use as motivation. Each of the children responded with a bicycle-like drawing, but each one symbolized it in a unique way, developing his own creative synthesis of what he had learned, what he had selected to see, and how he did his organizing and symbolizing.

Figure 6–1. Creative Responses of Sixth Grade Children to the Same Experience (Courtesy Fred Fraser, Eugene Public Schools Eugene, Oregon)

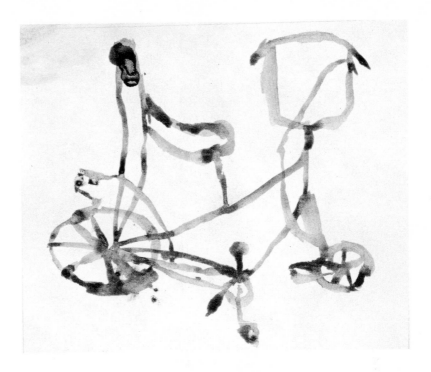

Some kind of creative activity is possible for almost everybody. J. W. Tilton, an educational psychologist, believes that most behavior is to some degree creative. He reasons that most situations people face are somewhat different from any they have faced before. They have to reorganize patterns or ideas, invent or borrow ideas, symbols, or objects to fill a void in a new situation.[1] For example, when two people are carrying on a conversation, each is creative as he tempers and adjusts what he is saying to the way he interprets the response of the other individual. He tries to find new words and new arrangements of words that will communicate his ideas more clearly. The creative child, in art, can likewise develop symbols to communicate his feelings and interpretations through his painting. The creative teacher changes and reorganizes ideas and symbols to meet the varied levels of understanding of the children in the class.

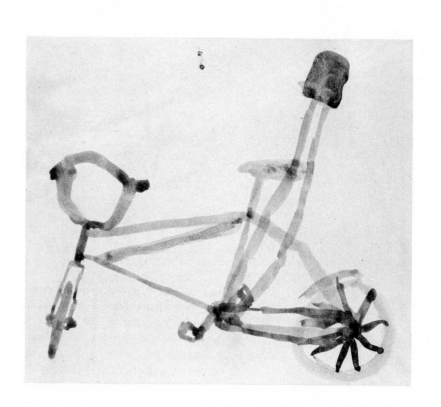

161   **The Creative Process**

As art educators we are concerned with two major questions: (1) What generalizations derived from research on the creative process can we use in organizing art activities in the elementary schools? (2) What can we do to help develop the creative potential of more children?

"Creative potential" is a person's capacity for developing creative behavior. Environmental influences appear to inhibit the development of the traits of creativity. For this reason we cannot adequately evaluate an individual's creative ability until he has had optimum opportunity to use it. Our question then becomes, "What kinds of experiences and what kind of environment can we provide to give children more opportunities to develop their abilities in creative behavior?"

Personality Traits Related to Creativity

Research into the nature of the creative process began with biographical and aesthetic studies of the lives of creative people. Studies have been based on artists' and scientists' own introspection into their creative activity.

Since 1950 considerable research has taken place. Studies of creative people have been made by Guilford, MacKinnon, Barron, Getzels, Jackson, and Torrance. Others now entering the field are searching for individual differences and more agreement on the dimensions tapped by the different tests. The key abilities that enable a person to be more creative (inventive, adaptive, and integrative) were identified by Guilford and are useful in helping a teacher to understand the research and relate it to classroom practice. These key abilities are originality, fluency and flexibility.

Originality

Investigators have identified originality as a trait of creative people. They have found that the creative person in the sciences and the arts is able to see remote relationships, is willing and able to make "unusual or uncommon responses"[2] and to be novel and clever.[3]

Originality in Children. In children's drawings there are different levels of originality. A child's immature perceptual development may account for an unusual representation of an object. If a child has not yet become aware of size relationships, he may draw people and trees the same height. If he has not discovered how hands and arms are organized, he may draw a tadpole-like symbol for a person. The originality he expresses does not result from a purposeful disregard for realism, but rather from his symbolic representation of his level of perceptual development. This kind of originality is different from that used by the mature artist who, for another reason, paints people as large as trees or distorts anatomical structure.

Originality in children may be described as the ability to make *unusual responses,* to organize things in *uncommon* ways, and *to be novel* at their present level of overall development. What might be called original in a child might not be original for an adult. What might be termed original within a given individual's experience might not be original for a larger group of people.

Fluency The frequency with which ideas or symbols can be expressed in a given time is called fluency. If a child is fluent, he draws more symbols in an art period and thus has more opportunities to make novel responses. Fluency is a trait often found in creative people, but fluency without originality may not result in creative expression. A child who paints twelve uninventive scribbles is probably being less creative than a child who is inventing symbols and organizing them in one drawing.

Guilford identifies two kinds of fluency, *expressive* and *associational.* In speaking and writing, expressive fluency means speed in bringing forth words and combinations of words that express ideas. Associational fluency is the ease in building subtle relationships, one related concept on another.

In art expressive fluency is probably evident when a child delineates many symbols without any great effort. Associational fluency can be seen in drawings in which the symbols are carefully related to each other. Some children notice small details and integrate them skillfully in their art work, probably because they live in a culture where subtle relationships are stressed. In Figure 6–2 a young Japanese child

Figure 6–2. Boys in Snow (Collection Al Zelver)

shows the effects of the rewards he receives in his culture to pay attention to visual detail, in this case space relationships.

In Figure 6–3 a Hawaiian child of Chinese descent shows how she integrates Oriental symbols with Western landscape form.

Verbal skills are not always an adequate measure of intelligence. A child may have a low score in the verbal part of an intelligence test, yet show high ability in the nonverbal part. The same child may not

talk freely, yet he may be able to express ideas fluently with paint. Another child may have found his verbal expression quite adequate and may not feel a need for expressing his ideas in pictorial form.

Fluency in art may be determined partly by intelligence and partly by culture, reward, and opportunity.

In her analysis of artists and nonartists Eiduson found that the most important single difference between the two groups was that artists had early recognition of their artistic talents. This recognition led to "... many gratifying experiences and relationships ... which tended to place a premium on artistic capabilities and help crystallize these ... activities in later vocational choice and performance."[4]

Flexibility   Flexibility, a trait often found in creative people, refers to a person's ease in changing his behavior, in meeting new situations, and in seeking new ways of solving problems.[5] *Degree of flexibility* means the level of ease with which a person responds to change. Where flexibility is weak we find *rigidity*. Rigidity describes behavior that is repetitious. The individual resists change in himself and in others. He stays within a narrow range of action, and resists moving into unfamiliar situations. *Flexibility-rigidity* describes a scale along which we measure behavior. Apparently some people are rigid in almost everything they do. Others are rigid in some situations and not in others, or flexible in most situations and rigid in a few.

Some of the experiences in academic training reinforce the trait of rigidity. If students are rewarded for conforming to the "right" as opposed to the "wrong" response, they will try to limit their behavior to what will get them good grades (being "right" on tests, using the "right" tool in the "right" way, saying the "correct" thing in class discussion).

If skills are taught in an authoritarian manner, the learner will probably be hampered in using them flexibly. If the skill is taught by the teacher as one of several "successful ways" people have found to use a tool or material, and if students are encouraged to explore other ways, more opportunity is given for flexibility to develop.

Types of Rigidity.   Rigidity can be seen in three types of behavior.[6] (1) *Slowness in reaction to familiar things.* Children who are hesitant in responding need plenty of time to formulate what they have to say, whether in words or in drawings.

(2) *Resistance to new or novel things.* This is related to "intolerance of ambiguity," an inability to respond to or accept that which is not understood. A person might respond quickly to familiar things, but slowly to the unfamiliar. A child who has appeared to be quite flexible when using familiar art materials may be quite rigid when working with unfamiliar tools and materials. A child might be very responsive verbally to familiar art forms, but be unable to verbalize about a new art form.

(3) *Difficulty in shifting from one type of motor-cognitive task to another*. A motor-cognitive task is one that requires the person to direct cognitively his motor skills — to use his body, his hands, his feet to achieve certain results. A highly skilled dancer has to use extreme concentration to make his body do just what he wants. A sculptor, working with a chisel, wants no interruption to interfere with cognitive control of his hands in his delicate operations. A child may have difficulty if he is taught one type of motor skill such as learning to write in neat rows, and then is asked to learn to control a large bristle brush. Somewhat different muscles and kinds of control are needed. If the teacher overstresses the value of orderliness in arithmetic papers, of staying in the right columns and keeping the borders clean, some children may find it very difficult to switch to the task of expressing an idea freely in art, when improvisation and exploration are goals.

Creativity Research

Studies of creative behavior have started with concern for creativity in science and in the arts. The assumption that creativity in these two domains is very different reflects the attitude that science is rational while art is emotional. Art, as defined here, and the range of activities involved include both rational and emotional behaviors. Research on both scientific and artistic creativity can contribute to understanding of "creative" behavior in the visual arts.

The following research studies have been selected as being particularly useful to classroom teachers concerned with children's creative behavior in art.

The relationship of creativity to intelligence was studied by Getzels and Jackson with students in the University of Chicago demonstration school.[7] This group was a limited sample. The researchers divided the students into two groups: (1) students who had exceptionally high IQ's (mean 150) but who ranked below the top 20% on a creativity scale and (2) students who ranked exceptionally high on a creativity scale but who were below the top 20% in IQ (mean 127). The creativity scale was a refinement of previous creativity tests and adapted to this age group. Comparisons were made of school achievement, teacher's assessment, fantasy production, and career aspiration. This whole sample is on the high side of the IQ and creativity scale. Within this narrow range there were family life style differences that were related to children's abilities. The less creative high IQ children had mothers who were more socially conforming, were more highly educated (more graduate work), and did not work out of the home. The more creative but more nearly average IQ children had mothers who spent more time out of the home and who were more interested in their children's internal values and interests than in social conformity.

Both groups of students measured very high on school achievement tests—but teachers unaware of test scores rated the high IQ students as more enjoyable and the high creative as less enjoyable than average students. The high creatives had more unconventional career choices and were considerably more creative in writing, with many more playful unexpected endings and much humor.

It must be remembered that this was a limited study, and that it did not report on the high IQ high creatives and lower IQ lower creatives.

A similar study was done by Klausmeier and Wiersma, who studied 240 seventh grade students, randomly sampled, from five public high schools in the same city who met the criterion of high (115–141), average (96 to 114), and low (71 to 95) IQ.[8] The students were tested on seven divergent thinking tests, adapted from Guilford, and four convergent thinking tests. Guilford defines divergent thinking as "the generation of a variety of items of information in response to given information," while convergent thinking "involves the generation of a well-determined 'right' answer from given information."[9] Using this typical range of students, the researchers found IQ and creativity to be parallel for each group—on the convergent and divergent tests, the high IQ group was superior to the average and the average was superior to the low group. This would indicate that increased IQ, measured by the Otis Quick-Scoring Mental Ability Test, and creativity, as measured in this study, may be related in a general way, but that when high creative and high IQ groups are studied as by Getzels and Jackson, the relationship is not as close.

Wallach and Kagan explored the question of the relationship of creativity to intelligence more exhaustively with 151 middle-class fifth grade children. They proposed that essentially the creative process involves *the ability to make abundant and unique associations combined with a playful permissive attitude*. Ten creativity tests and ten intelligence tests were given. In contrast to the results of the Klausmeier and Wiersma study, the correlation between the IQ measures and the creativity measures was extremely low, suggesting that the kinds of individual differences involving creativity are independent from those tested by IQ tests. The differences between these findings and the study above may well be the wide range of IQ tests used and the focus on creativity as a measure of associational and playful behavior.[10]

Wallach and Kagan then studied the social behavior and achievement-centered nature of the children in different combinations of creativity and intelligence.[11] They drew the following conclusions:

Highly creative, highly intelligent children were able to operate on both childlike and adultlike levels of behavior. They could exercise both control and freedom (perhaps related to Guilford's concepts of convergent and divergent processes).

Highly creative but less intelligent children did not fit into the school environment well, were likely to feel unworthy and inadequate; but in a situation where learning could take place without stress they were able to develop cognitively. (Could this mean that their modes of problem solving were not rewarded, so failure experience had become cyclical?)

Less creative but highly intelligent children were found to be devoted to school achievement and were most intolerant of failure.

Less creative, less intelligent children were bewildered by the school environment. Defense measures ranged from intensive activity with peers to regression and passivity.

On measures of anxiety, the highly intelligent, less creative children were lowest, the high creatives were intermediate, and those children lowest on *both* measures were the most anxious.

This last study indicates that teachers' understanding of the creativity-intelligence relationship is extremely important in developing art activities and study for children of these different combinations. All types of children need opportunities to understand art as it communicates and as it is used in our society, whether they produce creatively or not. They will respond in different ways to different tasks, different opportunities to explore, different motivation to be expressive. *Highly creative, highly intelligent* children can probably use more self-direction and a more open classroom environment in which to learn. *Highly creative, less intelligent* children need many opportunities for success and rewards in a nonthreatening environment. Art activities can allow them the creative freedom they need, yet with this activity their conceptual skills can be developed perhaps better than in other subjects where they have not done as well.

Less creative, highly intelligent children need a more structured program with less ambiguity about what is success, as their fear of failure could inhibit their most elementary attempts at innovation or projection of feeling through art.

The children low on both counts need art experiences at a manipulative and intellectual level they can handle without anxiety; they need opportunities for success.

Teachers need to experiment with art activities and art learning experiences to find more effective ways of reaching these different groups.

Bentley has studied the relationship of creativity to academic achievement with graduate students. Some of the differences that operate at the graduate level had already been identified in fifth graders.

Students were tested weekly on tests of Guilford's categories of knowledge (cognition, memory, divergent thinking, and ability to evaluate); Torrance's Test of Imagination, Form DX, a divergent writing task (seeking many ideas from a few concepts); and the Miller Analogies Test (analogical thinking with graduate-level subject matter mainly in the sciences, mathematics, classic literature, and history). There was little or no overall relationship between students' total scores on the Torrance creativity test and the Miller Analogies. Memory on the Guilford battery was not significantly correlated with creativity. But divergent thinking was highly correlated with creativity scores, and less so but still significantly with the Miller Analogies. Evaluative abilities and students' total achievement both correlated significantly with both creativity and the Miller Analogies.[12]

These results indicate, as Bentley observes, " . . . the student with creative talents is unduly penalized by tests like the Miller Analogies."[13] He believes that the use of such tests is particularly serious when the result is that creativity is not rewarded and is thus possibly suppressed. He further suggests that, assuming that "creative use of knowledge is an integral part of academic achievement," we need to develop means of evaluating and rewarding it.

Creativity and Use of the Environment

The relationship of individual differences in cognitive perceptual ability with creativity was studied by Mendelsohn and Griswold.[14] They divided college freshmen into three groups with three levels of creativity — high, medium, and low — as measured on paper-and-pencil tests. These students were given an interference experience — memorizing twenty-five words while twenty-five other words were played to them from a tape recording. Then they were given thirty anagram problems to solve. Unknown to the subjects, ten of the solutions had been given in the taped list (peripheral but incidental cues) and ten in the memorized list (focal-incidental). The high creatives used the focal cues (in the memorized list) significantly more than did the middle creatives, who used the focal cues more than did the low creatives. Only the high creatives used peripheral cues (from the taped list) to advantage.

The experimenters suggest that the reason for these differences may be that the high creatives are more effective in processing and receiving information — that individual differences in perception and cognition are readiness factors for creative ability.

For teachers, the research suggests that they must be aware that highly creative children are probably getting more information than others — even more information than the teacher, sometimes. One of the reasons creative children may be considered more difficult as pupils is that they are responding to and stimulated by many more peripheral cues.

This study may be giving us information that is helpful in understanding why so many people tolerate so much ugliness — they are not sensitive to peripheral information unless their attention is called to it directly. A man who attended a conference on urban ugliness problems was shocked to see a picture of his town's main street, exclaiming that he drove that street daily but had never "looked" at it before. Perhaps his awareness of peripheral visual cues was not strong; but the learning experience that brought these into concerned focus would probably change his awarenesses in driving down the street again.

Maddi, Maddi, Charlens, and Smith investigated the relationship of creative behavior to environmental influences. They tested four groups of creative writing students after three different environmental situations. One group was asked to evaluate twelve minutes of a monotonous tape before being tested. Another group was asked to evaluate a stimulating tape. Two controls waited for a period with neither tape. Then all the students were asked to write a creative description in response to a picture of people. Their responses were judged on (1) a desire for novelty and (2) novelty of imagery. The students in the group who had heard the monotonous tape showed more need for novelty or change, but they were much less creative and imaginative in their stories than were either of the control groups or the students in the group that had heard the stimulating tape. The investigators say the most plausible expanation of their findings is that monotony aroused a need for variation but depressed the ability to think in active creative ways.[15] Art teachers observe such a depression when students come from classes where conforming tedious activities have been going on. It is difficult for the students to shift to an exploratory active mode of responding. If pupils have opportunities to be creative only immediately after monotonous work, they may not be able to develop their potential. The stereotyped idea that art activities should come after the "work" is done may account for some of the uncreative work children do.

Sex Differences The above studies have been done mainly with male subjects. Helson has done an excellent study of women and their recall of childhood experiences related to creativity.[16] Two hypotheses were these: (1) creative women enjoyed activities as children that were related to creativity in adults;[17] (2) childhood tomboy activities will relate highly with intellectual ability but not with creativity, based on the assumption that intellectual interests are more masculine, calling for repression of creative spontaneity.[18] Helson made a survey of 135 Mills College women and 139 University of California women. They responded to a check list of childhood activities, indicating how often they had engaged in each activity and whether they liked, moderately liked, or disliked the activity. These activities were clustered into seven preference groups, and each subject was given a score according to her responses on the four most important clusters of preferences: imaginary play artistic expression IA, tomboy play T, social play S, and analytic impersonal A (that is, making airplane models, building with erector sets, and disliking dolls and dancing).

Creativity was measured by batteries of creativity tests of Barron[19] and Gough,[20] faculty assessment of students, personality inventories, the Myers-Briggs Type Indicator,[21] grades, and verbal and mathematical aptitude scores. The first hypothesis, that creative women enjoyed activities as children that were related to creativity in adults (pleasure in imaginary and artistic experience), was strongly supported.

The tomboy cluster was not negatively correlated with creativity as expected, but was positively related to both creativity and intellectual effectiveness. The tomboy cluster was negatively correlated to femininity, rigidity, and repression.

Personality Differences between the Sexes and among Art Majors

The same tendency was also found in a study by Getzels and Csikszentmihalyi,[22] who found that artistic women students were more independent and intellectual than less artistic women students. This study indicates that the pattern of personality development starts early in a girl's life. It could be inferred that social control, to direct girls toward a preferred sex role within a given culture, may permit fewer opportunities for creativity in women. The degree of this control is not easily measured, but strong differences between sexes in child-rearing practice are found in most social groups. Awareness of the effects of cultural patterns on behavior in creativity will help teachers evaluate their goals with a broader perspective.

Among students who select art as a career by choosing to go to an art school, differences in creative behavior and attitude can be found between the sexes and among students majoring in fine arts, art education, and applied arts (advertising and industrial arts). These differences in behavior and attitude are apparently long-standing traits, the beginnings of which are possibly prior to even elementary school.

Getzels and Csikszentmihalyi studied 179 students who were in their junior and senior years at the Art Institute in Chicago. Investigations were made in five different areas: cognitive processes, including creativity measures; perception; personality; faculty ratings; and art and academic grades. A questionnaire on personal and family structure data was also given.

The study is important in helping teachers understand artistically creative children. Almost 60% of the art students reported that they had worked in art during elementary school. More than 50% had considered art as a career by the ninth grade. The study gives insight into the developing personalities of children who are interested in the arts and other more independent areas whether career oriented or not.

One of the strongest findings was that art students vary considerably according to sex and choice of major area (fine arts, art education, applied arts) in several important ways; in other ways they are like each other and much like other college students.[23]

In perceptual tests of spatial visualization and in the Welsh Art Judgment Test, both men and women art students were significantly higher than average college students. According to the Allport-Vernon-Lindzey Scale of Values, both men and women art students were quite different from other college students. They were much higher in aesthetic values but much lower in social and economic values. The male students were farther in value pattern from the male sample than the female students were from the female sample. The female students followed the female sample pattern more closely in general but the variations were more extreme. Perhaps the male student is at a greater distance from average because he must show more resistance to or retreat from social norms.

On the creativity measure of the Sixteen Measure Personality Test, the art students were above the 89th percentile of the college norms.[24] On cognition the art students were above the general population norms, but male art students were somewhat below the college male norms and female art students were above the college female norms.[25]

These researchers believe that the strong sex differences point to complicated differences between males and females in becoming serious artists in our society. Perhaps different social expectancies require the different sexes to use different abilities to succeed. Boys' grades were strongly negatively related to visualization. Generally, women art students were more dominant than other women, men art students less dominant than other men.[26] Rau has found that high visual scores relate positively to aggression in girls and negatively in boys.[27] One might hypothesize that becoming an artist is an important decision for both men and women art students and requires of each a breaking away from more normative behaviors. MacKinnon in his study of high creative architects found the most creative more open to feelings and emotions and wide-ranging interests which in American culture are called feminine.[28]

To find out whether there were differences among art students between the high and low achievers and the different majors, Getzels made further study. The Allport-Vernon-Lindzey test clearly separated high-grade and low-grade art students. The higher the grades the more extremely high the aesthetic values, and the more extremely low the economic and social values. The low-grade students were much closer to average norms. Also the high students were the most theoretical but not as extreme.[29]

Differences between majors and sex on correlations between art grades and cognitive and perceptual abilities were most striking. Among applied art male students, grades and intelligence were significantly related. Among female applied artists the two items were not related. In other words, the higher the men's IQ the higher their grades, but the same relationship did not follow for women. Fine arts students had no significant correlations between the two items, though there was a small positive tendency for women. Differences in spatial visualization were even more dramatic. Applied arts women's grades were significantly correlated with spatial visualization while the fine arts men's grades were strongly negatively related. Fine arts women's grades also were correlated to high visualization but not as strongly as applied arts women. While these correlations between art grades and visualization were found, it should also be noted that the mean visualization score for fine arts men was higher than that for fine arts women.[30]

What seems to be suggested here is that a stronger element of success for women in fine arts and applied arts comes from visualization, while intellect is a strong factor in success for men in applied arts. Fine arts men may rely more on creative personality traits than on cognitive attributes.[31]

Differences in values were found among the different art majors. Art education students had the highest social values, a finding that probably reflects their concern for education. Art education women had the lowest economic values. Aesthetic values were highest for fine arts women, then fine arts men, then art education women, then art education men, then industrial arts and finally advertising students. But all were well above the college norms for aesthetic values.[32]

This study has helped me to understand some of the problems I have had in teaching design. Some students apparently design intuitively; they appear to be more creative and divergent. Analysis of design bothers them. Other students want to learn to design but lack what they call a "feel" for it. These students respond very well to analysis, using reason and perceptual discrimination to solve design problems. These are traits the applied designer uses most strongly. Children in primary grades have often been observed as "intuitive designers" but they appear to lose this ability in the middle grades when conceptual learning and categorizing become important in their other school work.

MacKinnon, who with Frank Barron and others has studied creative people in other fields,[33] says of the most creative people that they have most fully used their potential. They have little concern for impressing others, are freer to set their own standards, acceptant of themselves, and free to express their inner experience.

In his work with creative architects MacKinnon found that their childhood experiences gave them independence and opportunities to explore; they experienced neither rejection nor pressure to be dependent. Most high creatives had many opportunities to change environments as children and had many opportunities to be alone and to experience solitude. They were encouraged to develop their abilities at their own pace.[34]

Implications for Teaching

We have looked at creativity broadly. We have found that it is not a single kind of behavior but one in which many personal, environmental, and intellectual factors interact. Certainly it is clear that no one classroom environment, method of teaching, or kind of motivation will help the diverse kinds of children and youth develop their potentials to be creative. Creativity is not a cluster of characteristics needed by only the "gifted." Independent modes of expression and problem solving need to be developed by larger segments of our society. In a stagnant society, creative response to change is not needed; but in a period of great rapidity of change, most people need creative abilities to solve the problems of their visual environment, the renewal of their cities. The material in this chapter should be used to help the teacher understand the creative development of students in order to devise ways for them to be more creative. Also the teacher should recognize that there are multiple traits contributing to creativity, some of which almost every child should be able to develop, provided his environment encourages him to do so.

Working with this kind of material requires that the teacher be able to think through the meaning of correlations, because some of the data in even the same study might appear to be contradictory. For example, in this last study when all the arts students were grouped together, they were found to be like other college students in cognition; but when art grades were compared to their cognitive scores, there were differences among them.

Following, in Chapter 7, is a report of a curriculum in creative design in which students in ninth grade were tested on some of the same batteries discussed in this chapter. This is an exploratory course in changing creative behavior through art.

Summary

Creativity was defined as human behavior in inventing new patterns, forms, or ideas, rearranging established objects or ideas, and integrating a new or borrowed factor into an already established organization.

Fluency, flexibility, originality, and playful attitudes are traits that implement creative behavior. Fluency is the frequency of responses in relating or naming things.

Flexibility is the ease in changing behavior. Originality is the ability to make unusual and novel responses and to see remote relationships. These abilities in children are related to their overall experience, development, and opportunities and rewards. Exceptionally intelligent, less creative children tend to have socially conforming but well-educated mothers, while highly creative, less intelligent children have mothers who are less socially conforming and more interested in their children's internal values. Many teachers prefer the first group to the second, but the second group is more playful and humorous.

When a broader range of IQ was compared to scores on creativity tests the two factors were related—that is, the higher IQ groups had higher mean creativity scores than the average or lower IQ students.

If the creative process is defined and measured as the making of abundant and unique associations combined with playful attitudes, then intelligence and creativity were not found to correlate strongly. When children of various degrees of intelligence and creativity, by this definition, were studied as to adaptability to school, the highly creative, highly intelligent children could be both controlling and free. Highly creative but less intelligent children had difficulty feeling worthy in school. Less creative but highly intelligent children were most devoted to excelling and were intolerant of failure. Children low on both abilities had the most trouble in school and were the most anxious.

In a test involving environmental cues, high creatives were able to use peripheral information through a better information-handling process. Students who had just had a stimulating experience were more creative than students who had just had a monotonous experience; the latter showed a need for novelty but less ability to create.

In a test of college women's recall of childhood experiences the most creative women were high in memory of imagery and artistic experience as children. Tomboy behavior was positively related to creativity and intellectual effectiveness and negatively related to femininity, rigidity, and repression.

Art students grouped by major and by sex were found to have varied personality types. Male fine arts students with high art grades were low in spatial visualization, while female fine arts students with high art grades from the same faculty were high in spatial visualization. Fine arts men depended on creativity traits to succeed, while applied arts men depended more on cognitive abilities.

The most creative architects had the freest childhood experiences, were more independent, and had had more opportunity to explore.

These studies indicate that environmental experience, encouragement, early motivation, and freedom to be independent are important factors in the development of creative traits but that there are wide differences in the development of the pattern of traits among creative people and the different patterns tend to lead them into different activities.

The role of the teacher is critical in identifying children's readiness for creative behavior and then providing them with the experiences to develop from where they are.

References

[1] J. W. Tilton, *An Educational Psychology of Learning* (New York: The Macmillan Company, 1951), pp. 89–90.

[2] J. P. Guilford, "Creative Abilities in the Arts," *Psychological Review*, 64 (1957), 110–118.

[3] J. E. Drevdahl, "Factors of Importance for Creativity," *Journal of Clinical Psychology*, 12 (1956), 21–26.

[4] Bernice T. Eiduson, "Artist and Nonartist: A Comparative Study," *Journal of Personality*, 26 (1958), 22. Reprinted by permission.

[5] Guilford, "Creative Abilities in the Arts," and Drevdahl, "Factors of Importance for Creativity."

[6] K. Warner Schaie, "A Test of Behavioral Rigidity," *Journal of Abnormal and Social Psychology*, 51 (1955), 604–610.

[7] Jacob W. Getzels and Phillip W. Jackson, "Family Environment and Cognitive Style: A Study of the Sources of Highly Intelligent and of Highly Creative Adolescents," *American Sociological Review*, 26 (1961), 351–359.

[8] Herbert J. Klausmeier and William Wiersma, "The Effects of I.Q. Level and Sex on Divergent Thinking of Seventh Grade Pupils of Low, Average, and High I.Q.," *The Journal of Educational Research*, 58 (1965), 300–302.

[9] J. P. Guilford, N. W. Kettner, and P. R. Christensen, *A Factor Analytic Study Across the Domains of Reasoning, Creativity and Evaluation: II: Administration of Test and Analysis of Results*. University of Southern California Laboratory Report, No. 16 (1956).

[10] Michael A. Wallach and Nathan Kagan, "A New Look at the Creativity-Intelligence Distinction," *Journal of Personality* 33 (1965), 348–369.

[11] *Ibid.*

[12] Joseph Bentley, "Creativity and Academic Achievement," *Journal of Educational Research*, 59 (1966), 269–272.

[13] *Ibid.*, p. 271.

[14] Gerald A. Mendelsohn and Barbara B. Griswold, "Differential Use of Incidental Stimuli in Problem Solving as a Function of Creativity," *Journal of Abnormal and Social Psychology*, 68 (1964), 431–436.

[15] S. R. Maddi, D. A. Maddi, A. M. Charlens, and A. J. Smith, "Effects of Monotony and Novelty on Imaginative Production," *Journal of Personality*, 30 (1962), 513–527.

[16] Ravenna Helson, "Childhood Interest Clusters Related to Creativity in Women," *Journal of Consulting Psychology*, 29 (1965), 352–361.

[17] D. W. MacKinnon, "The Nature and Nurture of Creative Talent," *American Psychologist*, 17 (1962), 484–495.

[18] Helene Deutsch, *The Psychology of Women*, 2 (New York: Grune & Stratton, 1945).

[19] Frank Barron, "Complexity-Simplicity as a Personality Dimension," *Journal of Abnormal and Social Psychology*, 48 (1953), 163–172. (a)
Frank Barron, "Some Personality Correlates of Independence of Judgment," *Journal of Personality*, 21 (1953), 287–297. (b)

[20] H. G. Gough, "Predicting Success in Graduate Training: A Progress Report,"

rev. ed., *IPAR Research Bulletin* (Berkeley: Institute of Personality Assessment and Research, 1952).

H. G. Gough, "Imagination—Undeveloped Resource," in *Proceedings, First Annual Conference on Research Development in Personnel Management* (Los Angeles: University of California, Institute of Industrial Relations, 1956), pp. 4–10.

[21] Isabel B. Myers, *Manual (1962) for the Myers-Briggs Type Indicator.* (Princeton, N.J.: Educational Testing Service, 1962).

[22] J. W. Getzels and M. Csikszentmihalyi, *Creative Thinking in Art Students* (Cooperative Research Project E-008, University of Chicago, Chicago, Ill., 1964).

[23] *Ibid.,* p. 33.

[24] *Ibid.,* p. 40.

[25] *Ibid.,* p. 32.

[26] *Ibid.,* p. 47.

[27] L. Rau, "Interpersonal Correlates of Perceptual-Cognitive Functions." Paper read at meeting of Society for Research in Child Development, April 1963.

[28] D. W. MacKinnon, "Creativity in Architects," in *The Creative Person,* proceedings from a conference given by the Institute of Personality Assessment and Research, University of California, Berkeley, Calif., 1961, V-23.

[29] Getzels and Csikszentmihalyi, *Creative Thinking in Art Students,* pp. 63, 92.

[30] *Ibid.,* p. 79.

[31] *Ibid.,* p. 80.

[32] *Ibid.,* pp. 56–57.

[33] Conference on *The Creative Person,* 1961, The Institute of Personality Assessment and Research, University of California, Berkeley, Calif.

[34] D. W. MacKinnon, "Personality and the Realization of Creative Potential," *American Psychologist,* 20 (1965), 280.

Increasing Readiness for Art Experiences

Art educators as well as psychologists have begun the careful study of changes in behavior that increase the ability of children and adolescents to respond in and to art. Acceleration in development, increased perceptual analysis, increasing use of perceptual information in drawing, and the development of creativity are all involved.

Development in Art

An early but very significant study of preschool children's growth in art was done by Elizabeth Dubin. This study is important because it shows what the effects of early training can have on child development in art. Increased iconic differentiation—more details in children's drawings—was fostered by the experimenter's encouraging them to conceptualize about their own art work. Children aged two to four were divided into two groups, control and experimental, paired by age, sex, and interest in art (to the extent possible). In the fall the children drew and painted as they wished in a normal nursery school situation. The drawings were then classified by Marian Monroe's categories of child development, and each category was numbered: *scribble unnamed* (one point); *scribble named* (two points); *diagram*—lines, masses, colors with a sense of relationship between (three points); *design*—an obvious rhythmic pattern (four points); representation of a recognizable object (five points). The average score for each child was recorded.

During the winter the control group received no training, but the experimental group was given individual training. Scribblers unnamed were encouraged to verbalize about their drawings; scribblers named were encouraged to deal with the wholes and relations of parts in their drawings. The experimenter would say, "If you look carefully you can see that there are lots of parts to your picture and they make something nice all together." Children who drew diagrams were encouraged to describe the parts. Designers were encouraged to achieve more recognizable forms. Children who did representational work were encouraged to be aware of the aesthetic qualities, such as color and composition. The experimenter did not attempt to direct the nature of representation but allowed the child to represent as he wished. [It must be added here that representation should not be the only goal, that designing ability should also be encouraged.]

In the spring the two groups worked again under equal conditions in the nursery school. The drawings of both groups were then evaluated by the original criteria, and compared with the averages recorded in the fall session. Both groups showed improvement. The control group shifted from a mean score of 1.52 to a mean of 1.75. The experimental group shifted from a mean score of 1.70 to a mean of 2.48. In total the trained children *gained* almost three and one-half times as many score points as the untrained children. Even though a slight difference in groups existed at first, the rate of gain was much greater in the experimental group.[1]

A Classroom Study

The paintings of trees (see Figure 7–1) were made by primary grade children in a Saturday morning enrichment class. The teacher took the children on a "looking expedition," leaving their paints behind. She called particular attention to the acacia trees, encouraging the children to look as hard as they could, to touch the bark and the fallen petals, to smell the air, so that when they came back they could paint a picture of what it is like to see an acacia tree on a spring day.

When they returned to the classroom, the paints were all ready—with a variety of brushes and colors to choose from. Each child created different symbols of trees, of the feeling of spring air. They were particularly expressive of the *essence of spring,* of the tree's "being," not just static pictures of trees.

Figure 7–1. Children's Paintings of Trees

The teacher of this class was particularly gifted in getting children to become involved with the interesting minutiae of detail all around them. Because she was herself aware, she was able to inspire children.

This class represented a fairly wide cross section of society. Many of the parents wanted their children to learn to draw, and this teacher tried to help both parents and children set more creative goals for the class's work. She had them for only one hour a week, but her understanding and training in individual differences among children in art and her skills in motivation enabled her to help the children make important gains in creative invention and expression.

In terms of the P-D theory this teacher (1) helped develop the children's readiness by arousing their curiosity about an expedition and preparing them to look for certain things, (2) created a psychological environment of play and delight, (3) selected a stimulating environment in which the children as a group could find things to respond to, (4) helped them individually to understand the new stimulation by feeling, seeing, and smelling—giving them several ways to get information to stimulate their creativity, (5) had appropriate means ready for their creative expression, and (6) helped the children evaluate what they had learned about trees that would help them to be ready to see more the next time they studied them.

Perceptual Training Studies

An important study by Boger tested the effects of perceptual training on rural Negro and white children's scores on IQ tests in grades one, two, and three.[2] Much of such testing involves the child's abilities in perceptual cognition. This study does not deal directly with an art activity, but perception is a very important area of training for readiness in art.

Two experimental groups, one Negro and one white, and two similar control groups were tested on the Otis Quick-Scoring Mental Abilities Test and the Long Form California Test of Mental Maturity for primary grades. They were pretested, post-tested five months later, and check-tested another five months later. Both experimental groups had four and a half months of extensive training with pictorial and problem puzzles and exercises in visual discrimination (as in Figure 7–2), spatial relations, and judgment. Design problems and visual crossword puzzles were included. The teacher helped the children learn to use the games and exercises and helped them correct wrong responses. The control groups had regular classroom experience.

Figure 7–2. Is Figure *A* Most Like Figure 1, 2, or 3?

 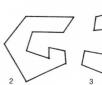

Significant gains for both experimental groups were found between pretests and post-tests both on total IQ scores and nonlanguage scores on the CTMM. The experimental group of Negro children had significant increases not only in total IQ but also in both verbal and nonverbal scores on the Otis. The white group's verbal scores did not change significantly on the Otis.

This study shows that perceptual training changes verbal behavior for some children and also that perceptual ability is related to general intelligence, as measured by intelligence tests. Test scores cannot be interpreted accurately unless perceptual abilities, which are trainable, are maximized.

Eisner's[3] study of drawing ability indicated that economically and socially deprived children lack discrimination in art. This study also indicates that until increased perceptual sensitivity and readiness for art are developed a child's artistic potential cannot be assessed. Unless we know a child's previous perceptual training — learned in his culture from his close adult relatives or learned in school — we cannot judge his potential.

Eisner's study, like other studies, suggests that adults should help children develop a broader visual sensitivity early in their experience so that their subsequent experience is not limited by lack of either perceptual discrimination or conceptual breadth. A balance of the two modes of learning — perceptual and conceptual — needs to be maintained if both visual literacy and conceptual literacy are to be maintained.

Covington[4] made a study of the perceptual abilities of kindergarten children who had either college graduate or high school graduate parents. Two groups were tested. The 36 children in Group one had college educated parents, and the 36 children in Group two had high school educated parents. Half of each group served as control, half as experimental.

The test, a form discrimination test, was a set of 30 problems in matching the right abstract form from a choice of three, similar to the problem shown in Figure 7–2.

All students were given a pretest. Group one children had a mean score of 17.94; Group two had a mean score of 12.83. Then, on thirteen consecutive days, the experimental sections were shown each of the 30 items of the test for five seconds. The control sections saw pictures of animals only and none of the abstract forms. The children were asked to "look at the pictures." Then the test of 30 problems was given again to both groups. The trained children who saw the abstract forms for thirteen days in the experimental Group two gained significantly in the post-test (mean 21.83). Though they had scored much lower in the pretest than the Group one trained children, they overcame their lag and almost equaled the mean score of the Group one training section (22.78).

Children whose visual environment is enriched and who receive adult help in responding to and gaining meaning from the visual environment are more perceptually literate before they go to school. But, as we found in the Bruner studies, concept-oriented educational systems tend to direct children's cognitive style toward more conceptual than perceptual analysis as they progress through the grades.

The children of high school graduates, according to this sample, tend to receive less early stimulation, less readiness training for perceptual tasks than do children of college graduates. Repeated exposure to pure form was necessary to increase scores on the form discrimination test.

The environment can be more drastically manipulated in experiments with rats than would be possible with human beings. Jensen reviews a long history of studies of rats raised in enriched, normal, and deprived environments.[5] His own study was of a training procedure in which the environment was designed to change behavior, just as teachers create enriched environments to stimulate learning in children. A rat raised in an enriched environment can use visual cues to solve the problem of finding its way through a maze to get food much faster than a rat raised in an open cage, in a laboratory, or in a deprived environment in which it does not see the outside world. The enriched environment included a large cage decorated with designs, containing ladders, runways, a small area like a maze, and toys to play with.

The effects of different environments on development are physical as well as behavioral. More favorable brain chemical conditions and increased weight were found in rats raised in the enriched environment. Rats raised in deprived environments who were later placed in enriched environments actually improved in physical characteristics of the brain. Inversely, such improved characteristics were lost to some degree when enriched rats were moved into deprived situations.

A perceptual training study in art appreciation was carried out by Wilson with fifth and sixth grade children. Three experimental classes were chosen from an experimental school and three control classes from a conventional school. Both groups came from the same socio-economic neighborhoods.

The Wilson Aspective Perception Test was used before and after the training of the experimental group. This test is a method of evaluating a child's written responses to paintings by determining whether he (1) analyzes a painting, (2) synthesizes the interrelations of a painting, or (3) responds by telling anecdotes about it. The test also identifies responses that tell whether a child has responded to the design relationships, sensory qualities, symbolic aspects, or literal qualities of the painting.

Untrained children tend to look at pictures as referents to verbal descriptions. Pictures in most of their books have been put there to amplify the meaning of the written word. Thus children respond to the literal and contextual aspects of pictures. Rarely do children have books in which the words are used to amplify the pictures.

In Wilson's study the experimental group had a series of lessons on some of the ideas in Arnheim's book, *Picasso's Guernica: The Genesis of a Painting,* which includes working sketches used by the artist in the development of the painting.[6] For twelve weeks, 90 minutes per week, the children were helped to analyze the processes of visual thinking Arnheim suggests that Picasso used. They looked at the prints and read the materials that were prepared for them that would help them attend to the qualities in the paintings.

The control group had the usual art activities program.

In comparing pretest and post-test scores of the two groups, Wilson found that significant changes were made by the experimental group, indicating that training can change the perceptual mode of elementary age children. The children gave a larger number of responses that showed analysis of relationships in the paintings; they paid more attention to sensory qualities such as color, shape, value contrasts, and formal aspects of the design. They were concerned with the symbolic aspects of the paintings, a response which Wilson had previously found was usually not given until late adolescence. Also their references to the literal qualities were reduced very significantly. The differences found were decisive enough to overcome the differences in schools.

This study raised questions about whether studio work in art was valuable as a means of teaching critical awareness and aesthetic judgment. An earlier study by Wilson indicated that children who had done art work all through elementary school knew very little about how to look at the art work of others.[7]

Perceptual training through art was also done by Salome, who studied what effect a specific kind of perceptual training would have upon the amount of visual information children include in their drawings. (See Figure 7–3.)[8] Two fourth grade and two fifth grade classes from the same school were used. Children were mainly from graduate student

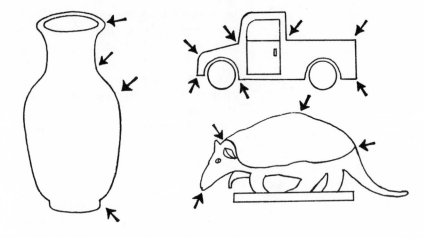

and professional families. Each grade was divided into a control and an experimental group. In the pretest and the post-test each child made a drawing of a table lamp, a model truck, and a mounted armadillo.

The experimental group worked in a "demonstration-participation" situation, in which they located points of maximal contour change. Two key concepts were used in each of the eight experimental lessons. The concepts were these: (1) contour lines describe the outer limits of objects and their component parts, and (2) contour lines include points of information, which, if properly located and connected with lines, can be used to produce representational drawings. Salome intended to find out whether perceptual training would be reflected in future drawings made by these children. Analysis of form in nature is used by artists who vary widely in their expression, whether they abstract from nature, transpose or change nature, or depict from nature. As a perceptual motor skill, drawing is basic to art expression.

The fifth grade experimental children significantly improved in their ability to draw recognizable details, to draw lines that followed the forms of the objects, and to make the proportions appropriate.

The fourth grade experimental group did not improve as much. Their original scores on the test were quite varied. Perhaps because of wide variation among the children, no significant change was found. This study needs to be repeated before we judge that fourth grade is too early for this type of training or that fourth graders are too variable for it to be useful for a whole class. On the basis of much of the previously received research we could assume that there would be considerable variability in readiness for such training depending on prior visual discrimination experience.

Kensler studied perceptual training and ability to do perspective drawing by sixth and seventh grade students from all socio-economic classes in a small midwestern city.[10] They were divided into three groups of two classes each. Group one learned a perspective system of drawing, Group two learned the perspective system and received help in learning to perceive in perspective, and Group three, the control group, worked in art that was not related to perspective.

Five drawing tests were devised:

Test I—To reproduce a photograph of two boxes. (The student would draw the foreshortening if he was able to recognize it.)

Test II—To draw the side of a box that would be seen by a doll who sat facing the box in a photograph. (This task required a transposition of space and ability to imagine that side from the information available on the side seen.)

Test III—To draw a simple box form that represented a photograph of a house, viewed in perspective, that was somewhat camouflaged by trees and decorative details.

Test IV—To draw a box from a verbal description.

Test V—To transpose from *known* shape to perspective shape. (The experimenter showed a box and commented that all the sides were the same size and shape, and the angles were the same. Then the students were asked to draw them.

Jackson's Hidden Figures Test—V was given to identify the more field dependent and the more field independent.[11]

When all the gain scores (that is, the degree the perceptually trained children changed their scores compared to Groups one and three) were analyzed, they were found to be not significantly different. The groups' responses were then divided into field dependent and field independent. When these scores were compared it was found that the field-independent students already had high scores and so had less opportunity to gain. When the final scores, rather than gain scores, were compared, the field independent were significantly higher than the field dependent on three of the tests, I, III, and V. These were the drawing tests where they worked from the pictures which gave evidence of perspective. Test V was used in the post-test only, and the children could ignore the description that the sides were all alike and could draw in perspective.

Again readiness played a role. Field independence-dependence has been related to child-rearing practices. The independent children profited from this training experience in terms of final scores. Other work needs to be done to find ways to reach the field-dependent children so they can learn from such experience.

Harold Cohen has done innovative research on the effects of studying environmental design on the behavior of students in the lower third of high school graduates.[12] He has worked with juvenile delinquents, who designed their own space and worked for pay to improve their visual environment. His results indicate that the two opportunities, to work for pay and to gain control over the environment, were strong rehabilitating forces.[13]

Developing the Creative Potential—A Research Study

The following study* was made in Palo Alto, California, in the public schools. Several research assistants and graduate students helped me to plan and carry out the activities.** The study is described in some detail to identify the complexities of studying art activities experimentally.[14]

The Question

Educators in art are involved with the kinds of experiences that might contribute to the development of the creative potential. The question explored in this study was the relationship of a course of study, including problem solving in design and the analysis of creative behavior, to the creative development of academically superior junior high school students. It was hypothesized that students who took such a course would improve more significantly in creativity, as measured by pretests and post-tests, than students who did not have such a course on standardized creativity measures.

The underlying assumptions of the study were (1) that creative behavior is a complex of abilities that most people have in some degree, depending upon both their unique potential and their opportunity for development; and (2) that environment does play a role in the development of these traits, but that much needs to be known about the effectiveness of varied environmental treatments on different groups of children of differing creative aptitudes and past opportunities.

Creative problem solving in design was used as the training for several reasons. (1) The arts have long been associated with "high creativity." An oft-repeated assumption in the folklore of the arts has been that participation in art produces creativity. (2) The arts are usually excluded from the training of the academically superior. If there is any validity

*Under a grant to the School of Education, Stanford University, from the Fund for Development of Education of the Ford Foundation.

**Warren Anderson, Arthur Efland, Guy Hubbard, Gordon Kensler, Frank Laury, Harold McWhinnie, Mary Rouse, Dick Salome, Ronald Silverman, Wes Williams.

in the first assumption, it needs to be demonstrated; the arts could be found to be a relatively untapped area for the development of the creative potential of superior students. (3) The study was motivated by a deep concern about the possibility that potential leaders of the country were being deprived of opportunities to grow in the aesthetic awareness and the perceptual skills necessary to help them improve the aesthetic quality of our civilization. (4) Design, rather than drawing and painting, was selected for the course because the researchers believed that the students would have less resistance to the "designer" than to the "artist" stereotype. Finally, the designing process appeared to be more easily analyzed, so that tasks could be formulated that involved the kinds of abilities identified in studies of highly creative scientists, the subjects of most of the prior research.

The Subjects

The subjects were ninth grade students who scored above the nine-tieth percentile on the School and College Ability Tests. An experimental group was made up of those students who elected to take the test, whose parents approved, and whose schedules allowed. The controls were matched by SCAT and grade scores. They included students who were eliminated by choice, by parents' concern about an art class, or by scheduling problems.

The Curriculum

A four-unit guide was developed for the course. The *first* unit introduced students to open-ended problem solving. The researchers presented some practical activities in order to stimulate initial involvement as the students discovered their need for flexibility in solving problems in unique ways. For example, students were asked to explore multiple goals while using limited tools and materials. In other instances the goal, tools, and materials were limited but students could explore the uses of the materials to reach the goal. In still other activities a specific goal was identified and multiple materials were made available for reaching it. Figure 7–4 shows varied attempts to solve the problem of constructing a structure of toothpicks that would support a textbook.

The *second* unit explored the dynamics of perceptual organization—
proximity, similarity, closure, continuity, and figure and ground—as
they are related to the interaction of form, line, and color in design.
Open-ended problems in design were assigned using these principles
of interaction.

The *third* unit was designed to increase students' awareness of three-

Figure 7–4. Varied Solutions to Structure Problem

dimensional space, to help them overcome the limitations of conceptual reality (seeing things in terms of their knowledge and conceptual stereotyping), and to help them to develop a more flexible awareness of changing spatial relationships, the size and shape of form, and the value and intensity of color. Tasks were assigned in which creative manipulation of space was the goal.

The *fourth* unit, more open-ended, drew upon abilities it was hoped had been developed in the three prior units. The final task was selected, planned, and developed by the students.

Another section in the guide was a supplementary source of information for the teacher. It consisted of specific materials from the research on creativity, which could be used for class discussion and student reading. The then current books on creativity were made available to

students. Twenty books of biography and autobiography of some of the men and women of recent times whose creative brilliance in the sciences and arts is generally acknowledged were made available, and reading assignments were made in these. (The books are listed at the end of this chapter.) The students examined these last materials in order to identify the motivations and behaviors that appeared to lead these people to creativity.

The curriculum included the guide and its assignments, the readings, and lectures by resource persons throughout the four units. These persons were selected for the excellence of their creative work. They

included an internationally known mathematician, a contemporary painter, a leading physician, a philosopher-chemist, and an electronics engineer who had made major inventions.

The tone of the class was somewhat academic; students kept notebooks of the teacher's and visitors' lectures and of their reading to use in stimulating their thinking for their own papers. Notebooks were kept in order to make this class more like their other classes, thus reducing discontinuities.

The Classroom Environment   It should be noted that this study was made in a university community where pressure for academic achievement is considered to be very high. The researchers were attempting to develop the creative behavior of these students during the first year in which their grades counted for college entrance—thus the pressure to conform to teacher standards to get good grades appeared to be very strong.

The teacher in this case was an excellent painter who was also trained as a social studies teacher. He was taking advanced graduate work in educational foundations as well as art education and the study of creativity. He was warm and acceptant of students, but dignified and reserved. To the research team he appeared to motivate students more through stimulating inquiry, activity, and study than through the force of his own personality. His technique reduced, in some degree, the chances of the results being mainly the effects of the teacher's personality.

This class was organized like many other classes. It met the first 70-minute period of every day, five days a week, and included a 20-minute home-room period. This class was interrupted with fire drills, loud-speaker announcements, assemblies, and special occasions. No regular art classroom was available so a home economics room was used. The layout of the room imposed an artificial grouping of four students to an alcove. After each session meticulous cleanliness had to be restored. Limited storage space curtailed the uses of some materials. None of these factors contributed to what is generally considered an ideal open classroom situation, where freedom of movement and choice are to be encouraged. The researchers assumed, though, that limitations of the physical environment were often found in other teaching situations, thus making the study related to more classroom situations.

Since the art class was an additional class for these students, the research team had to agree that no outside study would be required. Time for use of resource materials had to be scheduled within the class period. Students voluntarily did considerable work outside of class.

Evaluation of the Curriculum

To see if the course accomplished what the researchers proposed it would, there were pretests and post-tests of the experimental group and the control group over a six-month period. The experimental group participated in the creativity class, but otherwise joined the control group for classes designed for upper ability groups. The evaluation was made on the differences in degree and direction of change between the two groups.

Selection of Tests

J. P. Guilford helped us select from his tests of creative behavior those that would be appropriate for ninth grade students and that would tap a broad range of abilities.

The Palo Alto Public Schools, in which this study was made, were cooperating in the validation of the Myers-Briggs Type Indicator,[15] which differentiates between the more or less creative in more global personality types.

Results of the Study

The tests measured the students in the three traits of creativity: fluency, flexibility, and originality. In the *fluency* category, we found two tests in which the experimental group improved significantly more than did the control group. The associational fluency test requires speed in making meaningful relationships—a stimulus word is given and the subject gives as many associated words as possible. The word fluency test requires that the subject produce as many words as possible within a letter class.

Adaptive flexibility was the second general trait of creativity that Guilford identified in a factor analysis on all his tests with ninth grade students. Guilford found that his test *Match Problems II* was the most effective in identifying this ability. A great deal of flexibility is needed to overcome the sets that are presented so that the problem can be solved.[16] Our experimental group's improvement was very significantly greater than the control's.

In the third trait, *originality,* Guilford found *Plot Titles High* and *Alternate Uses* the strongest tests. In the *Plot Titles High* test (write unique titles to a paragraph story) the experimental group made a significant improvement; the control group did not. In the *Alternate Uses* test (many alternatives are identified) the experimental group again made a significantly greater improvement than did the control group.

It is interesting to note that, in some measure, in each of the major areas of creative behavior that Guilford has identified, the experimental group improved significantly over the control group. One of the important implications of these findings in this experimental class, in which a large part of the activities involved manipulation of tools and materials and the creation of visual symbols and organizations, is that significant changes on conceptual tests of creativity resulted. This result would lead us to consider that some degree of transfer of training from one kind of activity to another may have taken place.

With the creativity measures we also gave a personality inventory, the Myers-Briggs Type Indicator.[17] This inventory is designed to measure four dimensions of personality: introversion-extroversion, sensory-intuitive, thinking-feeling, and perceptual-judgmental. We did not find significant differences in the first dimension — shifts to or from introversion or extroversion.

In the second dimension of the personality test we did find an interesting shift. It concerns the use of sensation or of intuition as a preferred mode of becoming aware. The individual who uses sensory (S) cues depends upon direct evidence. The one who relates and associates in the perceptual process is more intuitive (called the N dimension). We found a significant increase in N with the experimental group in comparison to the control group. This result indicates growth in more open use of perceptions, allowing the student's visual awareness to become the means for his seeing remote relationships, more possibilities from what he perceives, than he would find if he used only direct sensory information.

In the third dimension, which concerns the use of feeling (F) in contrast to thinking (T), significant shifts were again found. The experimental group had a significantly greater increase in the use of feeling. The dependence on reason appeared to be strong in most of these students in the pretest situation. During this same period, the control group went down in the use of feeling.

In the fourth dimension the effects of the perceptual training in the experimental class seem to be evidenced. They increased very significantly while the controls decreased slightly. This dimension is an analysis of whether an individual becomes aware of an object by referring to its perceptual (P) qualities or by simply making a judgment (J) about it.[18] When the P trait is combined with the use of intuition (N) a more creative response to experience can be expected. On the basis of the second, third, and fourth parts of the Myers-Briggs test, the experimental group tended in the direction of becoming more intuitive, more dependent upon feeling, and more aware of perceptual qualities.

MacKinnon's comparison of creative and less creative architects is interesting in terms of the students in the creativity class. MacKinnon says of creative architects that they require both scientific and artistic creativity.[19] There may be some parallel with the experience of academically successful students going into a creative design class. Most of the students had little or no prior art training. According to their answers in a questionnaire, these students rated their preferences for classes in the following order: reading, social studies, science, mathematics, and languages. Art was their sixth choice. If these students showed increased strengths in the personality dimensions that are characteristic of the most creative architects, the study lends credence to the possibility that the students' problem-solving and perceptual experience in design contributed to their NP development.

The most creative architects had much higher preference for the use of perception than judgment in the JP area of the Myers-Briggs test.[20] This was the one area in the MacKinnon study of creative persons where a strong preference was found. In other groups in his study the proportion of J's to P's was about the same. The use of P more than J indicates an openness to perceptual experience, looking for possibilities and relationships rather than coming to a judgment which tends to stop the perceiving.

The second parallel found between the creative architects and the students in the experimental group was in the intuitive compared to the sensory response. The students increased significantly in the N dimension. MacKinnon found a high use of intuition in all of the creative persons in all fields he studied as well as among the architects.[21]

Myers reports that the N dimension is highly preferred by both male and female high creatives (97% men, 96% women).[22] In groups that Myers studied she found the greatest preference for perceptual (P) responses among creative men and women, the National Merit finalists, and gifted junior high school students.

Content Analysis of Student Evaluations

At the end of the experimental year the students in the experimental group were asked to evaluate the program in a paper that would not be graded but that would be used by the project in evaluating what had taken place. A content analysis procedure was used to identify what was contained in the papers as a whole. Two trained evaluators, not connected with the project or familiar with the students, read the papers for key concepts. The two readers then pooled and refined the concepts. Then each paper was read to see how many students responded to each different concept and in what directions. The ratings were checked nine weeks later to obtain a measure of temporal reliability, which was 89.7%. The percent agreement between the two evaluators was 87.8%. The students reported the following changes in their behavior and attitudes.

Attitudes toward Creativity Seminar at Beginning and End of Year
  Beginning of Year
    None were positive at the beginning of the year.
    Ten were negative.
    Six reported lack of information.
    Eleven made no comment.

End of Year:
  General attitudes:
    Twenty-six were positive.
    One made no comment.
  Flexibility:
    Nineteen reported that they felt they were more flexible in the use of materials.
  Reaction to people who are different:
    Eighteen reported that they were much more positive in their reactions to nonconformists.
    Seven reported that they already appreciated nonconformists.
  Changes in attitude toward failure:
    Nineteen reported that they had learned that failure was useful in creative work. A typical response is as follows:
      "Before this course I would have been completely stumped by failure, but now I think of it as a help in achieving my best goals."
    Five reported that fear of failure had been lessened or overcome:
      "My attitudes have changed considerably. I used to be scared to death to fail in anything."

      "My attitude toward failure has changed. Now I feel that if you have made an intelligent attempt, but you still fail it was worth it."

      "I have always been depressed by failure and still am; now I am more willing to try along a different line."
  Increased interests:
    Sixteen students reported increased and broadened interests.
  Difference in self-concept:
    Eleven reported more self-confidence.
    Eight reported they were less self-centered.

Implications

In summary we may say that we have made a global, exploratory study of the relationships between (1) a specific kind of art training (a somewhat structured but increasingly open-ended approach to problem solving in design) coupled with the study of creative behavior of people in the sciences and arts and exposure to creative individuals in these fields and (2) shifts in creative behavior as measurable by the Guilford creativity tests and the Myers-Briggs Type Indicator. The relationship was studied by comparing two groups of students, equally able in aptitude and performance as measured by the School and College Ability Tests (upper 10%) and school grades. The control group had the battery of tests administered and readministered over a six-month time lapse. The experimental group had the same testing but had the art and creativity experience, in addition to the usual program for students at this ability level.

It was found that the students in the experimental group generally performed significantly better in the post-tests than did the control groups in tests of fluency, adaptive flexibility, and originality requiring divergent production, but not in convergent production, nor in rate of emission of familiar cognitive responses. The students' evaluations gave some evidence that values, attitudes, and self-concepts can be changed; a student can learn to accept failure as a tool for exploration and to accept the nonconformist as a valuable member of society. Furthermore, there is some evidence that the designing process may be much more complex than the researchers had imagined.

Thus we may say that we do have support for our original hypothesis and that this particular type of training given to students of this ability level and general socio-economic level is effective in changing their responses to segments of tests designed to measure creativity.

We do not know which of the dimensions of the curriculum were most effective, nor do we contend that the same kind of activities would be effective with other ability level or socio-economic groups. In a group study such as this we do not know whether the treatment was effective for all students. A subsequent case study analysis may give more insight into this question. Probably the most important question, which can only be answered as this topic is further studied and defined, is this: Did we tap the most important functions of creative behavior that can be handled within the context of public school education? The results are strongly suggestive that an art program that focuses on problem solving and creative behavior does have important functions in general education of the academically superior.

Summary   In this chapter we have seen some of the ways certain types of preparation for art have been taught and evaluated. All of art teaching probably cannot be tested. Part of the problem is finding adequate criteria for evaluating art products. But a good beginning has been made in testing some of our hypotheses and assumptions about teaching art.

We have seen that children's performance in art can be significantly accelerated by their own conceptualizations about what they are doing. We found in the Boger study that increased perceptual training increases IQ scores, particularly among deprived children. From this we might assume that art activities might also be helpful in increasing IQ scores, as well as teaching children to understand art.

The Covington study showed that parents' educational level affected children's perceptual discrimination. It also indicated that perceptual exposure can help children improve their scores on perceptual tests.

According to the Bruner and the Dennis research and these last studies, it seems apparent that environment plays an important part in children's perceptual readiness, helping the advantaged children by the time they enter school. Yet the same children are conditioned by the concept-oriented curriculum to use their perceptions less.

Research with rats in areas where humans cannot be used strongly suggests that a stimulating environment has an important effect on subsequent problem-solving ability.

Increased ability to react to the perceptual qualities of art was demonstrated with children who were helped to analyze art.

Studies that have evaluated the effectiveness of perceptual training on drawing behavior indicate that analysis is effective in some cases.

A study of the creative behavior of superior junior high school students indicates that their attitudes toward failure and toward creative people and their own scores on creativity tests can be improved significantly as compared to a control group. A problem-solving-oriented design course that also gave them opportunity to study creative people was the treatment used.

This chapter, then, indicates that aspects of art or art readiness can be taught and that the results can be evaluated to see whether readiness has increased.

Bibliography of Paperbound and Other Books Used in Creativity Seminar

Andrade, E. N. da C. *Sir Isaac Newton, His Life and Work*. Doubleday Anchor Book, S42, 1958.

Barnett, L. *The Universe and Dr. Einstein*. Mentor Book, MD231, 1948.

Baruch, B. *My Own Story*. Cardinal Giant, GC52, 1957.

Blesh, Rudi. *Stuart Davis*. Evergreen Gallery Book, #11E-119, Grove Press, 1960.

Block, H. M., and Salinger, H. *The Creative Vision*. Evergreen Original, E224, Grove Press, 1960.

Duncan, David D. *The Private World of Pablo Picasso*. Ridge Press Book, 1958, Dist., Pocket Books.

Einstein, Albert. *Out of My Later Years*. Wisdom Library, Philosophical Library, 1957.

Ghiselin, B. *The Creative Process*. Mentor Book, MD-132, 1955.

Huizinga, Johan. *Men and Ideas*. Meridian Books, M-61, 1959.

Nijinsky, R. *Nijinsky*. Universal Library, UL-62, Grosset & Dunlap, 1934.

Oppenheimer, J. R. *The Open Mind*. Simon & Schuster, 1955.

Peattie, D.C. *Lives of Destiny*. Signet Key Book, K-306, New American Library, 1954.

Polya, G. *How to Solve It*. Anchor Book, A-93, 2nd Ed., Doubleday, 1957.

Roberts, Colette. *Mark Tobey*. Evergreen Gallery Book #4, E-181 Grove Press, 1959.

Roosevelt, E. *This Is My Story*. Bantam Book, #846, 1951.

References

[1] Elizabeth Ruth Dubin, "The Effect of Training on the Tempo of Development of Graphic Representation in Preschool Children," *Journal of Experimental Education*, 15 (1946), 163–173.

[2] Jack H. Boger, "An Experimental Study of the Effects of Perceptual Training on Group I.Q. Test Scores of Elementary Pupils in Rural Ungraded Schools," *Journal of Educational Research* 46 (September 1952), 43–46.

[3] Elliott W. Eisner, "The Qualitative Aspects of Children's Cognitive Development." Paper presented as an address at the National Art Education Convention, Philadelphia (1965).

[4] M. V. Covington, "Some Effects of Stimulus Familiarization on Discrimination." Unpublished doctoral dissertation, University of California, 1962.

[5] Arthur R. Jensen, "Social Class and Perceptual Learning," *Mental Hygiene*, 1966, 231–233.

[6] Brent G. Wilson, "An Experimental Study Designed to Alter Fifth and Sixth Grade Students' Perception of Paintings," *Studies in Art Education*, 8 (1966), 33–42.

[7] Brent G. Wilson, "The Development and Testing of an Instrument to Measure Aspective Perception of Paintings." Unpublished doctoral dissertation, The Ohio State University, 1966.

[8] R. A. Salome, "The Effects of Perceptual Training upon the Two-Dimensional Drawings of Children." *Studies in Art Education* (Fall 1965), 18–33.

[9] R. A. Salome, "The Effects of Perceptual Training on the Two-Dimensional Drawings of Children." Unpublished doctoral dissertation, Stanford University, 1964.

[10] Gordon L. Kensler, "The Effects of Perceptual Training and Modes of Perceiving upon Individual Differences in Ability to Learn Perspective Drawing," *Studies in Art Education*, 7 (1965), 34–41.

[11] D. N. Jackson, J. S. Messick, and C. T. Myers, *The Role of Memory and Color in Group and Individual Embedded Figures of Field Independence* (Princeton, N.J.: Educational Testing Service, 1962).

[12] Harold L. Cohen, "M. O. D. E. L.: Motivationally Oriented Designs for an Ecology of Learning." Paper presented at the American Educational Research Association Symposium on Application of Reinforcement Principles of Education, February 17, 1967, New York, N.Y.

[13] Harold L. Cohen, "Learning Stimulation." Paper presented at The Brooklyn Museum Conference, "The Role of the Arts in Meeting the Social and Educational Needs of the Disadvantaged," November 15–19, 1966.

[14] June K. McFee, *Creative Problem Solving of Academically Superior Adolescents*, Monograph, National Art Education Association, 1968.

[15] Isabel Briggs Myers, *Manual (1962) for the Myers-Briggs Type Indicator* (Princeton N.J.: Educational Testing Service, 1962).

[16] J. P. Guilford, P. R. Merrifield, and A. B. Cox, "Reports from the Psychological Laboratory: Creative Thinking in Children at the Junior High School Levels" (Los Angeles: The University of Southern California, September 1961), p. 22.

[17] Myers, *Manual*.

[18] *Ibid.*, pp. 58–59.

[19] Donald W. MacKinnon, *The Creative Person* (Berkeley: University Extension, University of California, 1961), pp. v1–v24.

[20] Myers, *Manual*, p. 16.

[21] *Ibid.*, p. 14.

[22] *Ibid.*, p. 16.

8

Child Development in Art

Art educators and psychologists have long tried to explain children's art. At different times teachers have accepted particular theories as being "true" and have taught accordingly. Some of these theories resulted from teachers' long experience with children in art. Others, particularly those developed in Europe, were derived from analyses of large numbers of children's drawings, without consideration of environment or past experience. Other observers recorded the development of children, singly or in small groups, over long periods of time and from their findings attempted to generalize about all children. Most of these studies were made in an attempt to find an age-based "natural unfolding" pattern of growth which the observers believed to exist.[1,2]

General trends in development in art research were not different from studies in child development as a whole. Large numbers of children of each age would be studied to see how the average six- or ten-year-old would perform in many kinds of tasks. Tests were given to measure vocabulary, reasoning, computation, memory, eye-hand coordination, and other variables. Height, weight, and skeletal and muscle growth were measured. Often the concept "average" was interpreted to mean "best," and a child too far from average, especially *below* average, was considered to have a disadvantage that would stay with him (his rate of change was not expected to vary). Averages for large numbers of children obscured the changes in rate of growth for any one child. This method of study did not give information about the interrelatedness of all the factors of growth in any one child.

Recent research in psychology and anthropology indicates that we must consider many factors to understand the complex process of a child as he responds to his environment and expresses his response in a drawing or painting. As early as 1936, Anastasi and Foley analyzed the cultural influence on children's art behavior and found that different environments produced different types of art in children of the same age—differences in the amount of detail, subjects, colors, complexity of organization, and the quality of the drawings.[3]

The Yale Development studies under Gesell were generally accepted as having established some norms of child development. Educational psychologists and test developers used the chronological age base for evaluating intellectual and social development. Since that time developmental and child psychologists have been attempting to identify the many variables that contribute to development.

Current Trends in Child Development Theory and Research

As we have already noted, heredity and environment are now seen as interacting influences on developmental behavior. The potential of a child is modified, accelerated, directed, or even left to atrophy or diminish by factors in the environment. If the environment is extremely homogeneous, so that most children interact with the same rewards, opportunities, and stimulation, then age (the same length of experience in the same environment) might be a common base upon which potential differences could be measured. With both the environment and the potential varying, all that age-based norms can measure are the differences at different age norms of the transactional behavioral results of "average" potential with "average" environment. As the number of variables of potential and environment is increased, the possible combinations of these are compounded. When we recognize that each variable in a child's potential transacts with factors in the environment, modifying each other, then the complexity of development becomes apparent.

To understand a given child in comparison to age-based norms, a teacher would need to know the many details of environmental influence and the ways a present behavior of a child was modified by a past experience. How was his potential to learn accelerated, decreased, or redirected? Such questioning does not mean that age-based norms should be abandoned, but that norms ought to be established only in situations where environment and potential are held constant and that they should be used only within that context.

The Draw-a-Man Test, developed by Goodenough and refined and extended by Dale Harris, is an example of a test that is well qualified by its constructors.[4] Harris indicates that even though the test is often used as a "culture fair" test because it allows for differences in language training and the content of test items is not bound to one culture, still environmental factors of dress and cultural attention to some body parts and not others can limit cross-cultural use of the test. He believes that for the most valid results norms need to be established for different cultures. This would mean that within the diverse cultures within one political society such as Canada, the United States, or Mexico, multiple norms are needed. One of my students had an opportunity to have the Draw-A-Man Test administered to North Vietnamese refugee children in South Vietnam.[5] Two quite consistent types of drawings were returned that could not be identified and were difficult to grade according to scores standardized in the United States. A Vietnamese exchange student identified two cross-cultural influences expressed in them. One figure was a combination of devil symbols attributed to the enemy. The other was a combination of the American sheriff of the West and "Zorro," the Robin Hood of Monterey. These children had seen no movies but were refugees of war and had received American soldiers' comic books. Both environmental influences were found in their drawings.

When a teacher recognizes an unusual trend in the drawings of a cultural group, then clues about cross-cultural influences are useful. But some of these drawings are most difficult to evaluate according to standards useful in measuring intelligence.

Intelligence tests do help a teacher to see how a child varies from the norms established by the middle-class culture. But he does not know whether a variation is a cultural or motivational factor, such as a lack of potential or a lack of development. Not only does a low IQ score tell us how far a given child is from achieving in school, but also *how far the school environment may be from stimulating his intellectual growth.*

Harris' work is commensurate with other trends in present developmental psychology. Developmental and child psychologists are studying many elements of environmental interaction that modify growth. The increased concern for minority groups in this country has led to a search for greater understanding of environmental influences on intellectual development of economically and socially deprived children. In the case of seriously impaired and retarded children, teachers are using techniques of behavior modification, such as changing the rewards systems in the children's environment, to help the children drop undesirable behaviors and develop constructive ones such as learning to eat and dress and read.[6,7] But behavior modification needs to be undertaken with the greatest concern for the total psycho-social development of the child to see if changing one behavior will produce dysfunction in his other behaviors.

The study of development in art cannot be separated from the study of child development generally. Perceptual growth, conceptual growth, and learning from one's culture all affect how a child will behave in art. For this reason it is important for the teacher to understand the relationships between these areas of research.

Longitudinal Studies of Child Development

The longitudinal study was developed to overcome the limitations of research that recorded averages alone. The observers in a longitudinal study record growth patterns of many children over a long period of time. Although some of these studies began over thirty years ago, their findings are just now becoming available.

Variations in Growth Patterns. The Berkeley Growth Research, at the University of California, was a study of children from birth through age twenty-one. Nancy Bayley, later director of Child Development at the National Institute of Mental Health, worked on the project throughout the years. Her summary of the findings is very important to the understanding of current thinking in child development.

In this study records were kept of forty children. Mental and physical development were measured consistently. After analyzing the patterns of change through these years, Bayley gives us these insights into the nature of development:

1. Few children follow consistent growth patterns with each factor developing at its same rate throughout the child's development.

2. Few children actually follow the age-based norms. A norm or average of height is found by adding all the heights for an age group and dividing by the number of children measured. Few of the children are actually at the norm. (Unless we know the deviation of the scores from the norm, we do not know whether the heights were clustered closely around the norm or whether many of the children had heights quite far from the norm.)

3. To think of a child's development as the sum of intellectual, psychological, and physical growth is inadequate. Each of these is in part dependent on all the others. Each is developing at a different and often fluctuating rate.[8]

A child with high verbal skills but with slowly developing motor skills is a good example. A teacher who does not recognize differences in growth patterns and their influence on each other may misinterpret his behavior. If the child's writing ability develops slowly but he reacts well orally, an uninformed teacher might assume he just is not working at writing and may punish him for his lack of effort. The child, unable to understand his difficulty, may react by being rebellious, by switching to a task in which he is more sure of success, or by retreating from the situation — refusing to try at all.

To understand such problems we need as much information as possible about each child. *By acting without knowing, we may be increasing a child's problems rather than helping him overcome them.* On the basis of the Bayley report we need to remember that a pattern of growth for a child at age seven *may not be his pattern at age ten.*

This newer approach to child psychology has been called "organismic." This term, borrowed from biology, means that the parts of the whole organism are in a sense independent and at the same time interdependent. Although growth or function of any part can be measured by itself, it can never be considered as truly separable from the other parts. The activity of the whole organism is the interaction of parts and is thus dependent on each part's stage of development. To assess adequately a child's development, a teacher should consider all the individual and environmental factors that may have influenced him, as well as the varying rates of his physical and psychological growth.

Intelligence and Personality Development. Another longitudinal study by Sontag at the Fels Research Institute on Human Development at Antioch College was concerned with relationships between IQ, personality development, and physical growth. One hundred forty children from various socio-economic levels were measured in their degree of dependency or independency, their need to achieve and enter competition, their IQ, and their physical development.

Dependency-independency measurements of children came from interviews with parents and observation of the children. Questions like these were asked: "How much help does the child need in caring for himself?" "Does he dislike being left with other adults?" "How early did he dress himself?" "How far away from home is he allowed to go?" Observations of a child with his parents gave cues about the dependency of the child on his parents. His need to achieve and his competitiveness with other children were observed in his activities with other children. Independence of his peers was observable in the degree to which the child was anxious to compete with other children, was self-reliant, and was not afraid of new situations.

These measurements were made every six months from age $2\frac{1}{2}$ to 10. The rates of IQ change and physical development were measured in the same sequence. In analyzing the individual children's patterns of growth the following general tendencies were found:

1. A child's rate of intellectual development is not necessarily the same through childhood.

2. Deceleration in his rate of intellectual growth is often found during periods of stress and anxiety in the home when he tends to become more dependent.

3. Acceleration in intellectual growth is related to periods of more independence and need to achieve.[9]

This study supports the organismic concept of child development, with environmental factors being shown as related to changes in the rate of intellectual development. It further points out that consideration of a child without awareness of the environment within which he is interacting gives us an incomplete picture of his development.

Bayley, in a 1965 review of her own and other longitudinal studies, shows that later work supports the organismic concept with even more evidence that parental behavior can be a strong influence on intellectual development. Boys are most influenced by mothers' attitudes toward them—loving mothers had boys whose IQ scores were lower in infancy but higher later. Girls' IQ scores correlated more with their parents' academic and professional achievement.[10]

Intellectual Growth as a Variable in Perceptual Development

One of the major variables in the perceptual development of a child may be his intellectual development. We have seen in the Sontag study that environment plays a role in the acceleration or deceleration rates of IQ increase in children. In any large sample of children at any given age a normal curve of scores on a Stanford-Binet or other intelligence test will usually be found. This means that, in an ungrouped classroom, scores are likely to be clustered around 100 with deviations in both directions. The mean IQ will vary from one classroom to another. The variation may be due to a real difference in average intellectual ability. It may also be due to differences in ability to respond to verbal tests. In some communities, such as those where professional people live, the development of language skills is necessary for a child to get recognition of his achievement. In other communities there may be a high proportion of children whose families do not stress reading or quality in verbal expression.

Intelligence and Ability to Handle Detail. A study was made of college students to discover the relationship between intelligence (as measured by the Wechsler vocabulary test) and the ability to handle visual patterns. In the visual test the students were shown forty patterns of white dots arrranged within the possibilities of a square subdivided into twenty-five squares. Half the patterns were symmetrical as in Figure 8–1; half were asymmetrical as in Figure 8–2. Each pattern was projected by a tachistoscope on a screen for $\frac{1}{5}$ second. The students attempted to reproduce the pattern on a grid sheet. It was found that the highest-IQ students made the fewest mistakes. The correlation between IQ and ability to reproduce the asymmetrical patterns was significantly high, indicating that the higher the intelligence the greater the probability that the person can handle less well-ordered (in this case asymmetrical) visual information.[11]

Art Training as a Variable in Perceptual Development

The education of an artist includes a great deal of perceptual training, careful analysis of visual details, study of subtle relationships between things, and discovery of ways to interpret details in one's work.

The Visual Habits of Artists and Nonartists. A bidimensional camera was used to measure the way a person's eyes focus on simple

Figure 8–1. Symmetrical Arrangement

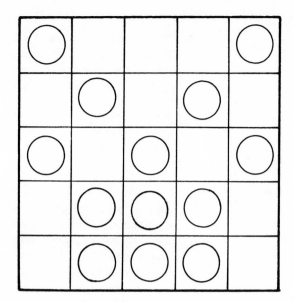

Figure 8–2. Asymmetrical Arrangement

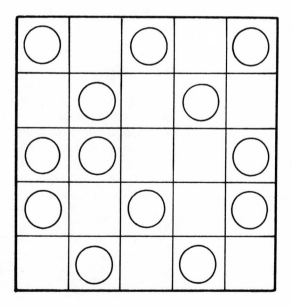

and complex patterns. Artists tend to make their original fixations on the complicated pattern; nonartists, including a sample of engineers, tended to fixate initially on the simple designs and to spend most of their time observing them.[12] Other researchers found that nonartists tended to prefer simple symmetrical drawings while those trained in the arts tended to prefer complex, asymmetrical drawings.[13] These studies reflect in part the differences in perceptual training of the two groups.

Development in Art

Theories of children's development in art have been mainly derived from normative studies of children's work in samples from Western civilization. The theories are based on the assumption that development in the structure of the content of drawing is more related to chronological age than to the transaction processes affecting a child's direction and rate of growth. According to older theories, drawing was a simple behavior not involving the many variables now recognized. Also drawing theories were based on collections of children's drawings of things they remembered but not on their abilities to draw when responding to something they could see.

The research technique of sorting by age and then looking for similarities among children of an age group hides what may be significant differences within a given age group. When we discuss children's art with emphasis on drawing we are talking about a much broader subject than the rightfully limited task in the Draw-a-Man test. Harris, in his thorough study of research on child development in art, says that "drawings do reflect a child's idiosyncratic view of his world and his experience." This statement might be further modified to read, "Drawings do reflect a child's idiosyncratic view of his interaction with his unique world as he has learned to express it symbolically."

Neither a child's experience nor his particular personality, which has developed as a transaction between his genetic potential and his environment, is dependent entirely upon age. Even if child art were strictly a muscular reaction, the effects of environment on physical development would have to be considered. Age, the length of time transaction has taken place, is only one of the variables of growth.

Lovano carefully controlled a drawing task for elementary school boys, grades two through six.[14] The task was for the boys to draw what they saw when presented with a slide-projected photograph of the front door of their own school. This task involves use of a present visual stimulus and does not rely on memory alone. The drawings were scored by a team of trained judges who rated and checked the drawings on their degree of analytical or global response in size, value, detail, and space relationships and the separation of figure and ground. Figure 8–3 is the photograph of the door, and Figures 8–4 through 8–8 are examples of the ranges found in each grade level.* Figure 8–9 gives this information in statistical form.

Figure 8–3. The School Entrance

*Figures 8–3 through 8–8 courtesy of Jessie Lovano.

Figure 8–4. The Range of Development
in Second Grade, from A to B

Figure 8-5. In Third Grade, from A to B

Figure 8–6. In Fourth Grade, from A to B

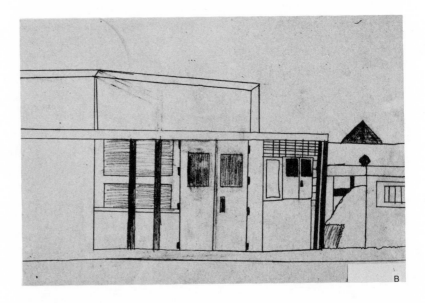

Figure 8–7. In Fifth Grade, from A to B

Figure 8–8. In Sixth Grade, from A to B

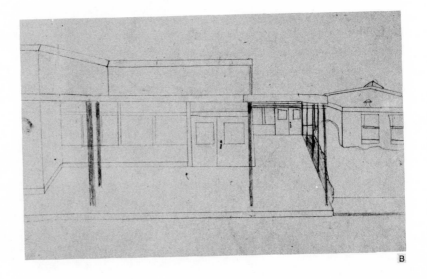

Figure 8–9. Ranges of Response to a Single Stimulus (Adapted from Lovano)

Grade	Means	Mean	Range	Standard Dev.
2		7.3	9 Points	2.09
3		8.5	10 Points	2.22
4		9.4	11 Points	2.73
5		9.9	12 Points	2.88
6		10.8	19 Points	3.27

5 6 7 8 9 10 11 12 13 14 15 16 17 18 19 20

Scores

There is evidence of progression as one looks at the mean scores as they shift upward grade by grade. There is also evidence of growth if one looks at the top scores of each grade. But when one looks at the range of scores for each grade level, it is clear that any given teacher in these grades has many children who do not change in their ability to respond to a single stimulus and to record what they see. Further, the higher the grade, the greater the diversity. No significant correlations were found between age and scores on this drawing task at any grade level though a low (.405) correlation was found when all grades were grouped together.

To understand a child's development one would have to go far beyond his drawing to estimate his particular variation from "age-based norms." One would need to understand how the following variables had influenced his work:

1. The way his culture has directed his attention.

2. His cognitive style in handling information, more analytic or global, more reflective or impulsive.

3. The ways he is learning to relate himself to three-dimensional space.

4. His developing use of and dependence on the perceptual constancies — seeing things as he knows them to be, as they appear in physical space, or in both of these ways.

5. The ways his home and school environment have encouraged him to develop the creative traits of fluency, flexibility, originality, playful attitudes, and independence of conformity.

6. The concepts he has learned and the degree to which he has learned to relate visual information to these concepts.

7. The percepts he is aware of; his ability to manipulate forms in space and analyze relationships.

8. The perceptual-conceptual skills of the adults from whom he receives his primary learning.

9. The richness or dullness of his visual environment.

10. His past experiences in art, whether supportive, encouraging, defeating, or inhibiting.

11. His adaptation to the school environment.

12. His attitudes toward art activities.

Normative studies tell us very little about the range one might expect in a given classroom. Often in reports of such studies a typical behavior is identified for a given age. But teachers also need to know the range of scores that the average was taken from and how the scores cluster around the mean.

The Meaning of Averages   According to educational psychologists, members of a class may differ in several ways. If you rate similar-aged children's drawings on an age-based scale you will, except in very rare instances, find more than one age norm represented. Let us assume that you are a fourth grade teacher. Your pupils come from various ethnic and social-class backgrounds. Their experience in art is varied. Some have had authoritarian teachers before, others have had permissive teachers. Some of the children think art activities are exciting; others, for various reasons, are fearful of trying. You may identify many other variables. If all of the pupils are given a similar drawing or painting task, you have the opportunity to see how much they are alike or different, on this particular day. You may use one of the age-based scales to see how your pupils are performing, and plot them according to Figure 8–10. Two of the children perform like second graders, three like third graders, four like fourth, four like fifth, three like sixth, and two

Figure 8–10. A Normal Curve

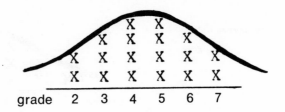

like seventh graders. If you draw a line over the top of the scores you will find you have a bell-shaped or normal curve, as this class clusters toward the middle. The normal curve usually appears when a mixed sample of people is tested on a behavior that they have had varied opportunities to learn or develop.

But you could have a class where the scores were clustered in the middle and the bell shape looked like Figure 8–11. If this is the case, it means that the children in your class are much alike, as the range of their scores from high to low is short.

Figure 8–11. Scores Clustered to the Center

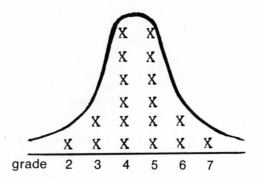

By contrast you could have a very low bell-shaped curve like Figure 8–12, which means that the children are quite different and the range of scores is wider than normal.

Figure 8–12. Scores Spread Out

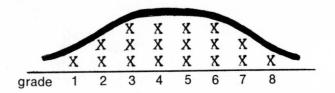

Each one of these groups could have the same mean score. That is, if you add all the scores and divide the total by the number of pupils, you will get almost the same answer. But the ranges of scores and the ways they cluster around the mean are very different. Distribution of scores makes a great deal of difference in the classroom. You would have to find out why the scores are so different and then find ways to motivate all the children to become involved in art.

If we were to test all the behaviors that children use in art, such as aspects of perceiving, symbolizing, designing, creating, problem solving, and conceptualizing, we would find similar ranges on each aspect and any classroom might vary in any or all of these ranges. Also the bell shapes could be skewed; that is, the scores might cluster below the mean or above the mean as compared to the mean on which the age-base stages were made. This is why it is so important for teachers to know more than the averages of any scale; they need to see how the children in the original research varied from the mean and in which ways. Then they can see how their pupils' variance from the mean is related to the larger study.

If we had measurements of average behavior on all the behaviors involved in art, we would find that a given child would be high in some and low on others. Occasionally a child will be high, low, or average on all scores. Each of these abilities varies with the child's opportunity to learn, as the cross-cultural studies have shown. Unless we know something about the opportunity a child has had, his present ability means only where he is now, and gives us little information about what his potential is or how it may be developed.

The studies of Dubin, Salome, Kensler, Covington, Wilson, and McFee, reported in Chapter 7, all indicate that children's levels and quality of work can be changed by educational processes. Furthermore, the behavior of children in different educational environments indicates how diverse experience leads to different learning, producing different kinds of development.

Experience in a social class, perceptual learning, and early experience in the environment are factors that shape the development of mental abilities. Jensen indicates that during the first months and the early years of life the effects of the environment begin to set the stage for subsequent learning, even changing the physical properties of the brain.[15] He suggests that readiness, which is in part affected by the length of time a child has had experience (that is, his chronological age), is perhaps *more* affected by the type of experience he has had. Jensen stresses that perception is foundational to all other learning. The early interaction the child has with his environment in learning to see creates the framework upon which his subsequent development depends. If a child has had a meager framework for responding, his information handling will be limited until this framework is changed. Certainly learning to respond and to create visually is foundational to development, understanding, and producing in art.

Perceptions of *depth, distance,* and *size* are probably affected by four classes of determinants: (1) the condition of the eyes, (2) the nature of the things observed, (3) the effects of learning, and (4) the aptitudes or readiness of the individual. Anyone studying perceptual development would need to consider all four classes.

Smith and Smith, in an extensive factorial study of age and verbal ability, made three assumptions: (1) that "perceptual development is a form of intellectual development," (2) that "maturation results in a proliferation of the capabilities for perceiving,"[16] and (3) that "the ability to make accurate spatial judgments is not a general trait in children or in adults."[17]

The researchers studied 97 children and 85 adults, ages five and one-half to 42 years, of varied socio-economic backgrounds and intellectual abilities. The subjects performed 37 perceptual tasks. Many different abilities were found. For example, the ability to judge the size of a familiar object was different from the ability to judge the size of an unfamiliar object. The ability to judge the size of a thing did not necessarily relate to the ability to judge its distance from the viewer. The ability to judge the distance of a close object varied from the ability to judge the distance of a faraway object.

Apparently the use of any perceived depth in everyday life is not necessarily constant but is variable in terms of the learned units by which it is judged.[18] Judgment of the depth of a curved surface was found to be more difficult than judgment of a flat surface, for both adults and children. No consistent effects of age were found. Perception and judgment change with experience, but the age at which a perceptual skill develops will depend both on maturation and experience. Since maturation patterns, culture, and opportunity to learn vary widely among children, teachers can expect children in any one age group to differ extensively in readiness to see.

Theories of Child Development in Art

Considerable effort has been made to identify children's developmental stages in art according to chronological age. This work started in Europe before 1900 when the child development studies began. Many of these studies were made by researchers who analyzed the drawings of one child or a group of children without knowing the conditions under which the drawings were made or without having enough samples to make valid generalizations about all children. Some attempts were made to study children's drawings from different cultures.

The widely used theories of Viktor Lowenfeld are age-based but they do allow for overlapping at ages four, seven, nine, and eleven. Lowenfeld postulated five stages:

Scribbling, two to four years of age, when the child is marking with various kinds of strokes.

Pre-schematic, four to seven years, when the child is developing his scribbles into symbolic representation.

Schematic, seven to nine years, when the child has developed symbols he uses over and over again to mean certain things.

Dawning realism, nine to eleven years, when the symbols are becoming more "realistic."

Pseudo-naturalistic, eleven to thirteen years, when the effort to achieve realism is accentuated.

The term "schema" is usually used to mean a flat drawing of a symbol that represents an object, and not a picture of the "real" thing as it exists in three-dimensional space. Actually all drawing is schematic; no drawing ever achieves "realism" as the eye perceives it. In dealing with children's drawings, we more specifically could call them *flat* schema and *perspective* schema (in which the symbol represents space).[19]

Another study of children's development in art was made at the Cleveland Museum. It is perhaps the most extensive research on child art development to be carried on in many years, but it has not had wide publicity. This work, directed by Thomas Munro with Betty Lark-Horovitz and Edward Barnhart, was exploratory and not extensive enough to generalize for specific ages. But it does raise questions that challenge some of our theories.[20]

The researchers studied dimensions of children's art more than symbolic development. A check list was developed from an analysis of the hundreds of children's drawings in the museum's files. The dimensions they found were (1) *representation,* the use of color and clarity of outline; (2) *representational unity,* the relationship of all the ideas presented as in a scene; (3) *thematic unity,* the organization of line, shape, and color; (4) the *quality of line* used; and (5) the *degree of completion* of all the areas of the drawing. Further analysis was made of the use of flat schemata, perspective schemata, and mixtures of both.

The different age levels were studied, using the children from the museum's Saturday morning classes as subjects. Sample drawings from each child were collected. Specific motivating subjects were used, such as "what you would like most to draw" and "children playing out in the snow in a park." The drawings were then evaluated according to the check list.

The researchers say of their study that the differences found do not lend themselves to an easy analysis. Too many differences in children and kinds of art are possible. They found that the stages were not the same in each of the dimensions they studied. The ability to achieve thematic unity—that is, overall design and decorative effect—increases to age eleven and then decreases so that fifteen-year-olds perform more like six-year-olds. In the study of the uses of schemata there is a great deal of overlapping between ages and "levels of artistic expression." In Barnhart's part of the study 50% of his sample, ranging in age from eight to twelve, were performing in the three stages he has identified—"Schematic, mixed schematic, and true to appearance." This finding suggests that the levels of development postulated by Lowenfeld's theory are too narrow in range and do not include all the dimensions of art behavior.

Traditional theories of child development in art are based on what a child can remember, not what he can draw from direct observation. Since sighted children are always perceiving in some way or another, a measure of their ability to handle information based on memory alone is grossly inadequate.

Throughout this whole dialogue on children's development in art, the assumption seems to be made by those who adhere to age as the primary factor that it is possible for a child to grow up without his experience affecting his readiness and performance in art; yet most of the behaviors used in art he also uses in other modes of learning. Perceiving, organizing, symbolizing, and expressing are all behaviors that develop through the individual child's potential to learn as it transacts with his opportunities to learn. Thus he can be taught to increase his readiness to respond to and produce art.

In his review of the history of research on children's drawings Harris stresses the effect of living in a culture on learning and the development of concepts as important variables that are often not considered by investigators. On the basis of his own extensive research and revalidation of the Draw-a-Man Test, he describes three broad stages of child art development. The first is the making of marks on paper and the gradual achievement of a degree of form. The second is the making of attempts at representation. The third is the use of graphic elements of design. Not all children arrive at the third stage.[21]

These three stages are identified as differences in psychological function. In the first stage the child is reacting to his own marks on the paper. The process is apparently central to his interest. A child's marks tend to take on form characteristics toward the end of this stage. Harris does not indicate whether this level is the beginning of relating perceived form to drawn form or a refining of form through the child's increased control in making marks. It could be both.

The second stage is described as the development of degrees of imitative and reproductive drawing, which Harris says is related to concept formation. (I now use the terms concepts and percepts to include perceptual learning as well.) Part of the process is gaining perceptual information, which can be remembered, organized, and translated into symbolic visual form, without having to be put into words. Most of us have experienced seeing something familiar without having words to describe what the perceptual qualities are that made it familiar. In this case we are remembering perceptual information that we have coded into some form so that when we see a similar phenomenon we can recognize it clearly. People with highly developed perceptual acumen can then verbalize about the relationships and differences even though up to this time the material has remained in perceptual coding rather than conceptual or word-based coding.

As we found in the Bruner studies, differences in experience in education affect the dependence on one or the other mode of information handling—perceptual or conceptual or both. People who have been trained to depend mainly on conceptual coding may be unaware of their perceptual coding, which is not dependent on word processing.

During this second stage of children's growth, when they are relating perceptual experiences, we can increase their readiness to perceive and to draw by helping them compare what they see and what they produce both perceptually and conceptually. We reduce the educational tendency to encourage conceptual development but not perceptual development.

The third stage is described as a broad phase in which children learn the principles of design and the use of graphics. Harris believes that many children do not reach this stage. It is dependent on some form of training within or without the school.

The work of Dennis with the Draw-a-Man Test indicates that the third stage is achieved in the earlier works of children who are in a rich art environment. My own reviews of children's drawings indicate that strong design qualities often occur in the work of primary grade children, indicating that the ordering process is available to some children without training. Some adults appear to design intuitively while others have to learn to design through comparative analysis of the interaction of the elements of design.

Until more research is developed, the status of theory on child development in art appears to be reducible to three stages similar to those described by Harris. Stage one is manipulation with little or no use of concepts and percepts. When it begins and ends depends on the opportunities the children have. Dubin's study in Chapter 7 clearly indicates that children as young as two years can change their levels of graphic expression by being encouraged to conceptualize about what they are doing. It would appear that if children are allowed to "scribble" as long as they wish all they will learn is that they can make marks on paper. But when they learn that their marks have meanings, they will develop more cognitive processes. We need a study comparable to Dubin's at this age level with emphasis on perceptual training.

Stage two, which through training can overlap with stage one, covers the processes through which a child responds to his environment and symbolizes his experience. In my work as a teacher, I have found adults who are still drawing as if they were just beginning to symbolize in drawing from their experience. In the cases where information was available the individuals were found to be conceptually very bright, but their experiences with art had been exceedingly traumatic at very early ages. Apparently this form of cognitive processing, translating experience into percepts and concepts that could be symbolized graphically, had remained undeveloped.

These two psychologically different stages are difficult to separate. A child may tell you conceptually that his drawing has a great deal of meaning to him. He may describe the same drawing differently at different times, yet for the viewer there is no recognizable symbolism. This discrepancy might indicate that the child is in one stage conceptually and in another symbolically. It is very possible that this child has perceptual information coded so that he can remember from one perceptual experience to another, yet he has not developed the capacity to symbolize the experience on paper. Most children are in the second stage in the first grade.

The third stage can be referred to as cultural "realism." The child is learning the styles of design and organization and the symbols that have meaning in his own culture. We can identify the drawings of American Indian, Japanese, or African children by differentiation in kinds of detail and style. Sometimes teachers forget that children in schools in Western culture are also learning a cultural style. Children whose only art forms come from mass media and popular arts have a different cultural "realism" than children who have an exposure to one of the artistic subcultures in their society. The children of experimental artists, whose friends are among the same group, are going to learn different things about art than the children whose art environment is basically interpretive of nature. How an individual child will respond to cultural influences will depend on all the factors of cognitive style, conformity training, motivation to innovate and so on.

Probably every child scribbles before he invents symbols; the symbols become more definitive as the child has more experiences; the symbols approach cultural "realism" when his motor, perceptual, and cognitive skills, as well as conditions in his environment, allow him to do so. The nature of the symbols the child invents is related to his total biopsychological-cultural experience.

The use of age as a criterion has been based on the assumption that biogenic growth patterns can be identified. Hallowell believes that we should abandon attempts to find relationships between art development and innate growth patterns, as the environment plays the major role in influencing the rate and direction of artistic development.[22] McCandless and Spiker suggest that any attempt to find a relationship between changes in behavior (such as in art) and a child's age must also consider past learnings, physiological changes, shifts in the kinds of rewards society is giving him, and the child's changing status, all of which are only "incidentally related to time since birth."[23] If an age-grading basis of modal development is necessary to conform to the age-grading system in schools, then Figure 8–13 is perhaps a helpful, but necessarily general, attempt to organize these variables on an age continuum.

Figure 8–13. Ages and Stages of Child Art

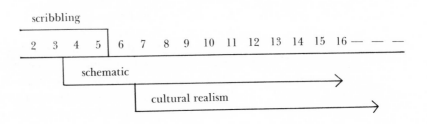

Summary   Most of the studies in this book deal with factors that relate to child development in art, intervening variables that direct and modify growth. Because of our habit of categorizing people by age we have used age as a basis for many of our theories about child art. Longitudinal growth studies show that the pattern is much more complex. There is little evidence to support the idea of a "natural unfolding" of child art growth based on age, because art behaviors, like all other behaviors, are modified continuously by environmental factors.

If one accepts the transactional point of view, then one's concept of development is that a child's present performance is the outgrowth of his potentials to respond as they have developed through his past transactional experiences. His future development depends on how much he is able to increase his habits of information handling and his abilities to differentiate, to analyze, and to express.

We do not know the degree to which any given child's potential at any given age can be activated through art education. We do know that early developed perceptual skills, an analytic cognitive style, and, when needed, a global one, as well as creative traits, can increase a child's readiness for art. The earlier he is able to develop them the more his growth will be accelerated, provided they are not forced on him before he can assimilate them.

Studies of child development—intellectual, psychological, and physical—support the transactional point of view, that potentialities are in large degree modified by experience and environment. Intellectual growth and perceptual growth are related, but environmental factors can encourage the growth of one over the other.

Theories of child development in art have mainly been devised with the use of drawings children have made from memory. Theories have been concerned with averages rather than ranges of development. The study of children's drawings based on responses to an immediate object indicates that drawing is not as easily categorized as the theories suggest.

Cultural patterns, cognitive style, dependence on the perceptual constancies, conceptual and perceptual development, creative traits, the visual characteristics of the environment, the iconic richness of the surroundings, rewards, values, and attitudes all influence the rate and direction of child development in art.

A tentative theory of developmental stages in art can be identified as the child (1) reacts to his own manipulative marks on paper, (2) attempts to symbolize concepts and percepts, and (3) produces culturally influenced symbolic realism.

We know that art is one of man's basic language systems and that the behaviors needed to respond to art—perceptual and conceptual discrimination, ability to respond to appreciative meaning, and the ability to design—need to be begun early in education and developed throughout life.

As was stated in Chapter 1, the purpose of the structuring of the research is to help the teacher deal with the complexity of child behavior in response to art, which includes much of his man-made environment, and to be able to use art for his own communication.

References

[1] Florence Goodenough, "The Intellectual Factor in Children's Drawings." Doctoral dissertation, Stanford University, 1924.

[2] Anne Anastasi and John P. Foley, Jr., *Differential Psychology: Individual and Group Differences in Behavior,* rev. ed. (New York: The Macmillan Company, 1949), pp. 851–855.

[3] Anne Anastasi and John P. Foley, Jr., "An Analysis of Spontaneous Drawings by Children in Different Cultures," *Journal of Applied Psychology,* 20 (1936), 689–726.

[4] Dale B. Harris, *Children's Drawings as Measures of Intellectual Maturity* (New York: Harcourt, Brace & World, Inc., 1963), p. 133.

[5] Susan M. Mayer, "Preliminary Findings of the Draw-a-Man Test as Administered to Children in South Vietnam." Master's thesis, Arizona State University, 1966.

[6] G. J. Bensberg, C. N. Colwell, and R. H. Cassel, "Teaching the Profoundly Retarded Self-Help Activities by Behavior Shaping Techniques," *American Journal of Mental Deficiency,* 69 (1965), 674–679.

[7] A. W. Staats and W. H. Butterfield, "Treatment of Nonreading in a Culturally Deprived Juvenile Delinquent: An Application of Reinforcement Principles," *Child Development,* 36 (1965), 925–942.

[8] Nancy Bayley, "Individual Patterns of Development," *Child Development,* 27 (1956), 45–74.

[9] Lester W. Sontag, Charles T. Baker, and Virgina L. Nelson, *Mental Growth and Personality Development: A Longitudinal Study,* Monograph for the Society for Research in Child Development, Inc., 23 (1958).

[10] Nancy Bayley, "Research in Child Development: A Longitudinal Perspective," *Merrill-Palmer Quarterly,* 11 (1965), 183–208.

[11] Norman Livson and David Krech, "Dynamic Systems, Perceptual Differentiation and Intelligence," *Journal of Personality,* 25 (1956), 46–68.

[12] Bernice T. Eiduson, "Artist and Nonartist: A Comparative Study," *Journal of Personality,* 26 (1958), 22. Reprinted by permission.

[13] F. Barron and G. S. Welsh, "Artistic Perception as a Factor in Personality Style: Its Measurement by a Figure Preference Test," *Journal of Psychology,* 33 (1952), 199–203.

[14] Jessie J. Lovano, *The Relationship of Graphic Style and Mode of Perception to Graphic Expression.* Unpublished Ph.D. dissertation, University of Oregon, 1969.

[15] Arthur R. Jensen, "Social Class and Perceptual Learning," *Mental Hygiene* (1966), 226–239.

[16] Olin W. Smith and Patricia Cain Smith, "Developmental Studies of Spatial Judgments by Children and Adults," *Perceptual and Motor Skills,* 22 (1966), 62.

[17] *Ibid.,* p. 20.

[18] *Ibid.,* p. 68.

[19] Viktor Lowenfeld and W. Lambert Brittain, *Creative and Mental Growth,* 4th ed. (New York: The Macmillan Company, 1964).

[20] Thomas Munro, Betty Lark-Horovitz, and Edward N. Barnhart, "Children's Art Abilities: Studies at the Cleveland Museum of Art," *Journal of Experimental Education,* 11 (1942), 97–155.

[21] Harris, *Children's Drawings*, pp. 229–230.

[22] A. Irving Hallowell, *Culture and Experience* (Philadelphia: University of Pennsylvania Press, 1955).

[23] Boyd R. McCandless and Charles Spiker, "Experimental Research in Child Psychology," *Child Development*, 27 (1956), 77 ff.

The Perception-Delineation Theory

The purpose of this chapter is to weld the content of the previous chapters into a workable framework for teachers in the classroom and to provide students of art education with a theoretical construct for their own continued inquiry. In Chapter 1 we introduced the skeletal P-D theory as it relates to teaching. In this chapter we amplify the theory in order to relate it to the new information presented in the intervening chapters.*

*In 1957 I formulated the Perception-Delineation theory to help teachers understand the relationships and differences among children as they interact with their environment and communicate their ideas in art. Now some years later I find the theoretical framework still viable but needing amplification because so much new research has been done.

A theoretical construct is a design, a way of finding a pattern, an order, a working relationship, among the parts of a whole. The construct is not the phenomenon itself but is rather a conceptual way of relating the order found. Our whole in this case is *the interaction pattern of developing child behavior that results from the transaction of the unique potential of the individual, his social and physical environment, and his expression and response in art.* This transaction pattern is the basis of individual growth and the collective growth of societies with distinct culture patterns.

A transaction is a process in which two or more factors interact and in the process each influences the condition and subsequent behavior of the other. A calm child who enters a class of anxious children may interpret their behavior as friendly. If he responds with increased friendliness, which decreases their fear of strangers, his overture to them may change their behavior, and his freedom to interact with others is reinforced by their changing responses. The two factors, anxiety and calm, transact, and the condition and the subsequent behaviors of the children are modified.

This is a simple situation to illustrate a point. In most situations there are many other variables that might change the direction of the transaction. For example, the behavior of the teacher with the new child or with the class could change the trend of the transaction toward other directions. The overt behavior of one extremely anxious child could also change the pattern.

Background of the Theory

As we stated earlier, this theoretical framework is derived from the theories and research of Witkin, Bruner, Attneave, Kagan, Dennis, Guilford, Getzels, Krech, Crutchfield, and others. Research materials were selected that were related to behaviors in art and that amplified our understanding of the ranges of individual differences that were involved in the transactional process of learning to respond and to perform in the visual arts. Special emphasis was placed on research that dealt with children and early adolescents.

Particular emphasis is given to the effects of early environmental experience. Some learnings can be generalized much more easily than others. The learning of specific things such as the names of people is not as useful in other situations as the learning of discrimination habits, seeing likenesses in somewhat dissimilar things, seeing differences in similar things, and using concepts to label visual experience. It would also follow that children who learn to see things both as they know them to be and as they appear visually are developing a framework for many other learning situations.

The primary visual perception abilities are *organizational,* seeing similarities, differences, proximities, continuities, closures, and figure and ground; and *spatial,* seeing objects in differing degrees of light, distance, and viewpoint relationship. These skills contribute greatly to learning about art and being able to evaluate, either intuitively or intellectually, what one has created. These abilities need continued development in order to be more widely transferable to other situations.

The degree to which perception is learned is clearly shown in the processes necessary in order for blind individuals who gain physiological sight to learn to see psychologically as well, to give meaning to what they perceive. It has been found that formerly blind persons must learn to see differences in form, size constancy, distance judgment, depth perception, perspective, and figure-ground distinction. Very intelligent subjects had to count the corners of triangles and squares to tell them apart. The ability to discriminate among people seen regularly had to be developed slowly.[1]

All of us learn by association. Familiar things when seen again suggest qualities we have previously learned with our other senses. Tactile qualities such as the roughness of sandpaper, qualities of smell such as the sweetness of carnations, or taste reactions suggested by seeing apple pie even when the odor is stopped by a glass cover come into conscious awareness. Some children not only lack percept-concept relation development but if they are economically deprived may have fewer associational learnings than the teacher and the more advantaged children have.

Add to these factors those of personality, cultural training, cognitive styles and habits, and creative behaviors and you will understand the complexity of the processes involved in a child's reaction to an art form and the reasons for the wide ranges of individual differences that are found in the classroom. To organize your information you may find that a working theory is useful.

The early development of creative attitudes, flexibility, and fluency, the use of postural kinesthetic cues, the ability to separate figure from ground, the use of analytic as well as spontaneous responses—all these factors contribute to the handling of information and to creative problem solving. These factors contribute to a child's readiness. A child who does not develop the ability to give creative responses until age ten has missed the learning experiences he might have had if he had developed this ability earlier.

Cognition Cognition is the process of thinking, becoming aware, solving problems, relating, differentiating, organizing, reflecting and innovating. Percepts and concepts are tools in this process. Percepts are mental images derived from sensory experience. Concepts are ideas derived from experience. Percepts and concepts can be remembered, expressed, or communicated to others through iconic or word symbols. A person's ability to experience, to think about what he experiences with language and mental images and then symbolize these to communicate to others, and to record his thinking for his own future use is the basis for his artistic and intellectual development. (See Figure 9–1.)

Percepts and concepts can be expressed in many ways—through gestures, through drawing, painting, sculpture, architectural form, poetry, and music, as well as through the written and spoken word. All these forms are means for man individually and collectively to

Figure 9–1. Cognition and Expression

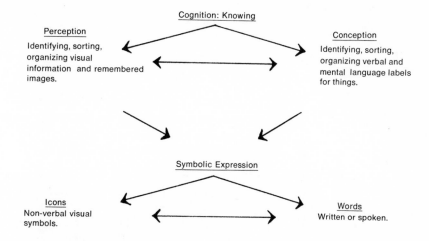

Cognition: Knowing

Perception
Identifying, sorting, organizing visual information and remembered images.

Conception
Identifying, sorting, organizing verbal and mental language labels for things.

Symbolic Expression

Icons
Non-verbal visual symbols.

Words
Written or spoken.

understand his reactions to the natural and the man-made environment and to other men. This statement is a simplification of a very complex process about which little is known or agreed upon. For example, we do not know how much man can think if he has not developed visual or verbal language—symbols for categorizing and manipulating what he learns from experience. We do not know how much individuals vary in the degree to which they use mental images, but we do know that a person's capacity to respond through language and visual images and to express them symbolically can be developed. This development leads to increased capacities to understand and use information effectively.

The Relation of Concepts to Percepts

Education in Western civilization has stressed conceptual learning at the expense of perceptual learning. As the Bruner studies show, children in schools where concepts are stressed tend not to use perceptual information in solving problems.

Percepts and concepts are transactional. The use of each conditions

Figure 9–2. Iconic Message

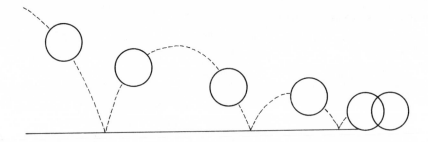

and influences the use of the other. Figures 9–2 and 9–3 illustrate the interaction. They relate to the same experience—seeing a ball bounce across the floor and responding to it. Both expressions give us information about a ball bouncing across the floor. Both expressions are symbols, created from perceptual information. The person who made each expression mentally processed an image he derived from careful observation of what he saw, then he symbolized his mental image into a visual image or verbal expression. An artist may be formulating the mental image as he draws, getting feedback from the drawing, and making connections as he works. The processing of information is not done by the hand that holds the pencil but by the mind that directs and coordinates the hands.

The term "eye-hand coordination" leaves out the sorting and organizing process that goes on. A person may symbolize an experience

Figure 9–3. Conceptual Message

The ball bounced across the floor in decreasing intervals of height and length and rolled to a stop.

through words or through a drawing. Both processes help him understand what he has seen. Both processes help the person with whom he is communicating learn what happened.

When a person's learning is chiefly perceptual or chiefly conceptual, he does not receive the feedback of both kinds of information. The person who has not developed perceptual skills in discriminating, in seeing forms move in space, and in relating one movement to another will not be able to describe in words what he has seen. The person who has a limited vocabulary may not be able to categorize all the things he sees into concepts to verbalize to others—though he may well be able to delineate through some art form what he has seen or experienced.

Research studies indicate that children who live in a rich iconic environment earn higher scores on the Draw-a-Man Test than do children whose society has simple visual symbols. Yet all children see men and have some kinds of perceptual information about them. Apparently exposure to iconic language is a strong factor in the development of the ability to express symbolically through drawing (iconic or visual images). The Orotchen children drew reindeer in great detail but drew men in a very immature style. Their society had little or no iconic forms, and in this case the excellence in drawing one item was derived from the children's having highly developed percepts of that item but not of others.

When children are given coloring books or are asked to fill in outlines of adult stereotypes, they are in some cases decreasing their use of perceptual information. The interaction of looking, then symbolizing in both words and icons, then looking again, then changing and amplifying the symbols helps to increase perceptual and conceptual development and to decrease stereotyping.

Perceptual Thinking   One of the factors that appears to be understressed in the psychological study of cognitive processes is the role of visual percepts that are used for thinking processes. Some individuals respond to at least three kinds of visual qualities in developing percepts. One is the abstract *affective* quality in things, including art, that arouses feeling — impact beyond the symbolic meaning expressed. A simple example is the design in Figure 9–4. Placed on the vertical it has one impact. Placed horizontally it has a quite different impact, because of the affective meaning we have developed toward things that push against gravity.

Figure 9–4. Position Changes the Message

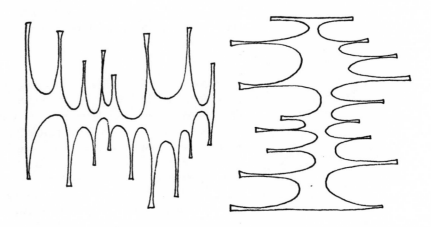

This design illustrates one of probably thousands of comparisons one can make of the different affective meanings to be derived from our attitudes toward various combinations of the elements of art (form, shape, line, color, texture, and space). A response to an affective quality is a cognitive response. It is built up through attention to direct experience; it depends on the cultural values and personality factors that encourage or discourage a person's paying such attention. As children learn from adults who are close to them *how to interpret information,* they build a reservoir of knowledge of affective qualities that have meanings.

The second kind of visual quality used to develop percepts is the abstraction of visual information into a symbol or icon which can be remembered or expressed. Figure 9–5A can be used as a sign or symbol for an apple. Figure 9–5B is an icon as it attempts to represent more of the visual reality of the object. People with limited visual development find it harder to remember. But it has a great deal more to communicate than Figure 9-5A. Some artists do not appear to be

Figure 9–5. Simple and Complex Symbols

A   B

very verbal; their cognitive processes appear to be dependent upon visual imagery and visual combinations. Instead of manipulating concepts to think in the abstract they manipulate lines, colors, shapes, spaces, and textures to organize what they are saying into meaningful symbolic or iconic expressions. They use their memories of these organized expressions for cognitive processes such as differentiating, comparing, relating, and identifying.

But most of us can have a more complete experience if we have a reservoir of concepts that relate to our percepts. For example, in Figure 9-5B there are areas of light, dark, and intermediate value. Shadows are cast by the form that is represented. Reflected light makes part of the darkest side have a light edge. These concepts help the viewer attend to perceptual information and develop richer visual percepts. The learning of concepts and the learning of percepts complement each other. When conceptual learning is fostered at the expense of perceptual learning, people's cognitive processes are limited and highly abstract. Each learning process based on perception changes the subsequent perception. Children whose opportunities to learn are meager tend to be meager in the kinds of responses they are capable of making.

The third kind of visual quality is the structure or organization, called in art the design or composition. The structure of art is based on human information handling as stated in Chapter 3: grouping by similarities of form, line, color, texture, or shape, grouping by proximity of any of these elements, finding closure or continuity through the use of the elements, and separating the design into figure and ground. The processing of information is similar in most art forms, but styles in art vary widely because of cultural standards of complexity and of meaningful symbols. Many artists reject structural analysis because they themselves use the process in a preconceptual cognitive state. They structure without putting the process into words. This reticence may account for some of the differences found in Getzels' study of fine and applied arts students. The two types may be operating at different levels of cognition—preconceptual and conceptual.

One time a Mexican architect and I found that we could communicate through design although neither of us spoke the other's language. I had a large white cardboard on the table and many sizes and variously colored shapes of paper. We played a game of adding and subtracting from the design with a great deal of amusement on both our parts when we found much agreement as to what "worked" and what did not. We were solving problems according to workable principles that we shared. This was surely cognitive processing and apparently based on our ability to think and communicate with visual symbols.

The perceptual thinking processes that are used in responding to the visual qualities—the affective quality, the abstraction, and the structure—are learned behaviors, part of the readiness an individual develops for art. The structural part of art, its design and composition, is apparently based on the sorting process we all use. Development of its use in art has to be learned by less intuitive people. The ability to recognize the functions conceptually is learned. Teachers who are intuitive designers need to understand design conceptually to communicate with their students.

Perceptual memory is another example of man's use of perceptual information that is not coded into words. When we see an object or an individual we have known remotely before, we are perceptually aware of a repeated experience, but would have a difficult time putting it into words. Yet we have received, coded, and remembered the information as percepts.

To summarize the background, we have found that perception is in large part learned, that it is basic to cognitive processes, and that personality, culture, and prior opportunities to learn modify present learning. Because percepts and concepts interact, it is possible to teach perception in the child's interaction process. In Chapter 3 we reviewed basic perceptual information processes related to art. In Chapter 4 we looked at children's individual differences that influence information handling. In Chapter 5 we looked at the functions of culture and social class in directing attention and contributing to the development of cognitive styles. All through the book we have seen how this process of perceiving and delineating, giving form to what is experienced is the *modus operandi* of experiencing and creating art. Now we will relate these materials to an overall theoretical framework suitable for the teacher.

Theory and Teaching   Teaching involves changing the environment to modify the interaction process of the individual child with the environment so that learning can take place. If the teacher is not somewhat aware of the present state of interacting growth of his pupils, he will not be able to choose wisely the more appropriate concepts and visual experiences for them to use new information or to change their transaction pattern so growth can take place. New concepts and experiences need to be introduced

Figure 9–6. The Perception-Delineation
Theory

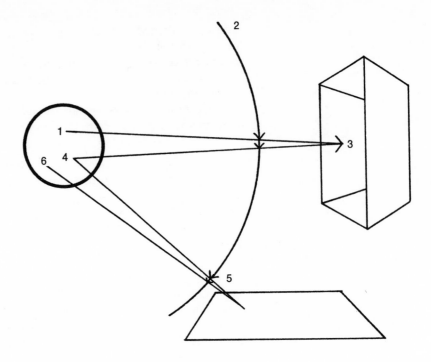

1. Readiness

    1.1. Perceptual-Conceptual Development

    1.2. Cognitive Style

    1.3. Cultural Effects on Perceptual Learning

    1.4. Prior Learnings

    1.5. Art Values of Child's Subculture

    1.6. Readiness for Creative Behavior

    1.7. Present Physical Condition

2. Psycho-Cultural Transaction within the Classroom

   2.1. Psychological Differences

   2.2. Cultural Differences

3. Visual-Physical Environment

   3.1. Affective Meaning

   3.2. Structure or Design

   3.3. Symbolic and Verbal Meaning

   3.4. Physical Condition of the Environment

   3.5. Tools and Materials

4. Information Handling

   4.1. Perceptual, Conceptual, and Symbolic Development

   4.2. Adjustive Learning and Cognitive Style

   4.3. Creative Information Processing

5. Creative Delineation

   5.1. Formalizing Understanding of Art

   5.2. Translating Percepts and Concepts into Communicable Symbols

   5.3. Giving Form to Design

   5.4. Choosing Appropriate Tools and Materials

   5.5. Programming Use of Media

6. Evaluation of Feedback and Transfer

6.1. Evaluation of Growth

6.2. Evaluation of Environment

6.3. Evaluation of Motivating Forms

6.4. Evaluation of Teacher's Roles in Information Handling

6.5. Evaluation of Symbolizing, Designing, and Using
Tools and Materials

6.6. Evaluating Transfer

gradually for children to assimilate them. The concepts and experiences need to be relatable to the children's cognitive styles and cultural backgrounds. Thus, the first question to be asked by the teacher is *"What are the areas of readiness of this class and what are the ranges of individual differences among the children?"*

Point One in the diagram accompanying Figure 9–6 is the overall *readiness* of the child to respond cognitively, both perceptually and conceptually.

The second question the teacher asks is *"What are the likenesses and differences between my values and those of the different children?"* *Point Two* is the *psycho-cultural transaction* of the child with his environment—the values, attitudes, and new information presented in the classroom, which the teacher manipulates to foster more learning.

The third question the teacher asks is *"What can I introduce into my classroom to help my pupils develop better percepts and concepts?"* *Point Three* is the complex of things from the *visual-physical* environment—the man-made, including art, and the natural, which the teacher provides to stimulate children. These things include the affective, structural, and symbolic qualities of the visual arts. Point Three includes those things from each child's past experiences in his home and community environments that he brings to the present through memory.

The fourth question the teacher asks is *"How can I help my pupils integrate these new ideas into what they already know so that new outcomes can develop?"* *Point Four* is the total of a child's habits of *information handling* and the teacher's efforts both to help him integrate new information into his established system and to expand his habits of information handling so he can increase his concepts and percepts. His expanding capacities give him more alternatives for creative problem solving and more sensitive reactions to art.

The fifth question the teacher asks is *"How can I help my pupils communicate what they are learning and what they are creating as a result of this learning experience?"* *Point Five* is the child's *creative delineation* of his response. Through invention or borrowing of verbal or iconic symbols he communicates his perceptual and conceptual responses to his experience through a designed expression. If his response is to art forms of others, his delineation involves his own unique analysis and abstraction of the message, its affective qualities, and its structure through the ideas he develops about the work of art.

The sixth question the teacher asks is *"How will the things my pupils have learned increase their readiness for another task?"* *Point Six* is the *feedback* the child gets from making his own responses, information that changes his readiness and his ability to *transfer* his learnings to the next similar task.

Learning is seldom an isolated event. The points on this theory of learning are interacting. Readiness operates at Points One, Two, Three, Four, and Five. The items are placed in this order because of the concerns of the teacher and because there is some evidence that they are cyclical. A child with a given readiness has an experience in an environment from which he selects what is meaningful and integrates it into his past experience according to his cognitive style and personal-cultural habits. From this assimilation he evolves a response—a perceptual image, a concept, or both—from which he delineates an expression in words or in art; or he may have an aesthetic reaction which is an internalized delineation of form and impact. Each experience he has, when carried through to a delineation of his responses, changes his readiness for the next related experience. It modifies his subsequent information-handling and problem-solving abilities and gives him a broader basis for being creative.

Point One. Readiness   Our first task is to identify which areas of prior experience have influenced a child's present development.

Point 1.1. Perceptual and Conceptual Development.   Readiness depends on a child's ability to handle visual information—the ways he is learning the perceptual constancies, the level of his dependence on percepts, concepts, or both, and the quality of his vocabulary of related concepts.

Point 1.2. Cognitive Style.   Readiness is influenced by whether the child is global in his responses or whether he can discriminate analytically, whether his mother encouraged or discouraged his exploratory investigation of his environment. His cognitive style also influences the ways he will use information. Is he becoming more reflective or more impulsive? Does he analyze? Can he use both analytic and impulsive responses effectively? If he is conceptually analytical, can he also succeed in separating figure from ground, and can he analyze differences and likenesses perceptually? Is his conceptual vocabulary developed in response to the visual environment and to art?

Point 1.3. Cultural Effects on Perceptual Development.   Cultural experience causes a child to develop habits of responding to some types of things and to particular qualities in these things. The child's habits determine what qualities remain unanalyzed because of lack of cultural motivation to attend. His anxiety level, his motivation to observe, and some inhibitions of perception may also be determined by the culture.

Point 1.4. Prior Learnings.   Readiness involves ways in which prior learnings influence a child's responses in school. These prior learnings are the results of his potential for interacting with his social class, his ethclass, and his subculture. Does he know why he is in school? Are his values similar to the teacher's? If not, how can both the values of the school culture and those at home best be served? In what ways does his background inhibit his use of materials? Has he used tools and materials before? How was he taught to use them?

Point 1.5. Art Values of Child's Subculture.   A child learns his attitudes toward art within his subculture. Has he received cultural conditioning toward art in relation to acceptable sex roles? A child who comes with negative or very limited attitudes about art or artists is ill prepared to succeed in art. His prior training in art through his culture and in school will cause him to form attitudes about what he considers art to be, how he is to respond to it and how he is to produce it. His readiness will depend on his prior experiences with all the points of the P-D theory—the environment he has worked in before, his information-handling experiences, and his opportunities to express through or respond to art.

Point 1.6. Readiness for Creative Behavior.   Readiness for creative behavior includes a child's established patterns of rigidity or flexibility, his openness to perceptions, his ability to make judgments and see relationships, his development of playful attitudes, his capacity to reflect, his willingness to try something new impulsively, his freedom from the fear of failure, his opportunities to be original, and his fluency in responding in school-determined time allotments.

Point 1.7. Present Physical Condition.   Handicaps may limit a child's present ability to cope with an art situation. Current research on visual physiology indicates that sorting, organizing, and modifying information begins in the *retina* before it is transmitted to higher processing centers. Soon other physical areas of individual differences may be identified.

Point Two. Psycho-Cultural Transaction within the Classroom

Point Two deals with the total psycho-cultural society of the classroom. Each child and the teacher are in transaction with the society in terms of their own interpretation of the behavior of others.

Point 2.1. Psychological Differences. The psychological differences children have developed may make the environment more or less conducive to learning and to being creative or exploratory. A growth-restricting teacher is frustrating to a child raised by a growth-fostering mother. A rigid child in the class of a flexible creative teacher may be confused by too many alternatives. A highly creative child may have difficulty functioning within the limits imposed by a rigid teacher and may become a "discipline problem." A highly anxious child who has experienced many failures may find the challenge to be "self-directive and creative" or to "express himself" highly threatening. He is experiencing a discontinuity in the way he is rewarded and punished.

Yet it is at this point that much learning takes place; the child is interacting in a total environment, which includes tasks, concepts, and percepts that he must become aware of. The teacher recognizes that the classroom is a dynamic system of transactions between teacher and pupil, between pupils and other pupils within the class. Because each individual has a somewhat different readiness to respond, the teacher will develop flexible ways of introducing art learnings and experiences to children.

Point 2.2. Subcultural Differences. When teacher and pupil have social-class and cultural differences, interaction is less direct. Discontinuity may occur when a middle-class child of one ethnic group comes into a class where the teacher or the other children are of another middle-class ethnic group. It often happens that economically deprived children of many different ethnic groups face a middle-class teacher of the dominant society. Thus, we cannot say that an environment is either hostile or friendly, but rather that for a given child an environment is more or less hostile or supportive depending upon how he interprets the clues he is able to get from his environment. His ability to respond to clues depends upon his readiness at Point One, which grew out of his past interactions in his own culture. A teacher who works with a rejected child may find it difficult to gain the child's confidence because he has learned to reject adults generally or adults of a particular skin color.

Children often are affected by more than one cultural difference. The Puerto Rican, Appalachian, or Negro child who comes to the city from an impoverished rural environment has to cope in some degree with an urban slum society and go to a middle-class school. In the art class still other values emerge which are not generally middle class. This child is interacting with four distinct subcultural value systems. For communication to take place between the teacher and the child some common values need to be found. The responsibility is placed upon the teacher because the child cannot recognize the reasons he is experiencing discontinuity. He is only lost in a very strange environment where few of his prior habits of thinking, of responding to adults, or of knowing how to behave to get personal rewards will work. So he resolves his conflict by retreating into himself or by reacting intensely to the teacher as he tries to find his way. With his peers of the same background he may develop a strong ingroup adhesion against the system he finds strange and hostile—the school. Fortunately, art can be found in some form in almost all background cultures. A teacher who searches for meaning in the subculture and who will respect the art forms that are familiar to the child has a beginning basis for reaching this child.

As shown in Figure 9–6, Point Two crosses the interaction at all points in the theory. A child's readiness is affected by the present psychocultural environment as he interprets it. His transaction affects what he is able to receive from the environment at Point Three, the effectiveness of his ability to assimilate information at Point Four, and his freedom to express at Point Five. His interaction will show up in the teacher's assessment of his growth at Point Six.

A teacher's understanding of the ranges of differences among children in their interpretation of the environment will give him insights into the behaviors he observes in children. He will then have more clues as to when a child is not progressing, when the tasks, concepts, or percepts are too foreign to him, which kinds of learnings he needs to help him develop, and what is threatening or supporting to him in the learning environment.

At Point 2.2 a teacher works with groups as well as with the individual. The cultural and ethclass similarities and differences in the class will affect the total transaction. If the teacher's goal is to establish mutual respect, he needs understanding of these differences in order to choose wisely the general art activities that can be adapted to the individual and still keep the class working together. If the class is from a culturally homogeneous neighborhood, more similarity in general tasks can be developed. If the class is made up of many cultural groups, the teacher may have to start with art forms of a culture different from any of them and then move to the art in the specific cultures. He might start with the art in mass media, which most children are exposed to, or with the buildings in their neighborhood. No one way is "right." The teacher's decision is based on the makeup of the class and the teacher's range of knowledge.

Children who come from closely knit extended families may find self-direction difficult. Children who are highly motivated for self-direction may be disruptive to group activity. The teacher needs to be aware of such cultural factors in planning for the group.

Point Three. The Visual Physical Environment

The transaction between the readiness of the child to handle the information in his environment and the support he receives in the psycho-cultural environment strongly influences what he will respond to in his environment. Two children with equal physical visual equipment may receive very different information from looking at the same object because of differences in perceptual readiness, range of concepts related to the object, and attitudes toward the object. For this reason the teacher needs to observe how effective the objects selected are in motivating children to respond to art.

Point 3.1. Affective Meaning.   A teacher needs to be aware of the possible affective meanings an object may have for different children. He must understand each child's cultural background and must be alert to a child's negative reaction or lethargy.

Point 3.2. Structure and Design.   The teacher must be able to analyze the structure and design of the specific things he introduces, to see whether their complexity level is appropriate for the class.

Point 3.3. Symbolic, Verbal, and Iconic Meaning.   The teacher must be sure that the symbols can be understood by the children. The level of abstractness or realism must be appropriate for the children in the sequence of tasks.

Point 3.4. Physical Condition of Environment.   It is important that the physical properties of distance from the object, effective lighting, and contrast with other objects make the stimulating objects as clearly visible as necessary for a specific learning.

This point is important whether the teacher is introducing new art forms for children to become familiar with or is bringing in objects to stimulate their observation of forms, textures, and colors, to stimulate their exploration of techniques, or to expose them to varieties in design.

Point 3.5. Tools and Materials.   New tools and new materials are part of the stimulating environment. If they are introduced rigidly with limited or "correct" uses stressed, the child will tend to use them rigidly unless he strongly resists authority. If tools and materials are introduced to a child at a level he is capable of using and if he is encouraged to explore the potential they have, he will develop skills in using them. The work of artists who use media in divergent ways can stimulate his own exploration.

Point Four. Information Handling

Point Four of the P-D theory deals with the various ways in which environmental reaction is responded to in terms of readiness and how each child adapts to the learning experience through his habitual way of responding to perceptual information.

Most children have the capacity to respond to the full range of visual qualities as well as the elements of art—forms, shapes, textures, lines, spaces, colors, backgrounds, foregrounds, relationships, and patterns—in myriad ways. But their readiness, their opportunity to learn appropriate to their achieved readiness, their cognitive style, their available percepts and concepts, their personality traits and their culture all direct which visual qualities they will respond to. Their ability to handle detail and their choice of what is important to attend to will further direct their development in art.

To help children learn more from their environment at Point Four, the teacher must (1) understand readiness as much as possible, (2) develop a supportive psycho-cultural environment, (3) select appropriate changes in the environment so that a particular group of individual children can learn, and (4) *help the children to recognize what is familiar, what is related, and how a new idea fits into what they already know as a basis for making their own creative responses.*

Point 4.1. Perceptual, Conceptual, and Symbolic Development. The teacher can help the child develop concepts, percepts, words, and symbols about an object as he responds to the visual qualities: (1) its affective meaning, (2) its structure or design, and (3) its symbolic or iconic meaning, as well as its cultural context. In other words: (1) how does this painting, this architecture, or this garden make us feel in comparison to other similar works? (2) What holds this art form together? What is its design? How is it composed? How are space, texture, color, line, and shape used to communicate to us? (3) What does the object say to us about our experience? What do its visual qualities tell us about the kind of place it is? Then the teacher needs to ask, "What is the relationship of the visual qualities to the values and attitudes of the people from whose culture it was created?"

Point 4.2. Adjusting Learning to Cognitive Style. The teacher's understanding of cognitive style is critical at this point. The analytical or reflective child will be receiving information that is different from that of the global or impulsive child. The teacher's understanding will help each child to use the mode of responding that he has developed, so that he can succeed. The teacher can also try to help the analytical child be more impulsive at times and encourage the impulsive child to take more time to reflect and comprehend more in his environment.

Point 4.3. Encouraging Creative Information Processing. At Point Four the teacher is concerned with readiness for creative behavior. It is here that each child's concept of the appropriateness of his response is important. And again individual differences are a concern. A child learning in a strange environment needs success. So the teacher must decide when a child needs to focus on learning a task, such as seeing likenesses and differences, and to learn that there are many ways to make comparisons and that these lead to varying solutions to problems. Too many alternatives too soon may make a small child experience failure; fewer alternatives may help him succeed. Continued success, though, without variation can lead to boredom. So the teacher's professional evaluation of these important variables goes on continuously.

Actual creative behavior is taking place at Point 4.3 if points 4.1 and 4.2 are being handled carefully by the teacher. One of the important points where creative problem solving takes place is when new learnings and past memories have to be adapted and changed in relationship to each other. At this point a child may conceive of a relationship or a difference that will influence his response to art or to his own production. He needs the support of the teacher and reward for his efforts.

As he learns to see in more detail and learns to relate and organize what he sees, he will have a greater reservoir for producing ideas. He may become more fluent. If he learns that there are many more alternatives and if he understands them, he will have more potential for making responses that are, for him, unique.

If the teacher has created a psycho-cultural environment that stimulates a playful attitude (at Point Two) to develop along with the exploration of new learnings at Point Three, then at Point Four creative behavior will be germinating.

Point Five. Creative Delineation

Point Four is a cognitive processing of information in which memory, innovation, reordering, and structuring can take place. At Point Five the child's response is given form.

Point 5.1. Formalizing Understanding of Art. If the task is one of understanding the visual qualities of art, the child can verbalize by operating as critic in terms of the affective (how it makes him feel), the structural (what holds it together), and the symbolic meaning (what the symbols say). Also he can learn the cultural meaning of art (what it tells him about what is important to the society it came from), beyond the affective responses his own cultural experience has developed in him.

Point 5.2. Translating Percepts and Concepts into Communicable Symbols. If the child's task is to produce his response in one of the myriad forms of art, then he must translate his percepts and concepts through experimentation and evaluation.

Point 5.3. Giving Form to Design. A child who designs intuitively or analytically needs to give form to his design. He needs many opportunities to try out combinations to compare the impact of one combination to that of another as he uses design to communicate ideas and feelings.

Point 5.4. Choosing Appropriate Tools and Materials.   The child must choose tools and materials appropriate to what he has to say and to his capacity to manipulate. He needs tasks that will help him to explore the potential of materials. As his creativity develops, he will need more avenues for expression. The media themselves as they are introduced at Point Three need to be explored along with the child's expression of ideas at Point Five.

In terms of the orientation of this book, what a child says through art is more important than the medium he uses to say it. Emphasis on learning to use media has often deterred growth in learning about and through art. Yet having an appropriate medium to say what one has to say is often critical to what is being said. Creative expression with tools and materials also depends on individual differences. A fearful attitude about a certain medium (torn paper, finger paint, sharp tools) can inhibit a child's use of it as a means of expression.

Point 5.5. Programming Use of Media.   The depth and breadth approach studies of Beittel and Mattil[2] compared ninth grade students' art work in one medium or many media. The depth approach, familiarity with one medium, produced the most growth, according to the researchers' criteria of aesthetic quality. Perhaps the use of one medium helped children go beyond the manipulation of it to concern for what they were saying through it. As they became more facile, the medium was less a hindrance to their expression. The use of many media may challenge children in a manipulative sense and may keep their attention, but it also may require less use of analytical and reflective abilities. Decisions about the number of media depend on the teacher's goals. Initial manipulative successes may be necessary for a child's initial involvement with art, but as he becomes more interested, concentration in one medium as a means of concentrating on depth of meaning and inventive composition would be more appropriate. Conversely, a child can become so skilled in one medium and one message that he succeeds by continuing his successes. In this case the teacher can encourage him with a new medium or introduce an enriched motivating experience in order for him to continue growing.

Point Six. Evaluation of Feedback and Transfer

This point in the P-D theory concerns the teacher particularly. It is the point where evaluation of what has gone on will help him make adjustments in his teaching on the basis of what he observes of changes in children's readiness to reach the content and instrumental goals he has for his class. He will be able to see what learnings are transferable to other situations. He will need to ask himself the following questions about the previous points in the theory.

Point 6.1. Evaluation of Growth. On the basis of this experience with these children, have I adequately understood their original readiness? What new understanding do I have? How has this activity increased their readiness? Am I stereotyping this class, or am I seeing the full range of individual differences that are important in art activities?

Point 6.2. Evaluation of Environment. How are the children responding to the environment that they and I create? Are some children still uninvolved? What kind of information do I need about the uninvolved children to help create a better psycho-cultural environment for them? Am I continuing to challenge the self-assured children?

Point 6.3. Evaluation of Motivating Forms. Have I analyzed the motivating art forms, the visual and tactile experiences, the new media I am introducing to children to see if they are appropriate to their readiness? Have I fully explored the structural, affective, and symbolic meanings of the art forms presented so that I can help children understand them? Am I bound to the art of my own subculture? What can I find among the art forms of the children's subcultures that will help them to understand art? Am I free, inquiring, and flexible enough in my own uses of materials so that I can encourage children to work flexibly with materials appropriate for their individual development? Am I stereotyping the children's ability, or am I watching to see who is ready to move into more depth with a material or who needs to change a tool or material because the present one is hindering him?

Point 6.4. Evaluation of Information Handling.   Am I presenting new ideas in varied ways so that global, analytical, impulsive, and reflective children can respond? Am I reaching the field-dependent as well as the field-independent children? Am I inhibiting the intuitive designers with too much analysis? Am I leaving out those who do not design intuitively, or am I providing them with working principles which they can explore in problem solving? Am I reaching all the subcultures of each ethclass represented in my classroom as I help them relate new ideas to what they already know and remember? Am I preserving a sense of playfulness in the conceptual work we do? Am I encouraging playful manipulation of perceptual information by planning for such activities as exploring the varied effects of changing the light, distance, or viewpoint of objects?

What are my own modes of handling information? Am I an impulsive, creative person who does not like or need to analyze in order to respond to my environment? If so, what do I particularly need to do to help the analytical child? If I am reflective and analytical, how can I encourage playful and impulsive behavior and not show discomfort with such behavior?

Do I need to understand more about design in order to help the intuitive children solve their design problems more effectively?

Do I need to understand art and the environment so that I have a rich reservoir of understandings to draw upon to help children conceptualize and see? Am I aware of emerging trends in the visual arts that may be meaningful to this present group of children?

Am I so bound to my own subculture that I find children from other groups difficult to teach? How can I learn more about them so that through understanding I can be more acceptant of them and thus be more flexible in finding ways to help them learn more effectively?

Am I aware of the impact these children are receiving from television, movies, advertising, and their changing society so that I can evaluate the effectiveness of my program in relation to their whole learning situation? Am I using these media as forms of teaching about art and the environment?

Point 6.5. Evaluation of Symbolizing, Designing, and Using Tools and Materials. Have I explored the potential of the many new and traditional art media so that the possibilities I introduce to children do not stereotype their work with these media? Am I responsive to the new symbols the children produce? Can I evaluate constructively the designs they develop?

Point 6.6. Learnings That Can Be Transferred. What do I see in the children's changed behaviors that will help them use in other situations what they have learned in this situation? In other words, what transferable understandings do they have about the visual qualities (affective, structural, and symbolic) or the cultural meaning of art that can help them understand these aspects in subsequent learning experiences?

What skills have they developed with one medium that they can use in exploring other media?

When the teacher has asked and answered these questions he is ready to introduce another task, growing out of the learnings from this one, that will lead to his goals.

All of the theory is for the purpose of helping teachers be more effective in reaching goals. In Chapter 10 we will discuss content goals (understandings about art that teachers want children to develop) and instrumental goals (abilities, attitudes, and habits that will enable children to be more effective in and through art).

Case Studies   To make these points of theory clearer let us imagine four children in the fourth grade. At Point One you identify some of the factors of their readiness as follows: The first child, a boy, has been raised by a growth-fostering mother who encourages exploration and independence in her son. She has encouraged him to look with her at all the exciting forms to be found in rocks, plants, small animal life, forms, shadows, colors, textures, and lights. Her vocabulary helps him relate his perceptions to new concepts as he learns them. She has helped him recognize many things and respond to many subtle variations in visual qualities. She has encouraged his exploration with art materials to recreate his visual and tactile experience. He is able to analyze how things function as well as how they look. He has a rich basis for being creative; he is flexible and not afraid of failing.

The second child, a girl, has a growth-restricting mother who is fearful of her involvement with bugs, plants, and found materials. The mother is highly educated and has filled her child's world with books, pictures, trips to museums, concerts, and music lessons. The child has learned many concepts about pictures, when they were painted and by whom. She has also learned habits about keeping clean, writing neat papers, and taking excellent care of her toys. This child is more dependent on concepts than on percepts. She is afraid of failing and will not try new things she is unsure of.

A third child, a boy, has a growth-fostering mother. He is free to roam a great deal. His learning about his environment has been mainly from other boys who have had little interaction with parents. His use of language in relation to his perceptions is stereotyped. He has explored tools and materials, traded equipment, and has rebuilt wagons and go-carts. There are few books and magazines at home. He has little motivation to relate percepts and concepts or to be analytical with words, but he is creative in working with real things in relating and manipulating them.

A fourth child, a boy, has a growth-restricting mother. The child is growing up with adults of limited vocabulary. He plays with a few books and building toys. He has been pushed to excel in school, but there is little in the home to reinforce or enrich his readiness for school. He has had few opportunities to develop analytical abilities so his responses are mainly global. He is quite rigid and not very fluent.

These four cases are not unreal. We have considered only a few individual and environmental factors. Four children with the same age and the same measured intelligence quotient could be quite different in readiness because of their interaction with each of their environments.

Now assume these children are in your fourth grade art class. Your task at Point Two is to help them accept the task you are going to introduce — in this case, react to a painting. You realize that they differ widely in their readiness for an art activity of any kind and in their cognitive styles. They will be responding quite differently. Their attitudes will probably range from curiosity to rejection. The kind of rapport you have with these students will have a great deal to do with your success in creating a workable environment in which they can learn. The first and second children will be less of a problem; each has a kind of readiness for responding to art even though their readiness is different. The third and fourth children will be much more dependent on *how* you introduce the painting and your tolerance for their initial somewhat negative reactions. If you punish or reject them at this point for inattention you have probably lost them for the rest of this activity. But if you accept their struggles and help them understand that you are aware of their reasons for rejection of the task at present, you have the opportunity to lead them into interest.

You as a teacher want all the children to learn to appreciate art.

Operating at Point Three, you introduce something into their environment. You select a reproduction of an original painting whose subject matter, color, and design you think will interest them and ask them to study the picture and write a description of what they see. The results should give you more clues as to the differences among the children that may not have shown before. Your new information should help you decide which areas of readiness they need help with and how you can help them integrate the new visual qualities into what they already know at Point Four.

The first child, who is used to analyzing perceptually and who has a rich conceptual background, not only would be better able to describe what the picture is about in terms of symbolic meaning, but would also be likely to describe details.

The second child would feel she was in a familiar situation and might write about the artist, describe the kind of paint used, tell where she has seen prints of the painting before, but give little information about shape, color, texture, or emotional impact except literal concepts of what was happening in the picture and what literal symbols of things she could recognize.

The third child might attempt to get out of responding or he might write something funny. To get him involved, you might encourage him to look for parts he likes best or least in the painting. His freedom has made him independent of situations. Facing an unfamiliar task he might exercise his independence unless you help him relate unfamiliar to familiar things. His behavior lets you know that the task you have given him has little meaning, and you will need to observe his behavior further to find ways to reach him. You are operating at Point Four with this child—trying to find ways to help him become involved with what is being presented.

The fourth child, who wants to excel, might work very hard to respond but would receive little information and would have inadequate concepts for sorting his information. His written response would be limited, describing little or no detail. You may have to give this child much more opportunity to learn to discriminate before he can respond to this kind of task.

Each of these children needs a very different kind of help from you at Point Four. The first child needs continued opportunity to relate percepts to concepts and to direct and evaluate his own work. You can provide him more choices in motivating subjects and media.

The second child probably would feel uncomfortable if you took away her familiar way of succeeding in art—her knowledge of artists. Your task will be to help her use her knowledge as a base for beginning to develop visual awareness. She might try to compare the works of the artists she knows something about. She might become aware of perceptual qualities in the works of other artists. This girl has developed many concepts but her capacity to relate perceptual information to concepts has not been developed. She can express these concepts first in words and then begin expressing them iconically by drawing and painting. When she has gained success she may not be afraid of responding emotionally to art.

The third child may be the most difficult for you to work with. Your best cue to begin with would be his ability to manipulate tools and to repair things. He might become involved with art-related tasks such as helping repair equipment, comparing how different tools work, or discovering how much better they work when they have been oiled or sharpened. He might see how many kinds of effects he can get by using tools in different ways. You may have to emphasize Point Five, creative delineation, in your work with him and then through successive tasks increase his perceptual and conceptual development.

You may show slides of sculpture made from automobile parts or machinery parts to help this boy see form in art, whether painted on canvas or welded from found material. All along the way you need to help him develop new percepts and concepts for relating and expressing new experiences. This child might wish to try taking pictures with a camera. His ability with equipment could be used to help him respond to the visual world and to the effects he could create by manipulating light.

The fourth child is motivated to excel in school but his "visual language" is underdeveloped. He does not easily respond to visual symbols nor to concepts about them. His written descriptions of familiar objects will give you clues as to where to begin to enrich his perceptual and conceptual vocabulary. You can try by giving him concepts and then have him search for percepts that are related, or have him explore visual things and encourage his descriptions. You may show him familiar art forms and other things in his environment.

Both the third and the fourth child could profit from developing light and shadow experiments such as watching objects move in space in a light box, casting shadows through a sheet of ground glass to analyze how shapes change, and tracing projections of slides of three-dimensional objects to see how they appear in space.

Using our model of the four children, let us consider their differences in production art activities. We know they bring a wide range of readiness to any task requiring perceptual responses.

Print-making is a suitable general task that we can use to show how children of varying degrees of readiness can work together. In print-making the teacher may use a wide range of tools and materials that allow for individual differences (cutting out cardboard, vegetables, or rubber tiles, cutting into linoleum or wood, masking out areas of screens to print images on paper or cloth). Photographic equipment also may be used for making prints, slides, and moving pictures. The process of manipulating light and form through time with projectors relates print-making to mass media forms children are used to. These activities are avenues for expressing experience through symbols. Unless such variety is possible, teachers might believe that the differences are so great that no curriculum in art could be carried out.

The first boy needs print-making experience because his developed skills should not be allowed to remain unused in school, where development of concepts receives the most emphasis. He can explore ways things in nature are symbolized in print-making. He can see how the visual qualities in objects can be expressed on a two-dimensional plane.

The girl can be helped to expand her interest from the painters she knows to another art form. The fact that many painters were also print-makers will help bridge the gap. New information can be more clearly related to past knowledge. Her contribution to the class can be a display of prints on which she writes descriptions of the different ways artists get effects that relate experience to expression.

The third child can become involved in the mechanics of the processes. He may sharpen cutting tools, oil and clean the press and the brayers, and help test some of the first boy's examples by making prints of his designs. Photographic experimentation might appeal to him most. Opportunities to produce effects in the processes of working with equipment could lead to quick involvement.

The fourth child could be given the task of experimenting, mixing colors of ink to get as many colors as he can. He can test these on different papers to see how they are absorbed. The task is simple enough for him to succeed, and the process itself leads to outcomes he has not found before.

The teacher could make the preparations and then demonstrate the process, but then the children might not become involved in ways suitable to their individual differences. When the methods, the equipment, and the experiments with color and paper have been tried by the individual children, they can be repeated for the class.

Further work in print-making can begin when everyone is to some degree involved in it. The teacher may bring into the classroom objects meaningful to children of different backgrounds. Operating at Point Four, the teacher will help the children select and examine them for visual qualities, shapes, textures, points of line change, patterns of light and dark that they have seen before. The class together can list the many words that represent the percepts they are deriving. The teacher can then encourage each child to select an object and explore its qualities, telling how it is similar to or different from other objects he has known before. Then at Point Five he can make several symbols of it until he finds one he likes. Considerable patience may be needed here. The girl may be very dissatisfied with her first attempts, and the teacher's role is to help her recognize her best efforts.

The third child may not be able to draw a symbol and could better cut rubber tile, or carve into wood, to make a surface that he can ink in order to print on paper. He could bend wire in outlines to create forms for relief prints.

The fourth child needs particular help in studying the qualities of the object and making the transition to symbolize it in some way. The simplest methods need to be used at this point, because achieving a symbol from increased awareness is the most important task. This child may need more help at Point Five than the other children. Fear of using a difficult tool or process could keep the child from the symbolizing activity entirely.

The teacher could ask the children to tell why they chose the symbols they did, why some symbols are more or less effective for different reasons. What symbol communicates most strongly? Again the reasons can be written down so each child's vocabulary can be increased to respond to affective qualities. The words used can help the child look for more perceptual qualities. The symbols can then be used to delineate and design an art form at Point Five. Creative organizations of the symbol can be used, varying color, overprinting, and rotating the position. Then at Point Six the designs can be discussed so that the children can see what they have learned. Both the children and the teacher evaluate at this point. The teacher will be able to evaluate his whole teaching strategy to see how he needs to change it at each point, for each child, and for the class as a whole.

It is extremely important to realize that this description of one activity, using four children as examples, illustrates only a few of many ways to solve the problems of getting different pupils involved. It is used to illustrate that perceptual-conceptual learning can be emphasized in productive art activities as a basis for increasing the depth of expression and that children of varying aptitudes can work together. Similar ranges of differences and aptitudes will be found among children of any age.

In relation to the theory each of the six points has been stressed. At Point One readiness was assessed. A mediating activity, getting ready for print-making, was used at Point Two to get diverse individuals involved by creating an environment in which they were able to work in a somewhat familiar situation. The teacher selected stimulating materials to tap different interests at Point Three. At Point Four the teacher helped the children relate the visual aspects of the materials to what they knew and learn new percepts and concepts to think about and symbolize them. Then the children were encouraged to express their ideas through appropriate media at Point Five. At Point Six they evaluated what they had learned in order to be ready for the next task.

Summary   The purpose of this chapter is to provide teachers with a workable framework for helping diverse children reach art education goals in the context of an organized classroom.

Learning behavior in art is seen as a continuing transaction between the individual developing child, his subculture, and his school culture. His behavior is the result of the interplay of his hereditary potential and his environmental opportunities to learn.

Cognition, thinking, solving problems, relating, and differentiating are based on the use of two tools, percepts and concepts. Percepts are mental images derived from sensory experience; concepts are ideas derived from experience. Both can be expressed or remembered through iconic or word symbols. Concepts and percepts can reciprocally enhance the learning of each other. But some cultural situations encourage the growth of one more than the other.

There are three kinds of visual qualities needed to respond to or create art: (1) the affective, (2) the abstractive or symbolic, and (3) the structural. These occur in a cultural context of values, attitudes, and beliefs.

The Perception-Delineation theory is a system for identifying the six points in which differences in behavior are crucial for learning. Point One is the overall readiness of any given child to learn. Readiness includes perceptual and conceptual development, cognitive style, cultural effects on perceptual development, prior learnings, the art values of the subculture, developed creative abilities, and the present physical condition.

Point Two is the psycho-cultural transaction within the classroom. Each child and each teacher comes to the classroom with a subculturally modified personality. As pupils and teacher transact with each other, their behaviors and readiness to learn are modified in the classroom milieu.

Point Three is the visual-physical environment. At this point, the teacher can introduce the three visual qualities of art and of the physical environment—the affective meaning, the abstracted and symbolic meaning, and the structural design and composition—into the learning process.

The teacher's role is the selection of appropriate materials in terms of the readiness of pupils in the psycho-cultural milieu of the classroom. He must also assess the physical conditions of lighting, distance, and separation of materials introduced. At this point the qualities and potentials of new tools and materials can be introduced as part of the new information to be assimilated.

Point Four is information handling. Here the teacher helps children integrate what they already know into what they are learning in terms of their perceptual, conceptual, and symbolic development. Differences in cognitive style and ability to handle information in creative ways must be considered.

Point Five is creative delineation. If children are responding to the art of others or criticizing their own work they need to give form to their analyses through written or spoken language. If they are responding to experience or remembered experience through their own work they need opportunities to create or modify symbols or iconic forms to express what they feel or know. These expressions need some design or composition to be clearly communicated. Appropriate selections of tools and materials need to be available for the children to make adequate choices. The media selection also can be changed to stimulate new exploration when new learnings are needed for motivation.

Point Six is the evaluation of feedback and transfer. It gives both teachers and children opportunities to evaluate their growth and to see what new readinesses have developed or how the teaching process needs to be modified to increase growth.

References   [1] Halden Keffer Hartline, "Visual Receptors and Retinal Interaction," *Science*, 164 (April 18, 1969), 270–278.

[2] Kenneth E. Beittel, Edward L. Mattil *et al.*, "The Effects of a 'Depth' vs. a 'Breadth' Method of Art Instruction at the Ninth Grade Level," *Studies in Art Education*, 3 (Fall 1961), 75–87.

10

Guides for Classroom Practice

The preceding chapters have been designed to help teachers understand more about behaviors children use in responding to and through art in its broad application to human experience. We have studied the ranges of individual differences among pupils and the ways in which learning can be developed and accelerated through the transactional process. A theory of these relationships, applicable to classroom practice, was developed to help the teacher recognize individual differences and activate learning.

Identifying Individual Differences in Readiness (Point One)

The professional teacher looks for individual differences in children, to identify the level where each child is in his development, not to classify each according to what can be expected of him.

The teacher asks,

Where is this child in terms of the possible development of his potential?

What are the factors that may have inhibited his development?

What can I do to help him increase his abilities to receive and to use information more effectively?

How can I help him express what he learns analytically and creatively so he can get feedback from his own learning and continue to grow perceptually, conceptually, and creatively?

What is there in my own attitude toward this child or in the attitudes of the other children or the administration that may inhibit his development?

How can I help him work within this group of children so that his behavior does not inhibit the development of the others?

Sources of Information

A teacher is fortunate if the school has a trained psychologist who can administer and interpret the results of tests. He can help the teacher get information on the creative, perceptual, and cognitive development and style of pupils, and can provide subscores on intelligence tests that may add to this information. A school sociologist or social worker should be able to give information about the background subcultures of many of the students.

A teacher who does not have this kind of information available in the school has to depend upon his own resources. If the purpose of the search for individual differences is to help find better ways to reach children and not to classify them, the teacher is less likely to make serious misjudgments. It is important to consider information about a child as tentative.

This chapter includes examples of *classroom inquiry,* a part of the teaching process to be used to help identify pupil readiness. Classroom inquiry is not to be considered research, although it can be used as the basis for detailed research. To use these techniques as research, in which the results are to be generalized to children as a whole, requires that careful measurement of the behaviors be made, that the criteria for measurement be specific, and that the class be representative of children of a given culture, regional area, or educational level.

A teacher is always making judgments about his pupils and then deciding how to teach on the basis of these judgments. *Classroom inquiry,* if carefully done, will help the teacher make better judgments, be more aware of the many influences on children's behavior, and be more acceptant of children as a result of this understanding.

Perceptual-Conceptual Differences

Development can be observed in several ways—through drawings, through the words used to describe what is seen, and through the kinds of responses made. A teacher can obtain some indication of children's ability to get perceptual information and then verbalize about it by asking them to tell or write what a painting means to them. Several types of pictures can be used to see whether the responses are different with different subject matter. This inquiry gives the teacher an idea of what has meaning to each child. The responses can be classified as to (1) the affective qualities, the feelings the child reports he gets from the picture, (2) the design elements and relationships— color, line, form, shape, texture, space—and the relationships of these by similarity, proximity, closure, and figure and ground, and (3) the symbolic meaning of the pictures as expressed in words.

The teacher can assess the response to *conceptual qualities* by counting the number of things the child recognizes and identifies by name. These responses may only tell the teacher about the child's vocabulary and not what he has percepts for. The teacher can obtain a separate score on each classification by counting the number of responses in each category. A total of all three scores gives an estimate of responsiveness as a whole.

The kind of response a child makes will have implications for teaching him to respond to art. A child with a high total score of affective responses is getting a kind of information that is different from that received by a child whose responses are mainly perceptual or mainly conceptual. A full response to the art of others uses all three ways of becoming aware. It gives a child or an adult more information and a much richer experience. Depending on the other characteristics of a given child, the teacher will try to expand each child's range of awareness and responsiveness to art.

A child whose number of total responses is low can also be helped to increase his responsiveness. The teacher should know which way or ways a given child is responding and should encourage him to use his affective, conceptual, or perceptual abilities to increase his confidence and involvement. When confidence has been established he can be encouraged to expand the ways he responds to include the others. The test can be repeated to assess how much growth has taken place and in which dimensions.

Changing the subject matter, art style, and degree of complexity may be necessary with less responsive children. Unless the teacher uses something that gets their attention, he will not know whether the lack of responsiveness is due to lack of interest or to undeveloped modes of attending.

Differences in Cognitive Style

Children's drawings of people can be categorized by the teacher using a simplified form of Witkin's Body Sophistication Scale. By sorting the drawings into three categories—sophisticated, global, and intermediate—a person untrained in this kind of evaluation can get useful and quite accurate information. Figure 10–1 indicates the differences among drawings representative of the categories as found in sixth grade.

Witkin has found that children who are low on the Body Sophistication Scale are not necessarily low in vocabulary or verbal skills (see Chapter 4). Apparently their perceptual analytical abilities are undeveloped. A teacher may find a bright verbal child whose drawings are quite global. Another child may not be very verbal but may show his analytical ability in his drawings. Such a child might not respond very

Figure 10–1. Examples of Sixth Grade
Drawings as Measured by the Body
Sophistication Scale (Courtesy Lovano)
A. Global B. Intermediate C. Intermediate
D. Sophisticated

A

B

C

D

well verbally to pictures he sees, but his drawings would indicate that he can learn perceptually and perhaps needs a great deal of help in developing the concepts he needs to express himself verbally about what he sees.

Classification of drawings needs to be repeated at short intervals if the teacher wants to be sure that the response a child gives is not the result of a temporary reaction. If a child's performance fluctuates a great deal in any classroom test, the teacher can conclude that other things are influencing the child's ability to respond. Possibly the child is very flexible and can respond in many ways.

In Chapter 4 the differences among children in cognitive style were described in detail. The teacher would probably be safe to assume that the more global child had had more restrictive relationships with parents. Such a child may be more dependent upon a teacher. A more analytic child may be more experienced in trying things on his own. A global child may be much more sensitive to the criticism of a teacher.

Reflective-impulsive behavior, as identified by Kagan in Chapter 4, indicates that the child who is reflective in perceptual tasks tends to be consistently so. He takes time to make responses and usually makes fewer mistakes than the impulsive child who responds quickly and makes more errors. A teacher can expose children to a box with a few assorted things in it, asking them to come up and look at what is there and then go back to their seats and make a list of the things they saw. A child who takes longer than most may well be more reflective. The teacher can then see how correct the responses were, in relation to the time each child took to look. Kagan also found that impulsive children who were highly verbal could make many mistakes visually. A child who made many responses, but many of them wrong, might be one who needs help in learning to analyze more carefully or he will miss much of the rich visual information in his environment.

Orientation to Space.   One way to identify extremes in orientation to space is to set up two kinds of motivation and observe how children respond to them. The teacher chooses two stories somewhat similar in appeal and interest to most of the class. For the first story, the children are divided into small groups, one group for each part of the story. They are to pantomime the action as they listen to the story. If the story is an unfamiliar one, it should be read aloud at least once before they try to act it out. Some of the children will be able to use their bodies freely in the action. These children have probably developed kinesthetic cues for relating themselves to their environment.

For the second story the teacher asks the children to paint a picture telling what went on. He will observe whether the children who were able to use their bodies freely also paint the second story as if they were personally involved in it. The teacher then observes the drawings made by the children who were inhibited about pantomiming. Children whose paintings are very literal, showing little action and little personal involvement, are probably field dependent. Many of the children in the class will probably be able to use both kinds of cues, and their familiarity in doing pantomime or enjoyment of reading will determine the ways they express their responses.

This experiment is far from controlled, but it can serve as a basis for identifying extreme differences in space orientation. Because two different activities are compared, the teacher has more information on the kinds of motivation that bring out certain kinds of responses in individual children. At the same time the children, by experiencing both kinds of stimulation, may have been motivated to expand the kinds of responses they can make. The two pictures in Figure 10–2 show two modes of response. Both are by ten year old children. *A* is a visual representation of a city. *B* is a dramatic expression of "being" in a city.

After the teacher has made some observations of the children's space orientation, he can use his knowledge in whatever ways he can to help the children to develop. The child who was too timid to take part in the pantomime may respond more easily with a hand puppet.

Figure 10–2. Two Modes of Response
  A. Visual Representation
  B. Active Involvement

He may be willing to make the puppet do things he would not do himself. The use of a puppet may help a child who has difficulty in using postural cues to get involved with story action. If he has made the puppet himself, he may feel more closely involved.

Creativity

Evaluating creativity in the classroom is one of the more difficult tasks. The teacher's own biases concerning what is creative have to be watched carefully. Personality variables can impair a child's opportunity to respond to a situation that the teacher may feel should stimulate creativity.

All the personality traits, including the style in which a child handles visual information, contribute to a child's capacity to make unique responses, relate unusual things, respond fluently to his environment so that he has more chance of producing a unique solution to a common problem. For these reasons it is very difficult to say that one child is creative and another is not. What we can say is that one child is, at this point, able to make creative responses because of his opportunity and reward for this behavior; while another child, who does not make creative responses, either does not have a potential for creative response or has not had an opportunity to develop it. Since we rarely give a child an optimum opportunity to develop his potential, we could rarely, if ever, say a child has no potential for creative behavior.

It is useful for a teacher to obtain some estimate of where a child may be in creative development as a basis for helping him extend the range of his experimentations with his environment. A child's drawings, observed over a period of time, will tell a teacher whether he is using the same symbols over and over again, or whether he is modifying and changing the symbols as he continues to draw. The way a child organizes space may stay the same time after time. The teacher can help children see how artists change symbols and how children can "say" the same things in different ways through changing or adapting their own symbols in art. The teacher can help children see that putting symbols on a line in printing is necessary, but putting symbols for people and houses on a line is not necessary in drawings. As children observe people and houses in space they will find other ways of organizing their symbols of people and houses.

To assess creativity, the teacher needs to compare drawings to see which children use the presentation of the task to take off in creative ways and which children tend to stay very close to the teacher's presentation. If the teacher's goal is to promote creative responses to what he is teaching, then the presentation of the material has to be flexible enough to stimulate the more highly developed children to take off on their own and give the less creative children a concrete experience to which they can respond.

A useful technique for comparing children's ability to respond creatively to visual or conceptual information is adapted from Guilford's Plot Titles Test. The teacher asks the school librarian to help him select a children's book that is appropriate to the general development of the class and is well written and clearly illustrated. The teacher selects a paragraph that describes a picture. The children are given copies of the paragraph to read and are then asked to write as many titles as they can think of to tell what is going on in the paragraph. Time is limited. The teacher collects the papers, then projects the illustration on a screen so that the print shows well. The children are seated so they can see the picture clearly and can see to write. The teacher again asks the children to write as many titles as they can think of to tell what is going on.

There will be four kinds of information. The teacher will get two kinds of fluency scores by counting responses to both verbal and visual information. He will get two kinds of originality scores by identifying and counting the number of unusual responses to either verbal or visual information. The teacher might ask someone else to help judge unusual responses in order to overcome his own biases. Or he may list all the responses for the class. Those that come up only a few times could be called unusual for that class.

The unusual response scores tell the teacher something about a child's originality and whether he is motivated more by visual or by verbal stimulation. They also tell which child can make the largest number of unusual responses and which child the smallest number. The teacher then has a basis for asking which kinds of responses are more developed.

The child who makes few responses may need much more time to respond. If he responds more to the words than to the picture or vice versa, then that avenue is probably a better one to help him achieve initial successes so his attitudes toward these kinds of tasks may improve. Later the teacher can encourage the development of the other avenue of response.

Dependence-Independence. The teacher can observe the degree of dependence of the children. A record needs to be kept over at least a two-week period. The first week of school is not a good time to observe children's behavior as the strangeness of the classroom may keep them from responding. Independent children will tend to respond to exploratory tasks on their own. They will seek out materials and tools that will serve their purpose. Dependent children will ask the teacher many times what tools to use and what to do with them. Some dependent children who feel alienated from the teacher will not do anything without the teacher, but will not be able to ask for help.

The teacher will want to observe how these different children perform perceptually, seeing how they are getting different information by the way they handle tasks.

Flexibility-Rigidity. Children are not necessarily rigid or flexible in everything they do, nor are they rigid or flexible in the same things at all times. The teacher should record his observations of children's behavior carefully during the first few weeks so that he can plan ahead. Each child's speed in adjusting to new tasks is recorded, with areas in which he resists new experiences noted. The teacher can watch how a child works with art materials, especially in new tasks. For example, with a new class, the art table is set up with assorted media such as finger paint, sponges, tempera, chalk, and pencils. Some children will use the freer media (such as finger paint), and the teacher can notice how long they take to get involved in it. Some children will persist in using the cleaner crayons or pencils. The teacher's record will contain information about which children need help in broadening their experience with materials. Later in the year, he can refer to the record to find out which children need more encouragement to become more flexible, and he can see which teaching techniques bring the greatest response. The teacher should always provide materials for (1) the general level at which most of the class can succeed and (2) the levels that include the abilities of extremes in the class.

Attitudes toward Art

Children in the upper grades can be encouraged to think about art and can respond to simple questionnaires about their attitudes. A general attitude questionnaire may include questions about art. Use simple questions:

1. Would you like to be an artist?_____
Why or why not?_____

2. Would your family like you to be an artist?_____

3. List some things artists do._____

4. Check which kinds of people need to be artistic and tell *why* for those you select.

Teachers _____   Mothers _____
Policemen _____   Grocers _____
Architects _____   Men _____
Actors _____   Children _____

5. Underline the art activities you prefer—drawing, painting, wire sculpture, constructing with wood, printing, mosaics. Can you think of others?

This questionnaire will give the teacher information about how the child perceives himself in terms of art and what attitudes he may have learned at home. Children may have acquired cultural stereotypes that separate art from everyday life. McDonald calls stereotypes "concepts of people, places, or events, which have not been formed on the basis of adequate experience with events. . . . Stereotypes are developed because the individual does not think critically, does not observe, does not analyze."[1] A stereotype is a conceptual average of similar but different things, just as visual information is an average of perceptions. The less opportunity the individual has to observe and to think critically, the more likely his stereotypes are to remain unchanged. The teacher's role is to increase the range of children's understanding, observation, and evaluation, so that limited stereotypes are broadened into more useful concepts.

A child may have stereotypes of art and artists, or he may have had opportunities to develop less limited concepts of them through direct experience. If he has not known any artists, his concept of the artist is likely to be developed by the values he hears about at home. If parents and friends refer to artists in negative terms, the child's stereotype is likely to be negative. The high value this society places on conformity and being "ordinary" may lead many children to forming a stereotype of the artist as a deviant, although many kinds of people are artists. Working in art requires children to relate themselves to their concepts of artists and what artists do. Limited and negative stereotypes can be the source of considerable conflict in art activities.

Creating a Supportive Psycho-Cultural Environment (Point Two)

In our study of individual differences we have found many ways in which the environmental experience of children modifies their behavior and development. The classroom is a planned environment in which learning takes place. The school is an institution that is expected to change a child's behavior in certain directions. The teacher does not always recognize the subtle concomitant learnings that influence a child's behavior. Curriculum is the whole experience of a child in school, including his behavior in the halls and the rewards and punishments he receives in the art room. What he learns depends in part on his background subculture, how well it has prepared him to understand the rewards of the school, how close the school's values are to those of his family, and how his own personality has developed through his experience.

The specific learning a teacher may be attempting to develop takes place in the broader school and classroom environment. One of the key factors of a child's responses to school is the teacher. The teacher's expectations for the pupils, the pupils' for the teacher, and the pupils' for each other all contribute to the classroom environment that modifies learning. When we think about how a child in another culture learns how to behave from his parents, his peers, and the social interaction of his subculture, we understand how important it is for the teacher to see his classroom as a unique subculture for learning. He needs to recognize the different value systems represented — his own in relation to the different children, his own in relation to the administration and other teachers, his own in relation to parents of the children.

In a provocative study of the effects of teachers' expectations on children's performance, Rosenthal and Jacobson randomly selected children in a mixed middle- and lower-class neighborhood school. The researchers then told the teachers that the children selected were most likely to accelerate in growth the next year.[2] The teachers knew that the children had all been tested the spring before and thought that these children had been identified by the test. Actually the tests were used as a basis to see whether the teachers' attitudes toward the children would affect the children's performance.

Those children whom the teachers were led to believe would gain the most actually gained over twice as much in IQ points as those not identified as potential accelerators. The teachers were asked to describe how all their children behaved in class. They tended to see the children they expected to gain as happier, more appealing, more curious, and more interesting. The children who were rated the most unfavorably were those children who *did accelerate*, but who were among the children who were not expected to do so.

The investigators speculated that the growth of the randomly chosen children was largely a result of each teacher's nonverbal communication with each child, the tone of voice used, and the facial expressions that showed acceptance and reward, which communicated to the child the teacher's expectations of him. Such communication is part of the classroom subculture. The important point of this research is that the teacher's attitudes toward a child's subcultural experience may be more important than what he actually learns in his subculture. This idea needs much further research. At this point we can probably assume that the teacher's attitude and the way it is expressed is a very important variable in the way a child learns.

The teacher who understands the child's subculture and is tolerant of cultures other than his own has a better chance of teaching children from many subcultures effectively. The teacher who is culture bound, who cannot recognize that other culture patterns exist with different values and attitudes, has a difficult time understanding the child whose behavior represents a culture different from that of the teacher. Apparently some children accelerate when they are not expected to. Possibly other children could perform at much higher levels if the teacher had higher expectations.

Reducing Discontinuity A major source of anxiety about art lies in the conflict in values between the children's home cultures and the standards of the classroom teacher. We found, in our analysis of American core values, areas of conflict and differences in the ways children are rewarded and punished.

If the children consider art as play, and if at the same time they are motivated by the traditional cultural value of hard work, the teacher can stress the work elements in art. The art activities should be a challenge intellectually and creatively. The children need to be made aware of the art professions, which require hard work. Intermediate grade children can begin to analyze the meanings of work and play in their society and the relative nature of the concepts. What is work for some persons is play for others. Do we work when we play? Do we play when we work? Is it all right to enjoy work? Such analysis will help children to overcome the idea that work should not be enjoyed and that anything one enjoys doing is of secondary value.

Children who want to rush through an activity because of the values on expediency need to be exposed to the value of the personal pleasure that can be derived from painstaking accomplishment. Field trips to observe superior craftsmen, movies such as those of Maria of San Ildefonso ("Pueblo Arts," University of Minnesota), who preserved the quality of Pueblo pottery by continuing to make high quality pots in the Pueblo tradition, stories of Eskimo craftsmen ("Eskimo Arts and Crafts," Canadian National Film Board), whose lives depend on the quality of their crafts, show the importance of artistry and craftsmanship.

Whenever possible the teacher should help parents understand the school's objectives in art. Children can be encouraged to understand that rewards are not the same in every kind of activity.

Reducing Threat and Anxiety   Threats, both real and imagined, can inhibit a child's ability to respond visually and to organize and use the information he receives. Anxieties may be produced by the environment at school or by prejudice in the dominant society, or the child may reflect conflicts from home. A tense, fearful child must be put at ease before he can perform up to his ability. Sometimes the teacher cannot eliminate all the threats in the classroom, but continued attempts should be made to make each child feel accepted by both the teacher and the class. Fear of failure, of getting dirty, of being "sissy," of discontinuity in reward, as well as other emotional disturbances from the child's own life, can contribute to his anxiety in school.

To help overcome fear of failure the teacher can assure children that their art work is exploratory and that they will have opportunities to try again if their first attempts do not bring what they want. Vigorous art activities need to be available for both boys and girls who may consider art "sissy."

Social Isolates

To identify children who are rejected by the rest of the class, socio-metric techniques can be used. Adaptations of Moreno's sociogram technique can be related to art activities.[3] Written answers to the question "Who would you like to have work on a mural with you?" may give insight into who the class thinks is "artistic." Another time the teacher might say, "We are going to visit a museum soon. We will divide into groups to study different things. Each of you write down the names of the people you would like to work with." Several interesting questions might be answered in this investigation. Are those children most often chosen to help on murals the same as those chosen as members of the study groups? What is the difference in the clusterings of who chooses whom in the two patterns? What children are not chosen in either group? What pairs of children stick together? Who are the leaders in the class?

Not every isolate is necessarily in need of acceptance by the group. Occasionally very independent, self-contained children are content to work by themselves or with one or two others. Sometimes they are the most creative children. But others, needing acceptance in order to get enough confidence to achieve in school, should be given special help. Classrooms that are made up of children from different ethnic, rural-urban, or socio-economic classes will interact differently depending on the numbers of each group represented, their aggressiveness, and the attitude of the teacher. Unless the teacher is aware of such subgroup reaction he cannot effectively develop mutual respect in his classroom.

Developing the Classroom Environment

I have found the following teaching technique very useful in developing a better classroom environment for individual creative work. Early in the year the class can discuss individuality, the importance of each one as a unique, creative person, and the importance of *this* group as being different from any other class because the members, as individuals, are different. A definite statement of one's orientation to art education, such as this, is helpful:

"As artists we all have different things to say with our art, different feelings to express. All year we will have opportunities to say important things through art. Each of you can grow in art in somewhat different ways. And all of us can learn from each other."

By encouraging individuals, by helping them gain respect in the group, and by emphasizing the uniqueness of the group, the teacher can develop a dynamic class. In such a group the timid, anxious children can build stronger concepts of themselves. Overconfident, self-assured children can make more accurate evaluations of their work.

The teacher's enthusiasm and his breadth of understanding of art will enrich the psychological and social environment during art activities. If the teacher does not value art, he cannot expect to teach children to value it. The teacher who values art and also understands the differences among children and the tensions that develop during rapid social change can have a tremendous impact on the children's creative development.

Changing the Classroom's Visual-Physical Environment (Point Three)

Up to this point the teacher has been trying to understand what *is* — the children's readiness to respond and their reactions to the classroom's psycho-cultural environment. Now the teacher must make decisions as to what experiences, what tools and materials, and what art forms would have meaning to them and would help them reach certain goals. The Perception-Delineation theory is an analysis of the relationships among the behaviors involved in learning through art activities. It can help a teacher work toward varied goals. By setting up different kinds of environments through which transactional learning takes place, the teacher modifies the children's direction and degree of change of behavior, and by studying the changes the teacher learns new information that changes his teaching behavior. The children also change the environment. The more aware the teacher is of the diversity in readiness and the learning ability of each child, the more flexible he can be about changing the environment — physical, visual, and social — to reach his goals.

In the child-centered school of progressive education the environment was left mainly to the children to develop. In the behavior-modification school the environment is controlled as much as possible by the teacher to change behavior in specific directions.

Using the Perception-Delineation theory, the teacher makes decisions based on the long-range goals derived from each child's uniqueness, the needs of society, and the learning potentials in the field of art. The teaching and the curriculum are continually being modified in order for the teacher to work with the children as they are changing.

The following questions should help the teacher evaluate the things being introduced into the environment:

1. What is the visual physical environment that exists in this classroom?

    1.1. Is the lighting adequate for different kinds of work?

    1.2. Are the work spaces flexible so that they can be adapted to individual and group work and diverse art activities?

    1.3. Are materials accessible to the children, or do they learn from the environment that materials are hard to get? Is storage adequate for children's own work, or must things be thrown away because there is no place to leave them? Do the children learn that the school values what they have made?

    1.4. Is the total room environment drab or exciting?

    1.5. How different is the classroom from the children's home environment? Do they understand why it is as it is, how it can be used, and how it can be changed? Some of the children may have had no experience in changing their environment and learning that such change has an effect on their experience. The classroom is a good place to begin.

2. What art forms would probably appeal to these children?

    2.1. What could be displayed that would help them to see the art in their own subculture?

2.2. What films, slides, and prints would be related to the backgrounds of these children and would introduce them to quality in art? (Lanier's review[4] is a good resource.)

2.3. What field experiences would increase their awareness of the broad functions of art?

3. What tools and materials are appropriate for the children to select from in order to reach the goals I have set for them and the goals they are setting for themselves?

3.1. What are the skills children have learned in past activities that would help them use these tools?

3.2. What tool or material is most easily used to help children in a learning task in design? What other tools will challenge more adept children with the same learning task, such as making order by the use of color?

4. Are the things introduced simple enough or complex enough visually? Are they related to the children's cognitive styles? Is there enough variety in the things introduced so that most children can respond?

All these questions need to be answered from the two sources—the readiness of the children to respond and the goals the teacher is working toward.

Helping Children Handle Information from the Environment (Point Four)

At Point Four we have identified the many ways teachers can help children learn from their environment. In the classroom a teacher will need to watch his practices to be sure he is doing as much as he can to help children handle information.

1. *Children need to develop concepts to use with the percepts they are developing.* Analyze the information you are presenting at Point Three. Do the children have enough vocabulary to respond conceptually to what they are learning?

2. *Children should learn to understand symbolism—the icons used in the art works presented and in their own work.* Are you increasing children's awareness that there is a symbolic language, and that artists (including themselves) express symbols in different ways, changing the meanings somewhat as they

do? Can you help the children respond to the affective as well as the conceptual meanings of symbols?

3. *Children should understand that the organization of a group of symbols affects their meaning.* (See Chapter 12 for information on design.)

4. *Children who are conceptually dependent* (as many school children are) must learn to understand concepts and the perceptual information that goes with them.

5. *Children should be aware of the constancies.* They should learn to see how objects change visually, although they do not change in actual size, shape, and color, as the viewer sees them in different lights and at different distances.

6. *Children can learn to relate the new things they are learning to what they already know.* Are you helping them understand that new knowledge sometimes makes persons change their minds about what they know? Are you doing this in terms of how art is organized, how it makes people feel, and the meaning of what is said through art?

7. *The less responsive or more global children should be identified.* The field-dependent children can learn to use more information from the things in the environment. Are you finding ways to get them to use kinesthetic cues more easily?

8. *The more impulsive children can learn to use more reflective behavior, and the more reflective children can learn to use more impulsive behavior.*

9. *The creative traits of flexibility and originality should be encouraged as the children learn to handle information.*

No teacher is watching all these things all the time. But he can review them, particularly when some children are not responsive or moving ahead as he thinks they could.

Providing Choices and Help in Creative Delineation (Point Five)

At this point in the teacher's analysis of his classroom practice, he is concerned with the media he can provide and the skills he can help children develop so that what they have to say through and about art comes about easily.

Both activities—giving form to one's responses to the art of others and giving form to one's own creative expression in art—take place at this point.

Giving form to one's response to the art of others means that the child can conceptualize what he has experienced in response to the emotional impact of a work of art, its design and composition, the way the parts go together, the visual elements (line, texture, color, shape, and space), and the meaning of the work of art as it transmits his own or another culture (interpreting values, concepts of reality, social organization, status, and roles). The traditional avenues of writing and speaking about art are useful. Children can also organize related art forms for a display to teach others; use overhead and opaque projectors to enlarge details; compare the ways two artists' works are alike and different; collect prints of the same subject expressed in many different ways; compare the design, the composition, and the expression of emotion of three artists of the same period; evaluate craft products for usefulness, design, use of materials, and impact on the environment.

Comparative processes can help the pupils understand more about art because they have gone beyond passive responses to it and have had to analyze, relate, and compare their responses. Analysis increases their readiness to respond to the next art form.

Art activities are so varied that any child can be helped to communicate nonverbally through art. Many media are suitable for the elementary classroom. There are many books with useful explanations of difficult media. Often they do not stress the kind of *experience* a child might have with art.

It is the experience the child has with a medium that is important for learning—not the medium itself. An art lesson leading to a goal can be taught with a difficult medium if allowances are made for different children's readiness.

The Techniques of Media

The techniques of media are beyond the scope of this book. A student who plans to become a teacher should keep a record of the processes he uses in art and art education classes. He needs to analyze the following:

1. The concepts that are necessary to the use of these processes.

2. The kinds of experiences he is having in his use of them.

3. The experiences he thinks children of different abilities would have in using them.

4. The information about art he gains by using them.

5. The possibilities for simplifying the processes to make them more appropriate for children.

6. The behaviors shown when a child has developed a flexible creative competence in using them.

Every art teacher should have a broad background of experience in the basic media and in newer media as used in drawing, painting, sculpture, crafts, construction, and photography. A broad background enables the teacher to have many alternatives in choosing appropriate materials and tools for his pupils.

In order to make the *introduction of a medium* more specific, we will analyze basic steps that usually allow for more effective learning by many kinds of children.

The new medium or tool can be related to something the children already know. The children can discover how the new medium differs from the old ones. Children who have had free exploratory experience blowing paint and using sponges and cardboards for getting quick expressions with paint can be provided with more choices and alternatives for their expression through the use of a good sable brush. The teacher helps the children transfer the attitudes and creative abilities they have developed with simple tools to the use of tools that require more skill but provide more possibilities for expression.

The boy in Figure 10–3 appears to be deeply involved and persistent in getting paint to move across a piece of paper by blowing through a straw so that air will direct the paint movement. To begin to help this

Figure 10–3. Persistence
(Ann Wills Photograph).
These photographs courtesy of
the Portland public schools.

boy become interested in using a brush, the teacher could show him briefly how he can make similar effects with a brush. Then he can be encouraged to see the exciting things a brush will do that a straw will not. This sequence of activity will encourage his flexibility in using tools and materials and in practicing creative use of them. The teacher needs to be particularly careful not to inhibit enthusiasm as he leads his students into broader experimentation.

As children increase the range of art processes that they can use successfully, they can make their own selections as to which processes will best serve what they want to say. The skill is secondary to the expression. The girl in Figure 10–4 may have some strong feelings about what she wants to say, but her facial expression suggests that she is having to work with a medium that is repulsive to her. The girl making the coil pot in Figure 10–5 appears to be intent upon her work, but from the way she is working, the task appears inhibitive. The girl in Figure 10–6 appears to be involved and enjoying her work. In each

Figure 10–4. Frustration (Ann Wills Photograph)

case the individual differences of the children need to be related to the ideas they want to express, their mode of expression, and tools and materials that enable them to succeed.

Once the child understands that exploration can lead to a new kind of expression and communication, he will be more willing to try new techniques. Reticent or inhibited children should be encouraged but not forced to try new techniques. Some substitute materials should be available. The children can learn new concepts and skills when they are ready.

Some of the experiences children might have with media are as follows.

For many children *easel painting* is a satisfactory medium, particularly when they are making simple symbols of things. At an easel children can paint direct symbols with the least physical effort. They can make

Figure 10–5. Involvement and Inhibition
(Ann Wills Photograph)

symbols fast, clearly, and in a variety of colors. For children who are more inclined to make detailed and complex symbols, the use of easels and large brushes may be frustrating. For these children, working at a table with paper tacked to a drawing board may be appropriate.

Figure 10–6. Anticipation (Ann Wills
Photograph)

Using smaller, shorter brushes and being closer to their work will help
them do the more detailed work for which they are ready. If a child's
paints run when he doesn't want them to, add extender or precipitated
chalk.

Clay is a material that children become involved with physically, like
finger paint. Some children will reject it as being "dirty." This is less
likely to happen if the clay is not too moist. Some children will find
that clay is drying to their hands and reject it without realizing why.
Have moist terry cloth to wash the clay off as they are using it. A drop
of lanolin on the hands before and after using clay will protect against
chapping and make working with clay more pleasant.

Children getting acquainted with clay may first manipulate it without
trying to make it into something. They need plenty of time for exploration. They may then try to make parts and put them together or squeeze
the clay and manipulate it into the forms they want. When they have
succeeded with one method, they should be encouraged to try others.

Printing offers an opportunity for invention and exploration in which most children can have some success. Printing processes are related to things they already know. There are direct uses for the things they make, products to show. Printing, like weaving, may cause less discontinuity for the child who has been trained to have something to show for his efforts. From more practical uses of printing, children can be led to more creative expression and more varied use of tools. Printing is particularly effective in the intermediate grades when creative behavior appears to decrease.

As in miscellaneous construction, tools and materials can be used in ways different from their original purposes. This shift can encourage flexibility in the uses of media.

If *crayons* are heavy enough in wax content, children can use them quite freely. A child's success with them will depend on his prior experience as well as on the medium itself. One limitation is that it takes considerably more energy to make an area of solid color with crayon than with tempera. Some children are inhibited in their expression if they have to stop and fill in; other children who like smaller detail and are more patient can find crayons a satisfactory medium.

Miscellaneous material encourages children to look at all things as objects with infinite possibilities for use. They can pool their discoveries and become increasingly observant of their environment.

Each child may see different possibilities in the materials. Encourage the children to look at the things not as objects but as materials to work with, to turn them upside down to get away from the accustomed view of them. Some children may find this kind of task quite difficult. If they are particularly rigid and want everything in its "right" way, if disorder disturbs them, they need special help. They may not accept the task at first, some not at all. Often, after seeing other children's solutions to the problem, they will follow along. They may copy at first. The ultimate goal for every child is that he develop the flexible capacity to see tools, materials, and objects in many possible ways.

A very few pupils may be at the other extreme and have little sense of order — anything goes with anything. Instead of encouraging the free action of these children, you can help them more by structuring the activity. They may experiment with only a few objects, perhaps placing them in categories (smooth and rough; big, middle-sized, and small; light and dark).

Sometimes *weaving* can be a means for getting a very practical-minded child to be more interested in art, particularly if he can see that weaving is an art form. For a child whose dexterity has not yet developed, a weaving task can be frustrating. If he learns that weaving is art, he may "learn" that he is not artistic, while in another medium he might have succeeded and learned a very different concept of himself.

Weaving requires considerable planning, even on simple looms. Once a warp is ready, a child can experiment by trying different weft threads to make different patterns, giving him an opportunity for creativity. Sometimes a task in which there are few choices to be made can lead a less creative child into more experimentation. In painting, where the possibilities for choices are so much greater, such a child might be afraid to experiment.

Torn paper allows children to explore different kinds of papers to see how they work and to combine textures and colors more freely than they might be able to do with paint. The rough effects may be pleasing to older children who are frustrated by their inability to draw. The use of paper helps them deal with large areas rather than with fine detail. Children who have been strictly trained about the care of books may feel strange about tearing paper, but if you explain that we are careful not to tear paper in some instances and that we may tear it freely in others, they may overcome their timidity about using it. Also children who are destructive of books can be given an opportunity to tear paper for art while they are encouraged to respect and care for books.

Except for a few children who find the dusty quality unpleasant, most children are able to use *chalk* effectively. It goes on smoothly and easily; it can be spread with fingers or with a dry sponge, erased, and overlaid more successfully than crayon. In some respects it can give the child more varied experiences than crayon can. It is limited because it rubs off easily and drawings must be sprayed. Some children find it "messy" because they get their hands dirty.

Children vary widely in their responses to *finger paint,* depending on their readiness, which may be affected by cleanliness training. It is unwise to insist that every child finger paint, but the freedom to work freely in this medium is an objective toward which the teacher can work.

Finger paint provides a child with a direct means of expression—his hands are his tools. If he is not inhibited, he can explore all kinds of effects, using fingers, palms, and the sides of his hands. Even his forearms are effective in manipulating the paint.

A child's behavior while he is finger painting will give the teacher more clues about the child's reaction to the paint than will an analysis of his work. If a child uses only one or two fingertips, is slow in getting involved with the paint, and tends to mix colors together when they touch, you may want to ask him if he would like to try something else. If he is strongly motivated to do what the rest of the class is doing and wants to stay with it even though he does not enjoy it, the teacher can give the child encouragement by participating in the work himself, by showing how much "fun" it can be.

These are among the traditional media used in elementary school. If they help a child learn without hindering his ability to symbolize and organize things, they should not be rejected merely because they have been used for a long time. But new media are being developed. They need to be studied to see what kinds of experiences they would give children. To use something just because it is new is not justified unless it stimulates learning for a particular group of children.

Children can use still cameras and movie cameras and learn a great deal about organization in design. They can compare, analyze, and learn to see with greater detail. The camera and the reproduction process should not be so complicated that their involvement is with the mechanics of the instrument rather than with the artistic expression.

Synthetic paints, oil paints, and plastics all have potential uses for children. The teacher may select these media if he believes they will be useful in achieving the goals he has set.

A teacher might believe that children need to become familiar with a wide range of materials so that they can have many choices about the way they express ideas and feelings in art. The selection of media also depends on the differences among the children. A teacher working with children who need security would select a new medium only if a prior one had given children experiences that prepared them to use the new one.

Evaluation of Feedback and Transfer (Point Six)

Looking at the art work of a child is only one means of evaluating changes in his behavior and his growth. The teacher must also evaluate the child's understanding of art, his ability to respond emotionally to art, his enjoyment of the design of art, and his understanding of the symbolic meaning of art to him personally and to his whole culture. These understandings are *content goals* for art education. A teacher can assess his teaching, the children's ability to respond, and the short- and long-range growth they are making toward these goals by using the evaluations at Point Six of the P-D theory.

Instrumental goals, abilities that children can develop that increase their readiness to respond to art and to create art, are also criteria that can be used to measure children's development.

Figure 10–7A is a drawing from memory by a second grade boy which was scored as global (2) on the Body Sophistication Scale. Only one IQ score of 78 (Otis group test) was available for this child, so it must be used with caution. Figure 10–8A shows this same boy's drawing with a score of 8 on the Lovano Drawing Scale when he was asked to draw from a slide projection of the picture in Figure 10–9. This indicates a higher level of information handling and detail than in Figure 10–7A.

Figure 10–7B is a drawing by a second grade boy which was scored as sophisticated (4) on the Body Sophistication Scale. His score on the group Otis was 122. Figure 10–8B shows his remarkable drawing when responding to Figure 10–9. It had a score of 15 on the Lovano Drawing Scale.

This comparison shows not only the range in a heterogeneous second grade but the differences in drawing ability when memory is not the main resource.

In this chapter we have described several means by which the teacher can identify and measure abilities and can assess readiness and reassess it as new learning is presented. Figure 10–10 A and B are examples of a teacher's record for the growth of an individual child. Figure 10–11 A and B shows how a teacher might analyze a group of children to see which children might need different kinds of experience at a given time. Figure 10–12 is an example of a teacher's record of observations over time. As the teacher watches these developments he obtains directives as to the changes he needs to make in his curriculum plan so that all the children in groups and as individuals can be moving ahead toward his long-range goals. Though these evaluations are specifically focused on art behavior, they will help the teacher in all his teaching.

The feedback that the children get in discussing their own growth in art helps them recognize their progress and feelings of success. Each of the avenues of learning and expressing through art needs to be

A

B

Figure 10–8. Second Grade Drawings of
Boy with Toy (Courtesy Lovano).
Lovano Drawing Scale
Scores: A. 8 B. 15

A

B

Figure 10–9. Boy with Toy

Figure 10–10A. Teacher's File Card–Observed Behaviors of Individual Children

		Name or code number

Weekly assessment															
Dependent															
Independent															
Free in movement															
Restricted in movement															
Flexible															
Rigid															
Playful															
Experimental															
Restrictive															

brought to the child's attention. He can compare what he said about a painting early in the year with what he said later. He can check to see whether he is seeing more and what kinds of things he is seeing. He can look back at his drawings to see whether his symbols are changing or becoming more expressive through the ways he organizes things. Intermediate grade children and young adolescents can write summaries of the things they have learned to help both the teacher and themselves understand what has had the most meaning to them.

Figure 10–10B. Assessment of Readiness

Perceptual and conceptual development: a frequency distribution of a child's own language to describe what he sees. Task: write a description of a painting.

	People	Cityscape	Abstract
1. Affective qualities			

	People	Cityscape	Abstract
2. Design elements and relationships			

3. Symbolic meaning			

Figure 10–11A. Assessment of Creativity

Numbers of Responses

Student's Name	Verbal Motivation		Visual Motivation	
	Fluency	Originality (Unusual)	Fluency	Originality (Unusual)
Totals				

Average scores (Add all the scores and divide by the number of students.)

Fluency ☐   Range of fluency scores   High ☐   Range of originality scores   High ☐

Originality ☐   Low ☐   Low ☐

Total average ☐

Figure 10–11B. Comparing Children's Readiness

	3 Points	2 Points	1 Point
Total responses to paintings	*Detailed* Henry James John Mary Ruth	*Intermediate* Linda Robert Pedro Gus Erik Margaret	*Global* Sara Jean Maria Carlos
Classroom behavior	*Independent* Linda James Mary Ruth	*Intermediate* John Henry Pedro Robert Erik Maria	*Dependent* Gus Jean Margaret Sara Carlos
Figure drawing from memory	*Sophisticated* Henry John Mary Ruth James	*Intermediate* Linda Robert Maria Pedro Erik Jean	*Global* Gus Carlos Margaret Sara
Figure drawing from a slide	Pedro Henry Mary Ruth James	John Carlos Robert Linda Maria Jean	Erik Gus Margaret Sara

Total points

12	James Mary Ruth	9	Linda Pedro	6	Jean
				5	Gus Margaret Carlos
11	Henry	8	Robert		
10	John	7	Erik Maria	4	Sara

Figure 10–12. Observation

Pupil: Pedro Jones
Age: 10 Grade: 5 Sex: M

Background

	Father	*Mother*
Occupation	Postal clerk	Nurse's aid
Ethclass	Mid. C. Multi-strain	Mexican-American
	European-American	Close knit, middle
Geograph. areas	Midwest-rural	Southwest-urban
Education	grade 12	grade 12

Notes: Multicultural family, Mexican-American heritage dominant but ambitious for son to achieve in American core culture. Some bilingual training.

Past achievement Grades: Low av. Test scores: Otis 105
Date: 2nd grade

Classroom behaviors

Response to perceptual stimulus

Painting: Subject: people

Visual characteristics	#3
Affective description	#7
Conceptualizing	#10
Total responsiveness	#20
Low	
Average	✓
High	

Cognitive style

Body sophistication:	
Sophisticated	
Intermediate	✓
Global	
Mode of responding:	
Reflective	
Impulsive	✓

Creativity

	Often	Average	Seldom
Traits:			
Fluency—verbal motivation		✓	✓
visual motivation			
Originality—verbal motivation			
visual motivation	✓		✓
Independence		✓	
Dependence			
Playful attitude			✓
Art products:			
Symbols: Repeats			
Modifies			
Changes		✓	
Use of space: Repeats			✓
Modifies			
Changes			
Uses kinesthetic cues			✓
Use of tools and materials:			
Flexible			
Rigid		✓	

	Positive	Neutral	Negative
Attitudes toward art			

Summary   Classroom inquiry gives a teacher working information or guidelines for identifying individual children's differences in readiness for art. Written responses to paintings help identify readiness to see affective, design, or symbolic aspects of art at Point One of the P-D Theory.

Children's writing about art and their own drawings give clues as to their analytic or global cognitive style and their orientation to space as well as their creative development. Their behavior in the classroom gives clues to their dependence or independence, their flexibility or rigidity. Questionnaires can give some information about their attitudes toward art, which may influence their willingness to become involved in art tasks.

The teacher can discover clues for developing a more supportive psycho-cultural environment in the classroom at Point Two of the P-D theory by studying the values and attitudes of the background subcultures of the children. Their overall readiness also helps to evoke their reactions to the psycho-cultural environment.

Children who are isolated in the classroom can be identified in a study of the social organization of the class. They can be helped in a classroom environment where more respect and understanding are given each individual.

The visual-physical environment at Point Three is developed and modified by the teacher to fit the perceptual and conceptual readiness and cultural interests of the class. This includes motivating objects, art forms, art materials, films, slides, prints, and art equipment as well as the design of the classroom itself.

The teacher helps the children to use the new information at Point Four by relating it to their ability to respond in accordance with their tolerance of new things, ability to handle detail, and cognitive style.

The creative delineation of children at Point Five can be in response to the art of others or by their own work. In each case the art of others or the medium provided for their own work needs to be selected in relation to each child's behavior at the points that precede. Then each child will have opportunity to express responses in verbal or iconic ways appropriate to his development.

The children need the evaluation at Point Six to get feedback about their progress and to help them assess their readiness for the next task. The teacher needs the evaluation to assess his effectiveness in the prior points and to modify or change the next task so the children can move easily from one cycle of growth to another.

All of these steps are described to help the teacher enable the children to reach the goals of fuller responses to and in art.

References

[1] Frederick J. McDonald, *Educational Psychology* (Belmont, Calif.: Wadsworth Publishing Company, Inc., 1959), p. 157. Reprinted by permission.

[2] Robert Rosenthal and Lenore F. Jacobson, "Teacher Expectations for the Disadvantaged," *Scientific American,* 218 (April 1968), 19–23.

[3] J. L. Moreno, "Who Shall Survive?" (Washington: Nervous and Mental Diseases Publishing Company, 1934).

[4] Vincent Lanier, *Final Report of Newer Media in Art Education Project* (Washington, D.C.: N.A.E.A.), 1966.

11

Establishing Objectives for Art Education

In an *ideal* democratic society the objectives of education evolve from the values and needs of *all* the people, and *all* segments of the society are represented through the democratic process in the administration of educational policy. Work toward this ideal is a continuous and difficult process. It is particularly so during a period of rapid social change and unrest. Minority groups and poor people are demanding their rights of equality in education and in representation in educational policy making. Differences in values between generations, between socio-economic and racial groups, and between political ideologies complicate the problem of interpreting society's needs. Increased geographic and socio-economic mobility have made localized education inadequate preparation for the children who move.

This chapter is presented as a working guide to help teachers and consultants identify their own basic assumptions about society and children in comparison with recent research, and to help them become less culture bound as they operate as teachers in a democratic society.

No measuring instruments are adequate in formulating a total picture of what contemporary society is or should be. Public opinion polls and census statistics give some information on what people think and how they live. Books are written by thoughtful social scientists, as well as by popular journalists, purporting to describe the condition of our culture. All descriptions, whether based on statistics, samplings, or critical analyses, are subject to varying interpretations, whether they are concerned with suburbia, central cities, ghetto areas or rural subcultures.

Those descriptions that are based on careful observation and analysis can be useful to a teacher who wants to understand the society; but it must be remembered that the picture is continually changing. What was a valid generalization three years ago may need to be discarded. Because of increased mobility, areas are losing their distinct characteristics. The structure of social classes is changing. Population increases. Rural areas are no longer far removed from urban. The world appears to shrink constantly in terms of time and speed of travel. Isolation of groups becomes much reduced, and social value contrasts are sharpened.

When cultures change rapidly, the identification of values to be maintained by the schools becomes more difficult. While a democratic nation has room for differing opinions on what the values are, a teacher must have some kinds of objectives in order to decide how and what to teach.

If a principal establishes the objectives within a school and if he does not understand the community, his objectives may be in strong conflict with those of the majority of parents. Some school boards who establish objectives tend to consider only the values of the segments of the society they represent. Interpretation depends upon how well the interpreter understands the functions of the society and culture.

One function of education is to maintain the culture — its values, ideals, and patterns for living — through the training of succeeding generations. In art, this maintenance is difficult because the arts have not been generally recognized as central in our culture. We must set up objectives for art education in a society that surrounds itself with art forms, but that is generally unaware of the aesthetic qualities. We must work with many people who have negative feelings about artists and designers, so we cannot derive all our values about art education from the general public. As we found in Chapter 5, the trend to depend on concepts more than percepts leads to disuse of percepts in solving problems. Persons who are deficient in use of percepts lack concern for the quality of the environment. They are ill prepared to evaluate the need for education in vision and the visual arts. In teaching the values of art we have to make art meaningful to people of very different value systems and perceptual readinesses.

Developments in educational research and philosophy do not always keep up with the rapid changes in our culture. For this reason we must proceed as logically and intelligently as we can, using the best tools we have for evaluating the function of art experiences in the development of children.

Sources of Objectives

One source of our objectives is our democratic society itself and the kind of citizenry needed to maintain and develop it. To identify the objectives we need to study our multicultural society, our form of government, and the basic assumptions, ideals, and realities of our complex social organization. Our second source of objectives is individual children as we understand them from the viewpoints of professional education, psychology, sociology, and anthropology. This understanding will help us to allow for individual differences in the learning process. The third source is our philosophy. We have varying conceptions about the nature of man and the universe, what man's purpose should be, and how his potential should be developed. Our fourth source is from the field of art, the contribution of art to civilization's accumulated knowledge and expressions.

The subject of art raises several questions: "What can the rich heritage of the arts contribute to the development of children? How can the study of art help children understand their culture? How can a teacher help them understand the language of art and 'read' their environment to discover what their society values?"

Goals of a Multicultural Society

The Visual Environment. In a complex society the quality of life of everyone is dependent on the decisions of others. Teachers attempt to educate children to take responsibility as citizens, to respect other people and their property, to obey the law, and to develop habits of self-government. Teachers *have not* helped children become responsible for their contributions to the visual environment, which everyone shares. To be able to take this responsibility children need (1) to be able to see what is going on in the visual environment, (2) to understand what is being communicated, (3) to understand that appearance is related to use, (4) to understand design so that they can evaluate their own and other people's decisions, and (5) to understand how changes affect the quality of the environment they all share.

The attitudes and values of a people are mirrored in the environment they create. What they consider to be important is shown in the scale of the things they build and the condition in which the things are maintained. The art teacher, who may be more visually sensitive than other people, can help children learn to understand the symbols in the environment.

The shared environment includes central cities, suburbs, rural areas, forests, waterways, deserts, and mountains. Children's grasp of the problems of environment can begin with the quality of the classroom, the school, and the neighborhood and then expand to the city and the country. Surface beautification and litter control are important first steps, but children can explore the relationships between the ways things are used and how they look. Then they will learn that the visual environment and the social environment are part of the same experience.

Education in a Multicultural Society. Two forces tend to make a political society have one culture, one system of values and attitudes. One of these forces is an educational system that stresses one set of values, such as middle-class values in the United States. The other is the mass media, which stresses values that arouse the least controversy. Yet any complex political society has many diverse subcultures within it. The art forms that subcultures use and develop help maintain their sense of identity. Children can learn to respect their own and other subcultures through their art forms. The upsurge in the use of African-derived dress and art styles by many of the American Negroes is an example of art functioning to clarify and maintain identity for people.

The Pan-Indian movement, which promotes the wearing of intertribal dress style and symbolism, is using art to support the identity of the American Indian as a national group as well as members of tribes. Revival and continuation of intertribal symbols help give more identity to the Indian within the Pan-Indian movement. (See Figure 11–1.) The middle-class American of whatever ethnic background who lives in a single-family ranch-style house with an expanse of grass in front and a place to "cook out" in back is also surrounding himself with symbols that tell who he is. The child whose slum environment is his source of feedback about who and what he is needs to learn ways to begin to control and change that environment. All these children need opportunities to understand and evaluate (1) the symbolic meaning in their own environment, (2) the symbolic meaning in the art forms of the other subcultures, (3) the art forms that come through mass media, as well as (4) the fine arts and crafts.

The child who does have familiar ethnocentered art forms that have meaning for him needs the reassurance that they are not excluded from

Figure 11–1. American Indian Dance
(Courtesy M. McFee)

the art he finds at school. If he is already rejecting his ethnic background, the teacher may be able to help him see its relationship to the arts of many people and the contributions they all make to the multicultured society.

Increased Leisure and Impersonal Work. Two reasons for the growing interest in art are the extension of leisure time and the increase in the number of people whose work does not give them a sense of personal reward because they do only a part of a job. One need of individuals in a mass society is to be able to find self-identification through meaningful independent work. To develop this capacity schools need to give pupils *opportunity to develop talent and skills in activities that contribute to their self-development.* The ability to organize and express ideas in art can give some people a strong sense of self-identification and achievement.

Leisure-time use of the arts is not limited to personal fulfillment. The improvement of homes and the appearance of communities depend on those residents who feel a personal responsibility and have time and skill to devote to the aesthetic quality of cities and towns. There is also a need for an educated critical citizenry that insists that standards for city planning include the aesthetic as well as the utilitarian use of space. Poorly designed suburbs become drab slum areas very quickly. Any area can become a slum if the people living there have never had the opportunity to learn that they can improve their environment and change the quality of their experience. There is little opportunity for individuals to take pride in improvement of their homes if little or no possibility is left them to contribute their own aesthetic judgments.

Lewis Mumford has observed that our emphasis on increased physical power and the production of goods has taken our attention away from the art of living.[1] Some people appear to be more concerned with having and doing the "right" things than with being able to make independent judgments from a wide range of possible choices. We have well-designed products, but many are so standardized that only a very discriminating person will take the time to look for a product that exactly suits him.

Sayers and Madden have suggested that work may have the satisfying qualities of "a deepening and broadening of purpose in . . . activity, . . . imagination and experimentation, . . . enjoyment of the activity from stage to stage, . . . 'pride of workmanship' [and] consequences . . . of deep and lasting significance."[2] In an age of automation millions must do work that has none of these qualities, work that has as its only purpose the earning of money to be spent. For this reason activity that is *not* a part of earning a living should have real purpose and meaning. We perhaps need to question the assumption that we should not work in our leisure time.

Art education can help to meet the needs of a mass society by developing the following attitudes in each pupil:

1. A capacity for aesthetic experiences in work and play. Skills to express these experiences.

2. An appreciation of art as a way of life, permeating personal, community, and national planning.

3. A capacity for independent aesthetic judgment as a consumer and a producer, based on experimentation in design.

The following kinds of experiences will help children to reach these objectives:

1. Aesthetic judgment (how things appeal to us visually, their design qualities) should be part of the children's evaluation of most of the activities of the school. It can be used to assess displays in science and social studies. It can be part of the understanding of many of the things studied: the art forms of our own and other social institutions, the home, community, state, nation, and world. Design qualities can be found in the pattern and structure of forms of nature, in the relationship of numbers, and in music and poetry.

2. Opportunities to make choices, based on familiarity with design qualities (shape, form, line, color, texture, balance, and rhythm) can begin at an intuitive level in the primary grades and at a more analytical level in the upper grades, when the quality of use is related to the quality of form.

3. Individual communication through art should be a continuous part of the child's learning experience to equip him to make cultivated aesthetic judgments as a citizen. Art activity, producing and appreciating, then becomes part of the way of life. The stereotype of art as only "play" can be broken down.

Citizenship for Democracy. Democracy is an ideal that needs constant renewal and development. It requires citizens who have the capacity as well as the values necessary for democratic life. Seven major assumptions about the nature of man are intrinsic to the functioning of a democratic society.

1. Man has infinite value. The state serves the individual.

2. Man needs and has the capacity for freedom of choice.

3. He has equal rights with others to develop his own potential.

4. He has the capacity for self-government.

5. He has the capacity to work with others in "a teamwork of equals."

6. He is able to use reason.

7. He works for the future—toward his ideals.[3]

A man in perpetual possession of all these attributes is, of course, an ideal. The major function of state-supported educational institutions in a democracy is to develop man's potential toward this ideal. The opportunity to develop their potential must be available to all children if a democratic society is to function successfully.

The teacher has to make decisions about the kinds of experience he should give children to promote the ideal. There are few guidelines from research—either on the state of current changing values in American democracy or on the effective teaching of values to children. Decisions concerning citizenship training have to be based on logical analysis rather than research. Counts writes that democracy "is more than institutions and ways of life. It is a great social faith . . . ."[4] Part of our obligation as teachers is to guide children into developing their capacities for self-evaluation and self-government; they must also learn respect for others and for the rights of the individual; they must have opportunities to see and experience democracy at work in the environment.

Values operate at ideal levels, as standards to work toward, and at actual levels, as practiced. For example, the ideal of equality of opportunity is held up as our standard, while in actual practice differences in geographic area, ethnic background, sex, and religion limit opportunities for many people. We know that children work toward ideals only as they learn them from those adults with whom they identify. The kinds of values the teacher actually exhibits by what he does in the classroom have more effect than those he only talks about. Unless children are able to identify in some degree with the teacher's attitudes and values, they are not likely to learn much from him.

As shown in Chapter 5, many children have not only had unequal opportunities to learn but they have been so deprived of preschool motivation that they require special training to be able to utilize equal opportunities if they are provided. Children who attend substandard schools are deprived of readiness training in perceptual and conceptual information, and so later they cannot take advantage of opportunities when they are provided.

By studying the assumptions about the nature of man that underlie the ideals of democracy, we can form an idea about the characteristics of people that are needed in this society. This idea can suggest the kinds of experiences in art that, we hope, will lead to the cultivation of such characteristics in every citizen.

1. Supporting the assumption that man has infinite value, our objective is to give each child the opportunity to develop his unique potential through creative activity and opportunity for aesthetic experience at his own readiness level.

2. As our society becomes more standardized, the areas for freedom of choice become more limited. Our objective is to give children the opportunity for independent decision making and action through art activity so that they may learn to respect the environment shared with others while creating a private environment that has meaning to them.

3. Children can have equal opportunities for developing their abilities because of the diversity of media and the flexibility of results possible in art activities, provided their readiness for art is developed.

4. By learning to evaluate their own work and the work of others, children can increase their capacity for self-government.

5. The art program can give children an opportunity to work together. The unique contribution of each child can be seen in group-planned and group-executed projects in art. The children learn to understand the role of their interdependent creativity in interdependent society.

6. The use of reason can be exercised along with expressive, intuitive activity. Self-criticism helps to unite the use of reason with the constructive use of emotion. One of our objectives is to help children become intellectually

aware of what they are doing — to be able to evaluate their own work and that of others.

7. The processes of art necessitate the anticipation of new outcomes. This kind of behavior supports the democratic ideal of hope and work for the future.

Objectives from Individual Children

A chief objective of art education is to identify a given child's readiness and find ways for him to increase his readiness to respond to art. A teacher helps a child to increase his ability to receive and react to perceptual and conceptual information, to modify, redesign, and create with what he learns at the time or remembers from past experience. The teacher helps the child to find appropriate means of giving verbal or visual form to his reaction to his experience. By reflecting on what he has done, he and the teacher can evaluate what he has learned and his increased readiness for a new task in art.

Children who are predominantly verbal can increase their ability to respond perceptually. Impulsive children can learn to reflect, while analytical children can learn sometimes to get global impressions. Children who look to others for directives can learn that their own responses are valuable as well. Children who have been deprived of opportunities for exploratory behavior can be encouraged to try unusual things and can be rewarded until they become confident. Children who are fearful of failure can learn that failure is a useful tool in exploring new ideas. Children whose art activities have been mainly manipulative can learn to think through art. Children whose responses to art have been mainly conceptual can be helped to learn through the manipulative process and by thinking about what they do. All these children can develop a broader basis for responding to and through art.

Teaching toward this chief objective requires continued study by the teacher to recognize the differences in aptitude, prior experience, personality, and culture that the children in a classroom represent. The teacher also needs broad bases of awareness to be able to create a working flexible environment for learning appropriate to the different needs of students.

Teaching is a profession. One cannot teach with someone else's lesson plans. Many professional decisions need to be made from many sources of information. Teacher education that is professional prepares teachers to deal with the complexity of the teaching situation and provides them with a breadth of understanding of the variables involved so that they can make their decisions from a broad base of alternatives. The teacher needs continual education to keep up with new developments in the field.

Philosophical Sources of Objectives

To the degree that we share the values of democracy we share in part a philosophical basis for education. Our freedom of religion and philosophy allows teachers to have differences in their own basic assumptions and values. The teacher who is aware of his own philosophical values is able to relate them to the values of the society and to his obligations to his pupils.

The ideas one holds about the nature of man also relate to one's ideas about beauty. Is the concept of beauty something that evolves through experience? Is it a universal "truth" that exists beyond man? Is it something man searches for but never finds in total? Is beauty in *things* or is it in the relationships and patterns expressed *through* things? Does everyone have the capacity to respond to beauty? Each of us should consider these questions to see how our ideas about teaching art relate to our basic assumptions.

These are broad philosophical questions. There is considerable disagreement among philosophers about their possible answers. But it is important for each of us, as teachers, to question and evaluate our assumptions, as the objectives we establish and the expectations we reward strongly influence the behavior of children.

In Chapter 1 we identified two extreme points of view about children and art as viewed by traditions in art education. We questioned these on the basis of contemporary research in genetics concerning heredity and environment. This book is based on a transactional point of view similar to that posed by Dobzhansky.[5] A child has a unique potential to learn, which transacts with his particular experience in a particular segment of human environment called culture. Behavior is the result of the interplay between potential and experience whereby learning takes place. The child's potential to learn is modified by each subsequent interplay and he in turn modifies his environment. The school is part of the child's experience. The child modifies the school and the school the child. What a child brings with him of potential and learned culture becomes part of the shared environment of the teacher and other pupils.

Objectives from the Field of Art

As used in this book the visual arts are concerned with much of the man-made environment, wherever perceptual or conceptual symbols are given visible form, wherever man modifies a tool or a product to enhance both its use and its appearance.

The quality of art is not determined by whether an object is or is not "art." The search for definitions of quality in art goes on continuously because art is a transaction between the individual and his culture, both of which are in transition. Art is an individually expressed reaction to a collective cultural experience. For this reason art is one of our best sources for understanding a culture different from our own, past or present, and gaining insights into the transitions in our own.

A child's art is his own reaction to his ongoing experience, and for this reason he can learn by reflecting on his own creations as well as on the art of other children and adults. If children can learn that art is a progressing, evolving thing and not a static "fine" art of some classic period—that it has been progressing and evolving through history—it will be more alive and real to them. Arithmetic is now being taught in terms of the patterns and relationships of numbers rather than by rote learning alone. This approach helps children learn to make many applications of arithmetic. Analysis of patterns and arrangements in art and recognition of the many places similar relationships can be found will help enrich children's responses to art far more than would memorizing names and dates of paintings and artists.

Another reason we have not used our art heritage more consciously is that our economy has been built on "conspicuous consumption."[6] To stimulate the need to buy, manufacturers each year introduce products "more lustrous and more dazzling" than the year before.[7]

How can awareness of the relationship of form and function affect the objectives of art teachers? Mainly, we are led to investigate art works, primitive and sophisticated, ancient and contemporary, not as single objects, but as parts of larger phenomena. This study can in itself be tremendously interesting. The arts, as they function in a society, can be made real to children by a study of American Indian groups and their costume design, pottery, basketry, housing, ritual, and religious service. On the basis of these concepts children can see the functions of art in contemporary culture. Their school, the library, the post office, their household tools can be seen as art forms of a kind.

Some of the values found in art that point up objectives for art education are these:

1. Art is a visual history of the development of cultures. The history of mankind can become more real to children through empathic learning of the art of other periods and societies.

2. Art is the basis of much of our communication system. Children should become aware of visual forms as communication. They should learn to be critical judges rather than passive receptors.

3. Art is a live reflector of our present culture. Children can see art as a growing, changing part of life through their own participation and study of art in its broad context — how man symbolizes his values in architecture, in the tools and products he manufactures and in the messages he gives out through art forms.

4. Art is one of man's means for reflecting on his individual and his group

experience. Art activities can help children objectify and organize their own reactions.

Curriculum Development

We have suggested some of the important goals that can be derived from the needs of society, from the field of arts, from philosophy, and from the needs of the individual child or young adolescent as he moves into adult life. Curriculum may be defined as a broad plan for helping diverse children achieve behavioral goals that enable them to reach educational goals. Education is more a spiral than a straight line. Some kinds of learning, such as developing increased visual sensitivity, need to go on throughout the educational process, but the teacher must decide which aspects to stress and which to review. The decision depends upon the readiness of the individual students.

Goals can be divided into *instrumental* and *content goals*. Instrumental goals are the perceptual, creative, and design abilities and the habits of curiosity that will help the students understand and use art more effectively. Content goals are the understandings about art the teacher hopes to help the class achieve. Both instrumental goals and content goals can be formulated into clearly identifiable behavioral goals that can be identified at Point Six in the P-D theory. Achievement of any of the goals leads the way toward further goals in the next learning situations.

Behavioral Objectives

A behavioral objective is a goal that can be described and measured as "visible activity displayed by a learner."[8] We may see the learner make choices, or he may increase or decrease in a given observed behavior. Objectives that are too broad cannot be measured and are rarely clearly defined. Woodruff divides objectives into behavioral and conceptual objectives. The only way we can test to see whether concepts are learned is through some form of written or spoken behavior.[9] Perceptual objectives can be measured only by the use of language, verbal or iconic. In this book we are mainly concerned with observable changes in readiness for art.

Having identified where a child is in his readiness helps us establish some behavioral objectives for him, and we can test to see whether he is learning. If little or no growth has taken place we will need to question which factors might be inhibiting his growth, what we are doing in the classroom environment, the things we introduce for him to learn, the ways we help him integrate them into what he already knows, the experiences we give him, and how effectively he gets feedback about his past accomplishments that involve his present learning.

Behavioral objectives that can be repeated for testing changes in readiness might be as follows:

Pupil A will increase his abilities to respond conceptually through writing from his first to his second observations of the same object, provided he had learned in the interim to look for (1) details, (2) relationships, (3) overall pattern, or (4) affective meanings.

Pupil B will increase the number of details in his drawings in response to looking at the same object after he has learned to view it in different lights.

Pupil C will symbolize separation of objects from the background in his drawing rather than drawing on one plane after (1) observing the sizes of the objects as they look in space, (2) observing the brightness of color of the objects in space, or (3) observing how objects overlap.

The teacher has established these objectives because of what he has learned of a child's readiness. If these objectives are not reached, the teacher will need to reevaluate his processes at the points of the P-D theory to see what may be hindering development. The teacher might ask of pupil A, "Is his lack of ability to respond caused by anxiety and if so what can I do to reduce his anxiety?" If pupil B has already shown he can respond with words but not with drawings, then the teacher might ask, "Are the materials he was using unfamiliar? Had he failed with these materials in the opinion of some teacher, and had the teacher's negative reward made him afraid of the material? Has he been rewarded for verbalizing so often that he is unable to communicate through drawing symbols? Or has he learned negative attitudes toward artists at home, and has this activity had negative connotations for him?"

If pupil C does not respond to any of the observing tasks then the teacher might ask, "Have I presented these ideas adequately? Were the objects clearly enough separated from the other visual information in the classroom? Is this kind of observation so new to this child that I must be patient and repeat the work often enough for him to overcome his resistance to the unfamiliar? Does this child have a physiological visual condition that makes it difficult for him to respond to the task? Is he more responsive to one kind of task than to others? Why does he respond to the one kind of task?"

Behavioral objectives that deal solely with the tasks needed to manipulate materials to produce some product in art do not allow for the individual differences children may have in responding to the tasks. Such objectives do not deal with what a child could be learning about art through his processing of art materials nor do they deal with the development of traits that can increase his readiness to respond to and through art.

If a child's readiness is identified, then the teacher can design behavioral objectives in a sequence that will guide him from where he is in his development to greater manipulative, perceptive, conceptual, and cognitive skills.

Traditions and Problems in Curriculum Development

The curriculum is the plan the teacher devises to reach goals. He develops tasks, problems to solve, and areas to explore with art media and with art forms and language that will give his pupils experiences that will help them achieve the knowledge or abilities needed to reach the goals.

There has been a long tradition in art education to structure the curriculum on the *media*. First children would work in one medium and then another. Teachers would decide which media were appropriate for some grades and not others. But media need to be selected in terms of the experiences children will have with them, what they can learn in the processes of using them, and the abilities they can develop. The media are only part of art, they are only processes and materials through which art can be expressed. The emphasis on media has also limited children's ability to analyze art—its form, its relationship to function, and its emotional impact. The road to art has been assumed to be mainly manipulatory.

It is difficult to establish a curriculum that will work for all classes of a certain grade. For example, an eighth grade art teacher may have a required art class. He has to decide which are the most important goals for his students to achieve. He may agree with our long-range goals, but he has his students for a fifty-minute period a day for one semester, and he cannot do it all. He has his own background of training to consider; he must judge what things the students need that he is best trained to teach. Most important, he has the readiness of his students to consider. If all his students have had excellent art experiences in elementary school, are well-trained perceptually, and have had both analytical and intuitive experience in design, his choices would depend on which direction he thought their abilities could best be extended in terms of the time and his ability to contribute. By contrast he might find that the perceptual skills of the students have been left to chance learning, that those few in the class who can design are the students who do so intuitively. The class's prior experiences with materials may have been limited to spasmodic free choice through the elementary years. Such a class would not be able to function with the same curriculum as the class that had received excellent art training.

This same comparison can be made in any grade, though the differences among children might be less in the primary grades because they have had less time to learn. When all the aspects of cultural and socio-economic variation among children and the ranges of individual differences are considered, the problems of establishing an age-based curriculum can be seen. Yet all of the people in society need to learn to cope, to evaluate, to control, and to create and modify art and the environment.

The following guide is proposed. First, a teacher must assess his students as early as possible to see where they stand in the development of those aptitudes and skills needed to achieve the instrumental goals. Without the achievement of these in some degree, the content goals cannot be developed very far. Having evaluated where the class as a whole stands and how the individuals vary within it, the teacher decides which goals are the most appropriate to work toward. Then he plans a series of problems and activities that he thinks will help his students get the experience they need to achieve these goals. As students develop skills in information handling, in perceiving, and in creating, he can begin to feed into the classroom information leading to content goals. He frequently reevaluates the readiness of the class in order to find out whether their behavior is changing toward the identified goals and to give himself feedback about the effectiveness of his curriculum.

Curriculum planning is assessing the best way a given teacher with a given class can work toward the long-range instrumental and content goals that prepare them to become more responsive, more critical, and more creative, now and in the future. The seriousness of this task is apparent when one realizes that the students who develop a broad basis for handling information are going to learn more and learn faster than are those who do not have such a basis. The art class may be the one place in the curriculum where perceptual, affective, and some aspects of creative development may take place.

Instrumental Goals

Instrumental goals are those that lead to higher levels of readiness to respond in and through art. Individual differences that encourage or inhibit their development have been studied throughout the book. Ways in which some of them can be analyzed by the classroom teacher are described in Chapter 11. The following list is not complete, but on the basis of the P-D theory and the research used these goals are most important:

Cognition

1. Develop a cognitive style that includes both perceptual and conceptual problem solving.

2. Be analytical or global, reflective or impulsive, as the art task demands.

Perception

1. Learn to see forms as they move in space and light.

2. Learn to see consciously how we organize visual information by similarity, proximity, continuity, and figure and ground.

3. Learn to discriminate between likenesses and differences.

4. Increase perceptual cognition and retention through increased perceptual discrimination.

5. Relate percepts to concepts.

6. Learn to respond perceptually to symbols and to retain awareness of details.

7. Learn to use both postural and visual information.

Conceptualization

1. Develop a rich conceptual vocabulary to reason consciously about the visual world.

2. Develop perceptual information to enrich concepts.

3. Develop a vocabulary for dealing with art media, design, and composition, the variations of light, color, form, shape, texture, and space, and the affective qualities of art.

Design

1. Use both percepts and concepts to analyze the interactions of shape, form, color, line, texture, and space in producing a whole art form.

2. Be flexible in trial and error and in analytical problem solving in design.

3. If more intuitive, develop some degree of conceptual understanding.

4. If more conceptual, develop more perceptual or intuitive designing abilities.

Creativity
1. Develop a more playful attitude toward artistic problem solving.

2. Increase independence and freedom from stereotyping.

3. Become more fluent.

4. Develop abilities for convergent and divergent problem solving.

5. Be more original; see relationships among unusual things; improvise, invent, and reorganize symbols.

6. Be flexible in use of tools and materials.

Motor Skills
1. Develop confidence in trying new tools and media.

2. Learn to see failure as a means of redirecting effort.

3. Develop a willingness to continue working with a tool to see how its use can be varied.

4. Coordinate motor skills with observation and improvisation.

Content Goals
The major content goals of art education are these:

1. Understand art as it functions in society to communicate, enhance, and identify.

2. Understand the perceptual world as it appears to us in light and space.

3. Understand design, the ways we organize our visual world and structure works of art.

4. Understand technicalities of media.

Preparation to teach in these areas comes from varied art courses and books. Some information is included in this book. Bibliographical materials will be helpful.

Summary
Objectives for art education come from four sources. The *first* is the needs of our society for citizens who can perform in a democratic society. The *second* is the range of social, psychological, and cultural differences in children and young people. The *third* source is our

philosophical assumptions. The *fourth* is art as a major part of man's civilization.

In a multicultural society with varied philosophical points of view, art education has a role to play in educating children to take responsibility for the shared environment, to use leisure more constructively, and to become more constructively critical citizens.

The assumption is made that every child has the right to develop his potential to expand his cognitive style, his perception, and his creativity. To help him develop these his teacher needs to understand his readiness to learn and his present stage of development.

A philosophical point of view is taken between the two extremes that children are a *tabula rasa* and that they are completely self-directive. Much can be learned and much depends on the uniqueness of the child.

Art is a major language system for cultural communication and development. Without art cultural development would be very limited and learning one's culture would be difficult.

Behavioral objectives help teachers identify specific learning patterns and assess their progress in art in the context of instrumental and content goals, goals that help children achieve and goals that help them understand.

The *instrumental goals* are these:

1. Developing perceptual skills in analyzing visual information, and seeing forms change in space and light.

2. Preserving independence in an interdependent society.

3. Learning to relate perceptual and conceptual information.

4. Learning to symbolize and organize in innovative ways.

5. Developing avenues for reflecting on one's own experience through one's own creations and the art of others.

6. Developing more comprehensive information-handling processes to respond in and through art.

7. Developing the capacity to react to the arts with critical objectivity as well as through emotional impact.

The *content goals* are these:

1. Understanding the communication functions of art in culture as it transmits values and attitudes through art, man-made products, the man-made environment, and mass media.

2. Understanding the simpler forms of the interrelationships in design as a basis for one's own work and the evaluation of the work of others.

3. Understanding the affective, structural, and symbolic meaning in the fine arts and crafts.

Goals that are both instrumental and content are these:

1. Developing respect for cultural pluralism in our society by becoming aware of the functions of art in different subcultures.

2. Learning to take qualitative responsibility for one's contribution to the public view.

References

[1] Lewis Mumford, *Technics and Civilization* (New York: Harcourt, Brace & World, Inc., 1934), p. 5.

[2] Ephraim Vern Sayers and Ward Madden, *Education and the Democratic Faith: An Introduction to the Philosophy of Education* (New York: Appleton-Century-Crofts, Inc., 1959), pp. 211–212.

[3] Ralph Gabriel, *The Course of American Democratic Thought* (New York: The Ronald Press Company, 1940).

[4] George S. Counts, "The Core of the Democratic Tradition," in *Readings in the Social Aspects of Education,* eds. B. Othanel Smith, William O. Stanley,

Kenneth D. Benne, and Archibald W. Anderson (Danville, Ill.: Interstate Printers and Publishers, Inc., 1951), p. 309.

[5] Theodosius Dobzhansky, *Mankind Evolving: The Evolution of the Human Species* (New Haven: Yale University Press, 1962).

[6] Thorstein Veblen, *The Theory of the Leisure Class: An Economic Study of Institutions* (New York: The New American Library of World Literature, Inc., 1953).

[7] Max Lerner, *America as a Civilization* (New York: Simon and Schuster, 1957), p. 868.

[8] Robert F. Mager, *Preparing Instructional Objectives* (Palo Alto, Calif.: Fearon Publishers, Inc., 1962).

[9] Ashel D. Woodruff, unpublished working papers for Behavioral Objective workshops, 1968.

12

Foundational Art Activities

In this chapter we will explore some of the foundational art activities that underlie more complicated expression of and response to art. Throughout the book we have dealt with the ways individual children and youths are prepared to see as a result of factors of culture and personality. Now we will be concerned with art learnings that can increase their capacities to respond.

The three foundational areas are (1) learning to see in space and light, (2) design, and (3) art in society. Children are involved in all three areas whether we are working with them or not. In some degree they are responding to objects in space and light, organizing what they see so they can respond to it, and "reading" their environment's symbols and icons to know where to go and how to behave. But they do not need to stay at whatever level of competence they haphazardly develop. They can begin to learn to increase their capacities at a very early age. Then they will develop capacities to evaluate the man-made environment, fine arts, cities, neighborhoods, man-made products, and nature.

Learning to See in Space and Light

In Chapter 3 we discussed the perceptual constancies and the ways in which they keep people from responding to the visual information that is in front of them. For example, when people know that things are the same in actual size they tend to see them the same size, even though one thing is far behind the other and much smaller in visual size. People tend to see the shapes of objects as they know them to be rather than as they appear to be in relation to the angle from which they are seen. People tend to see colors as they know them to be even though the light may change their lightness, darkness, or hue.

Perceptually skilled people can see things as they appear in space in varying sizes and positions and still recognize that they are the same actual size. The small boy who asked, "When are we going to get smaller?" on his first trip in a jet airplane had been very observant that planes become smaller as they fly away, so he assumed the people inside become smaller too. This boy's experience had not helped him differentiate between visual reality which varies in space and light and the reality of things as we know them to be in our immediate environment.

When a child shows concern for perspective and wants to place an object in front of or behind another, the teacher can show him how different artists use simple ways to show perspective. Overlapping, making distant things smaller, coloring them more lightly, or using all of these techniques together can make objects appear to be at different distances in a picture. It is important that the child learn to *see* things change, then to make meaningful symbols for perspective.

Seeing how sizes change is easy. Two boys the same size standing back to back appear to be the same size. If one boy takes ten steps toward the class and the other ten steps away from the class, the boy in the distance will appear to be less than half as tall as the one close to the class, as shown in Figure 12–1. To see this difference the children need to measure along a pencil held at arm's length.

Figure 12–1. Size and Distance Changes

When the children have seen this difference they can see how the doors along a school corridor become smaller the farther down the hall they are, and how their shapes change in space, as in Figure 12-2.

Figure 12–2. Shapes Change in Space

Turnbull's story of the adult pigmy who left his forest home could help children understand how past experience influences how a person sees.

Seeing shapes change is also a matter of learning to look. We tend to see in stereotypes and to *remember* what we see in stereotypes. To help children receive more varied visual information we must provide experiences that will help them compare the shapes of things in varied positions.

A large hoop, hung so that it will rotate in front of a blank wall, will help children observe the many shapes of a circle. It changes visually from almost a flat line when one edge is directed toward the viewer to a complete circle when it is perpendicular to the viewer's line of vision. In between are many oval shapes of varying width (see Figure 12–3). The children must learn to transfer this learning to the many

Figure 12–3. A Circle Changes in Space

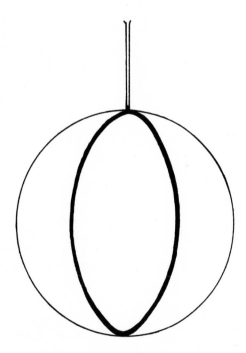

places they can observe a circle from an angle so that it appears elliptical. They should be shown the difference between a circle and a sphere. A sphere looks round from any angle but a circle changes. A hinged door changes its shape from a rectangle when closed (if the viewer is directly in front of it) to a straight line when the door is opened toward him (see Figure 12–4).

Figure 12–4. What Shape *Is* a Door?

Children can learn to see color change in light and distance through the use of artificial means in the classroom or through outside observation of nature. In the classroom the teacher can use a large three-sided black box or a darkened room to view things in, a spotlight with clips to hold colored gelatins, some white and colored boxes, some sheets of white and colored paper, and a table to work on where the children can stand around to see.

The class might first analyze a white box with the light shining directly on one side, then on top. They may compare the varieties of whiteness (see Figure 12–5). Where is the box whitest? Where is it greyest? The pupils may then put in a red gelatin and show it on the white box. What happens? They may try various combinations of gelatins and colored boxes so they can see how colored light changes painted colors.

Figure 12–5. Value Changes in Light

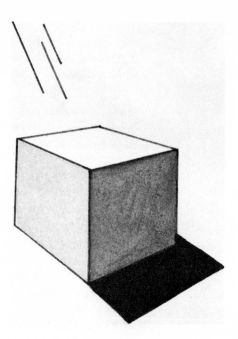

The children may then put white light on a white box and observe how sheets of colored paper put under and alongside the white box reflect their color onto the box and change the way the box looks. Colored light changes the appearance of the box but not the actual color. But colored paint changes both the appearance and the actuality.

There are very simple color transitions that can be observed in nature. Brilliant flowers against a white wall are reflected on the wall if the light is directed toward them and if the viewer is in a position to see the reflection. Colors are lighter and contrasts between colors are weaker the farther they are away from the viewer. All the leaves of a tree, even if the same actual color, are different as light goes through them or shadows are cast on them. The teacher can encourage children to experiment with light. They may cast light on different textures and forms with different curvatures, shine light through forms with different transparencies, reflect light off different backgrounds and surface pigments to see how light can change the way things appear.

These are fundamental experiences children or adolescents need to develop perceptual discrimination if they have not learned it before. As we learned in the studies of cognitive style, children's perceptual development is decelerated in school. Anderson has devised a text-book for teachers that will help them in the classroom. His many inventive ideas for encouraging perceptual development can be easily adapted for a particular class.[1]

Understanding Space

Understanding perception, learning to see in detail, and dealing with the constancies are important. Children need to observe the ways space is used in order that they may use their increased perceptual abilities in responding to the qualities of cities. Man's ability to ignore ugliness and blot out visual confusion from his conscious concerns stems from his lack of ability to see how the quality of the environ-ment is actually affecting the quality of his life.

Now let us look at the city to see what concepts and percepts we can use to help these diverse children understand the city from the point of view of how space is used.

We can help children understand that space is an area bounded by things that separate it from other spaces. The character of a space depends on how it is used and on the things that made it a space. It is different for each individual, depending on how he has learned to see it. But some things are common about spaces for all of us (see Figure 12–6).

A space may be used in different ways. For example, people may stroll or people may hurry; people may go in one direction, two directions, or many.

Figure 12–6. Spaces for Different
Activities

A space is different in light and dark, in rain and sunshine, in wind and
calm, night, morning, noon, or afternoon.

A space may be surrounded by natural things or man-made things. A
space is different depending on the quality and condition of man-
made things.

A space may be monotonous, chaotic, completely ordered, or ordered
with variety by the way people use it or the ways men create things
around it or both. A chaotic space such as an uncoordinated city
street is ordered by repeated Christmas decorations or a long parade
of marching people.

371   Foundational Art Activities

The experience we have within a space is different according to whether its use is related or unrelated to its size, its color, its light, its shape, or its temperature. A small windowless room with low ceiling, drab walls, poor lighting, too much heat, and too little ventilation, full of children and adults who do not know each other, can be changed by modifying any one of these variables. If the people know that this is an elevator and that they soon will get out, expectation of release modifies their experience. If they know that they will have to wait a long time the environment has more effect on them. Their experience in waiting would be changed if adequate air and normal temperature were provided, if the ceiling were raised, the color brightened, the light increased, or the wall opened.

Sometimes the quality of a space does not allow any choices in what a group of people can do. If the space is small, teenagers cannot dance and children cannot play. If the space is so small that people cannot move, panic may result.

The character of a space is identified by size, shape, temperature, and many other qualities. In addition, visual symbols might let us know that a space is a public waiting room, someone's home, a church, or the entrance to a theatre.

Children can do action research. (1) They can study how a space is used, such as the space defined in a chair or a busy sidewalk. (2) They can study how changing the shape, size, light, or color of a space affects the use of a space. (3) They can study how changing the appearance of a space makes it function better. The classroom may serve as an example. (4) They may study how the use and the look of a space affect each other. (5) They may study what the symbols in a space do to make the space workable. Do the shape, size, and color of the symbols help them serve their function better? What do the symbols in a space tell us about what people value? What do litter and disrepair say to us? What do fences do? What do they say? How does the entrance to a space tell us what goes on inside? The teacher who watches children respond to these tasks will get more information about how they see the city.

Children can learn to be more aware of the spaces they use at school. What is their space and what do they do with it? What spaces do they share and how does the behavior of one child in these spaces affect the ways others use the spaces?

In a school where the children are all from the same economic background and subculture, the teacher can study the environment to look for topics that would help the children understand that they can control their environment in some way. They can plant trees, pick up litter, and do other surface work that gets them involved and helps them discover that they can change the environment.

If the students come from mixed neighborhoods, the teacher will have to search for environmental problems they *all* share. They may work on public areas, school halls, grounds, classrooms, or parks.

If the administration sees the school as an instrument for social change rather than for maintaining the status quo, then the teacher can help slum children learn why their neighborhoods are as they are and also give them the tools they need in modifying their environment.

After studying the quality of space, children can deal with the networks they create between spaces—between rooms in a school, from the classrooms to the office, the playground, and the cafeteria. In the newer open-space schools the children make their own networks between the spaces they want to go to.

Children can study their neighborhood and the routes they use between their homes and the school. They can study patterns of transportation and find out how well the city operates its systems of getting from one place to another. They can study how these networks and the people using them all get along together.

Here we, as art teachers, must help children reflect on how these networks affect the experiences people have and how some networks are so designed that they make an area exciting, while others make an area quiet and pleasant and still others suggest monotony and drabness. A network may be a confusing place or a well-landscaped, well-marked, well-divided freeway, an open pleasant place designed for speed.

One of our stereotypes seems to be that we consider the quality of specific places and things and not the effect of the spaces between things nor the experience we have going around, in, through, and between things. The networks of a city are perhaps ignored because they are not considered things to evaluate.

Older students can study the environment, listing examples of orderly and disorderly uses of space. They can evaluate and study what alternatives might make better solutions to the uses of the environment. Other students can study a particular space, noting the uses people make of it and suggesting how the design can be improved. Then the work of the two groups can be compared to see how the findings of one group influence those of the other.

These are just some examples of areas for study. The study of the city brings the art of design into direct relationship with the study of man as a social being and of his relation to the natural environment.

There are different ways of dividing up the key elements of a city. Doxiadis divides them into five:[2] (1) the natural environment, (2) man as he has evolved, (3) the social organizations men have developed to interact with each other, (4) structures, and (5) networks of transportation, power, water, and communication. All of these are essential to a city.

The five key elements interact, giving qualitative aspects to the city. The natural environment is evident even though it is filled with man-made things. The relationships between the man-made and the natural environment can be studied by children.

The form of the land determines the form of a city. Rivers and bluffs divide it, lakes and shorelines outline it. Spaces between hills allow light to come into crowded areas and let people see farther.

Children can study their town to see how the natural landscape gives the city form. They can look at the different ways man works with or against nature. Does he build so that the best qualities of nature are saved and used? Are there places for people to walk, to find shade and softness instead of only the hardness of buildings and glaring reflected light? Some merchants put trees in pots outside their stores to show that they are doing the latest thing in beautification. Others plant trees to create a more leisurely place for shoppers to stroll by. Children can study ways that people use trees in a city. They can understand and respect the value of growing things in a city, and they may see that plants are useful in helping them to modify the environment themselves. They can look at trees and shrubs to see how well they divide or enhance space in relationship to how it is used.

People need to understand that the natural environment is still in a city in many ways, though it is modified by the city. Pavement intensifies heat. Smog is the result of an interaction of man-made gases and weather conditions. Heated buildings modify outside temperatures and redirect wind patterns.

People can have respect for rivers, seeing their banks as natural park areas and their water as a contributor to the quality of the environment. A river can be seen not as an intrusion on a city but as a part of it.[3]

The development of curriculum in these areas requires that teachers identify constructs which children can use as a basis for looking at the city. One aspect of the city cannot be learned alone; it must be seen as it functions with other things. The teacher's task is to select groups of interactions that children can understand.

Design

One of the key factors in the way things look is the way they are designed and the ways people sort and organize what they see of them. We cannot help children become perceptually literate without helping them understand design.

When people organize objects they use their perceptual information-handling processes for grouping them. We can see order in a group of objects if some of their qualities are the same. This kind of design is grouping by similarity as shown in Chapter 3. We can make order by (1) grouping objects that are the same *size* but different in color, texture, or shape; (2) grouping objects that are the same *color* but different in size, shape, or texture; and (3) grouping objects that are the same *shape* but different in size, color, or texture.

Trees, evenly planted along an otherwise conglomerate city street, make some degree of order. The same color used behind notices of varied size on a bulletin board holds them together—a simple form of order.

The variety is produced by the qualities that are not alike. Variety can be planned. A very little variety in a well-ordered arrangement creates interest. Four rows of four identical squares, the same size and the same color and placed at equal distances from one another, are about as orderly as order can be. If one of the squares is changed by size, color, texture, perspective, or position, the whole design is made more interesting. Such a simple variation "catches" the viewer's eye. See Figure 12–7.[4]

This same design could be changed in many ways and still maintain some order. Varying the spaces between the squares would produce a sense of movement. The squares could be made different shades of the same hue. All the squares could have different colors or textures,

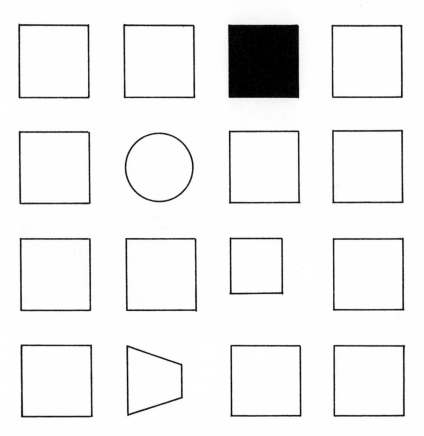

Figure 12–7. Effects of Variation

but as long as the sizes and spaces between were the same we could see the order. The squares, while occupying the same space, could be varied in perspective as if they were doors open at different degrees. The squares could all be different sizes but if grouped together, would be ordered, because they were the same shape and color.

Order and variety are dependent on each other. Order can exist alone but is made more interesting by variety. Variety cannot exist alone.

It is very difficult for an artist to make something completely varied. Look at Figure 12–8 to see what order was inadvertently left in. Although all the forms are jumbles, they are based on rectangles and so they are somewhat alike.

Figure 12–8. Extreme Variation

How much order is needed in a design depends on the use that is going to be made of the objects being ordered. A chair with too much variation on it sometimes does not look like a chair to sit on. But if the chair is a status symbol the ornate variation is useful to communicate an idea.

In teaching design the teacher should first identify the children's readiness. Most primary grade children can have experiences that will enable them to see how order is made out of disorder. Many children design intuitively, particularly if they have had things to organize and manipulate. Other children may never have learned that they can change the organization and appearance of objects.

The simplest tasks need to be taught for transfer. For example, making

order out of cut paper shapes is like making order on a bulletin board —
putting the same size or same color notices together so that the viewer
can see what is there. Organizing a science display helps children
look for the sizes, shapes, colors, and textures of objects so that they
can order them in interesting ways and show the relationships
among them.

Teaching for transfer is a two-way street. Design can be studied in
nature to see how nature creates order, and then children can try the
same kind of organization in their work. Or children's work in design
can help them see design in nature.

Intermediate, middle school, and junior high school children can
explore the more complex forms of design. They can compare the use
of an object with its appearance, so that the effectiveness of the design
for the use is clear. Then they will be able to make evaluations of the
design in cities, in furniture, clothing, crafts, painting, and sculpture.

The design problems suggested here can be solved in hundreds of
ways. They can be repeated by children of different grade levels without their becoming repetitious, just as certain axioms in mathematics
can be used in multiple ways.

Suggested Design Problems

Work with three elements at first — size, shape, and color — to create
order and variety. Cut shapes from assorted colored paper. This is an
excellent medium as it does not require a great deal of skill.

1. Keep the *color* and *shape* the same, vary the size of the shapes.

2. Keep the *shape* and *size* the same, vary the color.

3. Keep the *color* and *size* the same, vary the shape.

4. Keep the *color* the same, vary the size and shape.

5. Keep the *size* the same, vary the color and shape.

6. Keep the *shape* the same, vary the color and size.

Texture, line, and variations in color values can then be individually added to the problems. These problems deal with the principle of similarity.

A second series of design problems deals with proximity—the way things can be ordered by grouping together. Cut an assortment of different shapes with different sizes and colors and mix them. Then make order out of the diversity.

1. Separate all the things that are alike into clusters, first by size, then by color, and then by shape.

2. Create variety in these clusters by varying the color or the size or the shape.

3. Relate the clusters to each other by repeating some of the colors or shapes or sizes in each group.

In problem 3 similarity and proximity are being dealt with together.

Use continuity to create order in these problems:

1. Use the shapes from the proximity problem above. Use the edges of shapes of one group to continue along the same line with the shapes in the other.

2. Create closure by arranging the edges of forms so that they suggest a larger whole shape.

In all these problems, figure and ground separations were made.

Work through these problems so that many solutions are easy to find. The capacity to develop very complex designs can be developed by some children, and almost all can work through the beginning steps. Very analytical and creative children can start with complete order in design (all things alike) and keep adding variety until they feel that an ordering system is no longer in operation. Then they can start working back toward order by creating more similarity, proximity, or figure and ground separation.

Children of different ability levels and cognitive styles can work with these problems at their own readiness level. The problems have been successfully taught to primary children and have been challenging to teachers in training and graduate art students whose prior work has been mainly intuitive. With colored shapes on a felt board, with cut paper, with transparencies on an overhead projector plate, children and adolescents can explore the many possibilities for making order and variety.

In two-dimensional design, students can explore how changing the size, shape, or color of a form affects how it looks with other forms. Then they can see how the form is changed by being more distant from us, how the light reflects off it. They can explore the kinds of feelings they get from different combinations of shape, line, color, light, and distance.

Understanding the ways in which we make order out of confusion can give young people tools for environmental problem solving. The perceptual processes of relating objects that are alike are used by the designer to make the environment more easily read. Complete repetition of shape, line, texture, size, and color is usually monotonous, but the control of one of these elements through repetition creates order. Order is not an absolute but a relative quality which can be modified by adjusting one or many of the visual elements.

After students have solved two-dimensional problems, they can work on three-dimensional problems and the ways the spaces created would affect how they are used. Then such learning could be applied to studying the city. One might start with a real space problem such as the ways the space on sidewalks is designed for the ways people use them. See Figure 12–9.

Figure 12–9. Children Study the City. (Courtesy M. J. Albright)

This study of design fits into the pattern of transactional learning discussed throughout the book. When one thing in a group is changed everything else in that group is changed in some degree. It is this kind of problem solving that is so necessary for living in today's world, seeing how different things influence and change the effects of other things when they are brought into a transactional relationship. Our task as teachers is to find interacting clusters of objects that children can learn to evaluate in terms of the ways the parts interact.

Teachers should be alert for highly intuitive children or young adolescents who have trouble conceptually analyzing design when they are so successful designing at a perceptual rather than conceptual cognitive level. Experienced teachers have been successful in encouraging such students to work on their own unless they wish to participate in the design activities. In most cases the students have joined the class work when the task of design analysis was not forced on them.

Art in Society   Art is a major language system through which the people in a society transmit their culture from one generation to another, symbolize and maintain their values and belief systems, and identify the social structure through styles of architecture, dress, and product design. Since communication through art is so necessary for man's maintaining a social organization it should be a central rather than a peripheral part of the education of every child.

In Chapters 1 and 2 we identified the range of what the visual arts include and their functions in maintaining culture. Many of these ideas and concepts can be used with children. The bibliographies in Chapters 1 and 2 contain other sources of information.

Presentation of the functions of art in society can be correlated with social studies in primary, intermediate, and middle school classes. Art as it functions to maintain a society can be studied in relation to the neighborhood, the community, the town or city, the state, and the nation. The art forms of the many groups who contributed to the nation's overall culture can be studied in American history. Art can be studied with the histories of other nations and other societies. If pupils can relate one aspect of their study to another, they will remember and understand more about the study. If all subjects are taught by the same teacher the correlation is easy. In team teaching situations, particularly in intermediate and middle schools, one art teacher can work in time blocks with several social studies teachers to help children see the connections.

If the art teacher works alone, then he needs to relate what he is doing to the subjects most of his pupils are getting in social studies. He can teach design for transfer by helping students see that the way their environment is designed affects the way they live.

The teacher can look for art forms in the area. If the children are studying the community, they can start with the school itself. It is designed to let many people use the same space. How is the order of children coming and going helped or hindered by the ways halls and classrooms are put together?

The children can study the way the halls are laid out. They can describe what it is like for them to walk down the halls. Are the halls dark and congested or light and roomy? Are they orderly, yet interestingly varied? Children can learn to see that the way things look and the ways they are used are related.

The following questions may help children relate good design to their own experience: Is there enough variety in the way the school is formed and the way it looks to make it an interesting yet orderly place? How could the children make the school a more pleasant place by creating variety in halls and classrooms? If the school is disordered by things children leave around, how could it be made more orderly?

Children may wish to seek a design to relieve the drabness of the dark end of a hall. They might design an individual door cover for their classroom so it will identify them and relieve the monotony of having all the doors the same. Children can become involved in criticism of what they have done. How does a new design change the experience they have in walking in the hall or entering their own classroom? How does the design make other children feel about their school? Many children have yet to learn that (1) they can change their environment, (2) environment affects the way they feel, and (3) they tell others a great deal about themselves by what they do to their environment.

Such activities can extend to the school yard and to the neighborhood, unless the neighborhood is in such decay that trying to relieve the drabness would only make the children feel more despair. In such cases the children should work in the classroom and change its environment. Each child can then begin to learn that he has a responsibility for how his environment looks and how it works. The teacher needs to use great patience with the child who has never made anything, has never had a tool to use, or has rarely had to share his space with others.

If children are studying other groups of people, they can learn a great deal from the art the people have created. What did they symbolize about? What was important? How were their houses designed to fit the way they lived? How did they communicate status and roles by the way they dressed? What characteristics of the art of these people are clearly different from the art of others? Has their art changed often through history or has it remained much the same for many generations?

These questions about another society give children, particularly middle or junior high school students, a basis for looking at art in their own society. Is our art changing fast? Has it always changed fast? Is our society changing too? How do we learn about our society and what its values are by the cities we build and the ways we maintain them? What are the important arts of different people in our society? What are our present artists saying about us today?

Art as Social Communication

Social Role of the Fine Arts.   Much emphasis has been placed here on understanding the environmental arts, mainly because the neglect of the environment has caused the quality of life in it to decline. Emphasis has also been placed on education in aesthetics in relation to the fine arts and crafts.[5,6] Still more emphasis needs to be placed on the social roles of the fine arts as people observe their aesthetic qualities. When children go to museums or artists' studios they need preparation to increase their readiness to respond in all the domains of art. They need experience in asking questions of themselves as they respond to art.

1. What is this artist of a past century saying to me about what was important to him in the time he lived? What is he saying about what was real to him, and about other people? What is this present-day artist saying about the world we both live in? How is the way he sees it different from the way I see it? Is he showing me new ways to see beauty?

2. How has the artist organized his message so we can see the relationships among the things he is saying?

3. What are the familiar symbols he uses? What are the new ones and what might they mean?

4. How does the way the parts are put together relate to the message? Does the design help me feel the quality of the message more strongly? How do color, line, texture, form, shape, and space work together to convey the message?

5. How has the medium helped to convey the message, its quality, and its impact? Is the wood, stone, paint, metal, film, light or other material related to the message?

6. How can this artist be compared with other artists? How creative is he with the symbols he uses? How does he use design? Is his technique similar to that of other artists of his period or is he quite different? How?

7. What is the total effect of the work of art on me? Do I feel a different effect when I have seen it several times and have asked myself more questions? What are the feelings I have about this work of art that I cannot put into words?

In Chapter 1 we defined aesthetic judgment as a transaction between the individual viewer and the work of art. The teacher who agrees with this definition of aesthetic judgment will not try to impose a certain taste on his pupils, because each young person is unique in his readiness to respond. The teacher can increase readiness through perceptual activities and through increasing concepts, knowing that the cultural backgrounds and the inherent potentialities of the children will vary widely. The teacher can increase individuals' readiness to respond to many aspects of art through both conceptual and perceptual intellectual processes and through transactions with the affective qualities in the work of art itself.

Because the place of art as a subject central to education has not been established, we cannot realistically set up a curriculum for a specific year. Until there is some year-by-year consistency of teaching for the development of instrumental goals, and until teachers reach agreement on what the content of art should be, children will come to middle school classes no more ready to respond in and through art than they were as primary grade children.

A teacher can divide the work in art into three categories to ensure that pupils are covering the major aspects whether they are in the primary, intermediate, or middle school grades.

Art learning activities include understanding art in society, understanding the affective qualities and the symbolism of art, learning to see, designing, studying design in nature, and learning to use tools and materials.

Self-directed art activities give the individual child continual opportunity to relate his learning to his own unique potential, to express his reactions to his experiences. He needs a place, a range of materials to select from, and enough time to get involved so that he can get feedback from what he does.

Integrated art activities help the child transfer his learning about art to many of his other subjects. He uses design as he arranges a science display or learns about natural form. His understanding of history and society can be enhanced if he understands a period and a culture through the people's art. As he learns to take civic responsibility he can also take responsibility for the shared visual environment.

Flexible-Sequential Programming

In Chapter 1 two extreme traditions in teaching art were explored — child-centered and curriculum-centered. In the first, the sequence comes from the emerging expression of the child with little or no concern for the possibilities of learning. In the second the sequence comes from the nature of art itself, with little attention given to differences among children. A third type of program is proposed—a flexible-sequential program, which allows for individual differences and recognizes that much of behavior, including art behavior, is learned. The materials in this book, emphasizing the growing child as he learns from his transaction with his environment, indicate that flexible-sequential programming is a necessity.

When visual arts education becomes a central subject in public schools, when it is recognized as a major language system, there will be more time given to it. Then we will not have as many children visually or aesthetically impoverished in the upper grades as we have now. Children will arrive at each grade level with a shared background of preparation to respond in and through art. Until that time arrives, curriculum development, within a framework of content and instrumental objectives, based on the readiness of a particular group of children in a given classroom situation, will continue to be the main basis for developing sequence.

Flexibility in planning, in classroom practice, and in working with individual children is crucial, even in the most ideal school where everyone has had optimum opportunity to learn and where a grade level sequence has been devised. Each child should have opportunities to learn to handle information and to be creative.

Summary

In this final chapter we have identified some of the foundational content areas of art, content upon which much further learning and development are based.

1. Learning to see how the visual qualities of forms change as they are seen from different viewpoints and distances and in different lights, as contrasted to the ways we know them to be in terms of measured size, pigment color, and front view, is a basis for both analytic and creative art work.

2. Learning to manipulate design relationships as based on perceptual organizations of similarity, proximity, and continuity is necessary for nonintuitive young people and helpful to intuitive ones in evaluating their own work.

3. Learning to understand art as social communication is important, whether it is called fine art, crafts, or environmental arts.

We have ended the book with a proposal for a sequential schedule of art education based on the readiness of any given group of children at any grade level. Until art becomes a central subject in schools we cannot assume that perceptual literacy or design awareness has been developed unless prior opportunities to learn have been provided. For this reason the readiness level of children and young people as modified by their environmental experience and learning has little relationship to their grade in school.

References

[1] Warren Anderson, *Art Learning Situations for Elementary Education* (Belmont, Calif.: Wadsworth Publishing Company, Inc., 1965).

[2] Constantinos Doxiadis, *Science*, 162 (October 18, 1968), 326.

[3] June K. McFee, "Visual Communication" in *Educational Media: Theory into Practice*, eds. Raymond V. Wilman and Wesley C. Mierhenry (Columbus: Charles E. Merrill Books, Inc., 1969), pp. 195–216.

[4] Manuel Barkan and Laura H. Chapman, *Guidelines for Art Instruction Through Television for the Elementary Schools* (Bloomington, Ind.: National Center for School and College Television, 1967).

[5] Edmund B. Feldman, *Art as Image and Idea* (Englewood Cliffs, N.J.: Prentice-Hall, Inc., 1967).

[6] June K. McFee, *A Book about Cities* (Washington, D.C.: American Institute of Architects)(in production).

Suggested Readings

Art Education

Anderson, Warren H. *Art Learning Situations for Elementary Education*. Belmont, Calif.: Wadsworth Publishing Company, Inc., 1965.

Eisner, Elliot W., and Ecker, David W. *Readings in Art Education*. Waltham, Mass.: Blaisdell Publishing Company, 1966.

Faulkner, Ray; Ziegfeld, Edwin; and Hill, Gerald. *Art Today*. New York: Holt, Rinehart and Winston, 1969.

Feldman, Edmund B. *Art as Image and Idea*. Englewood Cliffs, N.J.: Prentice-Hall, Inc., 1967.

Hastie, Reid, and Schmidt, Christian. *Encounter with Art*. New York: McGraw-Book Company, Inc., 1969.

Hubbard, Guy. *Art in the High School*. Belmont, Calif.: Wadsworth Publishing Company, Inc., 1967.

Kepes, Gyorgy, ed. Vision and Value Series. New York: George Braziller, Inc., 1965.
  Education of Vision
  Structure in Art and in Science
  The Nature and Art of Motion
  Module, Proportion, Symmetry, Rhythm
  The Man-Made Object
  Sign, Image, Symbol

Lanier, Vincent. *Final Report of the Uses of Newer Media in Art Education Project*. Washington, D.C.: N.A.E.A., 1966.

Lansing, Kenneth M. *Art, Artists, and Art Education*. New York: McGraw-Hill Book Company, Inc., 1969.

Lark-Horovitz, Betty; Lewis, Hilda Present; and Luca, Mark. *Understanding Children's Art for Better Teaching*. Columbus: Charles E. Merrill Books, Inc., 1967.

Lowenfeld, Viktor, and Brittain, W. Lambert. *Creative and Mental Growth*, 4th ed. New York: The Macmillan Company, 1964.

Lowry, Bates. *The Visual Experience: An Introduction to Art*. New York: Harry N. Abrams, Inc., 1967.

Mattil, Edward L., Project Director. *A Seminar in Art Education for Research and Curriculum Development*. University Park: The Pennsylvania State University, 1966.

Munro, Thomas. *Evolution in the Arts*. Cleveland: The Cleveland Museum of Art, 1963.

Schinneller, James A. *Art: Search and Self-Discovery*, 2nd ed. Scranton: International Textbook Company, 1968.

Smith, Ralph A. *Aesthetics and Criticism in Art Education*. Chicago: Rand McNally and Company, 1966.

Wachowiak, Frank, and Ramsay, Theodore. *Emphasis: Art*. Scranton: International Textbook Company, 1965.

Behavior   Anastasi, Anne. *Individual Differences*. New York: John Wiley & Sons, Inc., 1965.

Bowers, C. A. *The Progressive Educator and the Depression: The Radical Years*. New York: Random House, Inc., 1969.

Bruner, Jerome S.; Olver, Rose R.; Greenfield, Patricia M.; *et al. Studies in Cognitive Growth*. New York: John Wiley & Sons, Inc., 1966.

Dember, William N. *The Psychology of Perception*. New York: Holt, Rinehart and Winston, Inc., 1960.

Dennis, Wayne. *Group Values Through Children's Drawings*. New York: John Wiley & Sons, Inc., 1966.

Dobzhansky, Theodosius. *Mankind Evolving: The Evolution of the Human Species*. New Haven: Yale University Press, 1962.

Getzels, Jacob W., and Jackson, Philip W. *Creativity and Intelligence*. New York: John Wiley & Sons, Inc., 1962.

Harris, Dale D. *Children's Drawings as Measures of Intellectual Maturity*. New York: Harcourt, Brace & World, Inc., 1963.

Henry, Jules. *Culture Against Man*. New York: Random House, Inc., 1963.

McDonald, Frederick J. *Educational Psychology*. Belmont, Calif.: Wadsworth Publishing Company, Inc., 1965.

Moles, Abraham. *Information Theory and Esthetic Perception*. Urbana: University of Illinois Press, 1968.

Segall, Marshall H.; Campbell, Donald T.; and Herskovits, Melville J. *The Influence of Culture on Visual Perception*. Indianapolis: Bobbs-Merrill Company, Inc., 1966.

Taylor, Calvin W., and Barron, Frank, eds. *Scientific Creativity: Its Recognition and Development*. New York: John Wiley & Sons, Inc., 1963.

Wilman, Raymond V., and Mierhenry, Wesley C., eds. *Educational Media: Theory into Practice*. Columbus: Charles E. Merrill Books, Inc., 1969.

Witkin, H. A.; Dyk, R. B.; Faterson, H. F.; Goodenough, D. R.; and Karp, S. A. *Psychological Differentiation*. New York: John Wiley & Sons, Inc., 1962.

Environment

Norberg-Schulz, Christian. *Intentions in Architecture*. Cambridge: The M.I.T. Press, 1965.

Sommer, Robert. *Personal Space: The Behavioral Basis of Design*. Englewood-Cliffs, N.J.: Prentice-Hall, Inc., 1969.

Spreiregen, Paul D. *Urban Design: The Architecture of Towns and Cities*. New York: McGraw-Hill Book Company, 1965.

Glossary

Abstract. To separate out certain elements from a whole.

Acculturation. The process by which individuals or groups of individuals learn more than one culture.

Aesthetic response. The transaction between the individual's capacity to make qualified responses and the characteristics inherent in the object.

Analytical–global responses. The degree to which individuals discriminate and identify parts in detail or in overall impression.

Art. That form of human behavior by which man purposefully interprets or enhances the quality or essence of experience through the things he produces.

Asymmetrical balance. Unity that is achieved without repetition of the left-to-right or top-to-bottom pattern.

Basic research. A study of phenomena made without concern for its possible application. *Applied* research uses basic research for specific purposes.

Behavioral sciences. Studies that deal with human behavior: psychology, sociology, anthropology, social psychology.

Categorize. To put into units of similar things, concepts, or percepts; in perception, to organize stimuli into categories of information that can be handled cognitively.

Clue. An idea, information that gives directions for behavior.

Cognitive. Consciously aware, thinking, knowing, perceiving. *Precognitive organization* is the sorting of visual information that occurs before the information is brought to a conscious level of thought.

Cognitive style. Differences in mode of responding to the environment: analytical or global, impulsive or reflective.

Concepts. The ideas with which we categorize, relate, describe, and differentiate things, processes, behaviors, conditions, etc., through thoughts, written words, or spoken words.

Creative traits. Traits that enable a person to be creative: fluency, flexibility, originality, playfulness, divergence.

Creativity. The behavior of a person when he invents, rearranges, and integrates ideas and objects.

Cues. Stimuli that give bits of information. *Postural cues* are stimuli obtained from the body about one's relationship to vertical and horizontal space. *Visual cues* are stimuli obtained through the eyes.

Culture. The attitudes, values, beliefs, patterns of behavior, social organization, and concepts of reality of a group of people that persist through time. A *subculture* is a group of people who share in part the culture of a larger group to which they belong nationally, socially, or ethnically, but who have identifiable differences as a group. The *core culture* is that segment of a larger culture that is central to the culture, least deviant from it.

Delineation. The production of symbols and ideas through iconic or conceptual expression.

Design. The pattern of relationships between shape, line, color, texture, and space that results in organic unity.

Deviant. One who is quite unlike the average or mode. A group that is different from a majority (or what is considered to be the majority) of other groups.

Discontinuity. The experience of a child who does not receive the same reward or punishment for the same behavior in two different situations.

Dynamic unity. The tensions created by contrast in value and color, between the degrees of depth in space, the varying directions of angular line contained within the whole of a design, maintaining a state of equilibrium. One of the factors that contribute to organic unity.

Enculturation. The process of an individual's learning his own culture.

Ethclass. A group of people who are part of a socio-economic class but who are in some degree different from the rest of the class because of variations in the culture pattern of their ethnic group.

Eye-hand coordination. Ability to coordinate the directives gained from visual cues to the appropriate movement of the hand.

Field. *Visual field* is the area a person sees without moving his eye. *Psychological field* is the totality of the factors in a given situation that influence the individual's behavior (field theory). Field dependence means reliance on visual cues to get information.

Flexibility. An ability to accept change in the environment, to change one's behavior as needed, and to try new solutions for problems.

Inhibit. To hinder responses. *Inhibition* is the blocking of a response by other learnings.

IQ. Intelligence quotient. The IQ is computed by dividing the mental age by the chronological age. Mental age is determined by a test that measures an individual's present general scholastic ability.

Kinesthetic response. Conscious awareness of bodily reaction to one's perceptions.

Mean. The arithmetical average, the sum of the scores divided by the number of scores.

Medium (art). The material used to communicate. Pl., *media*.

Motivation. A factor or a combination of factors that change behavior; basic and learned needs that lead to goal-seeking behavior.

Motor skills. Skills that require movement and muscular control.

Objectify. Traditionally in art, to attempt to make things seem more real through representation or symbolism.

Objective. A goal to be worked toward.

Organic unity. The effect of completeness when all parts contribute to the unification of the whole.

Organismic growth. A concept of child development that deals with the child as a whole being in which all factors are interdependent.

Orientation. The process of relating oneself to the environment.

Percepts. The visual images one develops when one categorizes, relates, describes, and differentiates processes, behaviors, conditions, etc., through visual memory, symbols, and icons.

Process. A continuation of behaviors—a sequential operation.

Punishment. A form of penalty for less than acceptable behavior.

Readiness. The sum of all the factors of growth, learning, and capacity that contribute to an individual's ability to perform a given task.

Reinforce. To strengthen learning through further experience.

Rewards. Acceptance, recognition, and praise for a behavior.

Rigidity. A tendency to persist in familiar problem-solving behavior; resistance to novelty and change.

Schema. A rather habitual way to symbolize a concept or a percept.

Significant. A statistical term that indicates that a given result could have happened by chance only five in one hundred times (.05), one in one hundred times (.01), or one in one thousand times (.001).

Society. A group of people who are organized into a political or social unit. A society may have many cultures within it but all are held together by government, religion, or social organization.

Stereotypes. Limited concepts that are often assumed to be complete. *Cultural stereotypes* are particular stereotypes about people that are part of a group's cultural tradition.

Symbol. A sign, a mark, a drawing, a form, or a style which has cognitive meaning to a group of people.

Thinglike. Perceived in terms of the observer's experience.

Threat. A condition of impending bodily or psychological danger, which can arouse fear and anxiety.

Traditions. Customs, practices, art forms, and language that are handed down from one generation to another.

Transaction. The result of the interplay and modification of two or more elements, such as man and nature, man and man, color and form, as they react upon each other.

Value. A people's culturally supported judgments of worth and importance.

Value. Lightness or darkness.

Visual information. Cues received through the eye.

Visual perception. The process of selecting, sorting, categorizing, and remembering visual information.

Visual qualities. Characteristics of an object as it is seen, rather than as it is known.

Index